Releasing the Imagination

Releasing the Imagination

Essays on Education,
the Arts, and Social Change

Maxine Greene

JOSSEY-BASS
A Wiley Company
www.josseybass.com

Published by

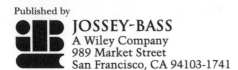

JOSSEY-BASS
A Wiley Company
989 Market Street
San Francisco, CA 94103-1741

www.josseybass.com

FIRST PAPERBACK EDITION PUBLISHED IN 2000.

Jossey-Bass books and products are available through most bookstores. To contact Jossey-Bass directly, call (888) 378-2537, fax to (800) 605-2665, or visit our website at www.josseybass.com.

Substantial discounts on bulk quantities of Jossey-Bass books are available to corporations, professional associations, and other organizations. For details and discount information, contact the special sales department at Jossey-Bass.

We at Jossey-Bass strive to use the most environmentally sensitive paper stocks available to us. Our publications are printed on acid-free recycled stock whenever possible, and our paper always meets or exceeds minimum GPO and EPA requirements.

Wiley also publishes its books in a variety of electronic formats. Some content that appears in print may not be available in electronic books.

Library of Congress Cataloging-in-Publication Data

Greene, Maxine.
    Releasing the imagination: essays on education, the arts, and social change/Maxine Greene.
        p. cm.—(The Jossey-Bass education series)
    Includes bibliographical references and index.
    ISBN 0-7879-0081-8 (cloth)
    ISBN 0-7879-5291-5 (paperback)
    1. Education—United States—Aims and objectives. 2. Education—Social aspects—United States. 3. Educational change—United States. 4. Arts—Study and teaching—United States. I. Title. II. Series. LA217.2.G74   1995
      370'.973—dc20

95-14659
CIP

Copyright page continued on p. 217.

FIRST EDITION
HB Printing   10 9 8 7 6 5 4 3
PB Printing   10 9 8 7 6 5 4

Contents

The Author

MAXINE GREENE is a professor of philosophy and education and the William F. Russell Professor in the Foundations of Education (emerita) at Teachers College, Columbia University, where she continues to teach courses in educational philosophy, social theory, and aesthetics. She earned her B.A. degree (1938) at Barnard College. After a decade of work and child rearing, she took her M.A. degree (1949) at New York University and her Ph.D. degree (1955) at New York University. She has honorary degrees in the humanities from Lehigh University, Hofstra University, the University of Colorado at Denver, the University of Indiana, Goddard College, Bank Street College, Nazareth College, Misericordia College, McGill University, and Binghamton University. Teachers College awarded her its medal of honor in 1989. Before joining Teachers College, Greene taught at Brooklyn College, Montclair State College, and New York University and also taught during the summer at the University of Hawaii, the University of Illinois, and Lehigh University. In 1990, she presented some of her work in New Zealand on a three-week Fulbright lecturing fellowship.

Releasing the Imagination reflects Greene's primary research concerns: contemporary philosophies of education and social thought, aesthetics and the teaching of the arts, literature as art, and multiculturalism. She has written more than one hundred articles in these fields and about forty chapters for collections and anthologies. The most recent of her five books is *The Dialectic of Freedom* (1988). She is a past president of the Philosophy of Education Society, the American Educational Studies Association, and the American Educational Research Association. She has also served on various state and municipal commissions for curriculum and assessment. Her present overriding concern is the establishment of the Center for the Arts, Social Imagination, and Education at

Teachers College. Her interest in the center stems in large measure from her continuing two-decade-long involvement as philosopher-in-residence with the Lincoln Center Institute for the Arts in Education.

Releasing the Imagination

Introduction: Narrative in the Making

It has been said that if we as individuals are to determine what our relationship is to some idea of the good, "we must inescapably understand our lives in narrative form, as a 'quest'" (Taylor, 1989, p. 52). To me as well, despite or perhaps because of the fragmentation and relativism of our time, it appears that we must reach for conceptions of the good that will affect the direction of our lives. Therefore, the essays in *Releasing the Imagination* may be read as a narrative in the making. We who are teachers would have to accommodate ourselves to lives as clerks or functionaries if we did not have in mind a quest for a better state of things for those we teach and for the world we all share. It is simply not enough for us to reproduce the way things are. Now in the midst of my life, I view my own writing in terms of stages in a quest, "stages," as Søren Kierkegaard put it, "on life's way" (1940). The quest involves me as woman, as teacher, as mother, as citizen, as New Yorker, as art-lover, as activist, as philosopher, as white middle-class American. Neither my self nor my narrative can have, therefore, a single strand. I stand at the crossing point of too many social and cultural forces; and, in any case, I am forever on the way. My identity has to be perceived as multiple, even as I strive towards some coherent notion of what is humane and decent and just. At the same time, amidst this multiplicity, my life project has been to achieve an understanding of teaching, learning, and the many models of education; I have been creating and continue to create a self by means of that project, that mode of gearing into the world. And that project has crucially shaped the effort that has resulted in *Releasing the Imagination*.

The dimension of education that concerns me most has been teacher education. I have come to that concern out of a background marked by absorption with the liberal arts and by social action as well. The values and visions of the civil rights movement of the 1960s and the peace movement of that decade still permeate my quest. Without any claim to the heroism of a Resistance fighter in the Second World War, I nevertheless quote the French poet René Char's view that Resistance fighters like himself "lost their treasure" when they returned to the "'sad opaqueness' of a private life centered about nothing but itself" (Arendt, 1961, p. 4). Char did not feel loss because he yearned for war or violence but because he recalled a time when people took initiatives, became challengers, and embarked on new beginnings. Similarly, even though our world has changed and become more complex over the years, I believe that what existed for many persons in our country in the 1960s and early 1970s was a comparable treasure; and I am convinced that, in the domains of education today, people can choose to resist the thoughtlessness, banality, technical rationality, carelessness, and "savage inequalities" (Kozol, 1991) that now undermine public education at every turn.

In *Releasing the Imagination* I hope to connect my own seeking with the strivings of other teachers and teacher educators who are weary of being clerks or technocrats and equally weary of that sad opaqueness of a private life centered about nothing but itself. I hope to stimulate a kind of silent conversation that may move readers to discover what they have to say once they attend to their own situations, to the actualities of their lives. In doing so, I want to be conscious of diversity of background and perspective. I want to attend to and express regard for difference as well as for what is conceived to be common. I want to acknowledge the resemblance of what lies around us to "a jumbled museum" (Smithson, 1979, p. 67). Yet I also feel deeply dissatisfied with what postmodern thinkers describe as "bricolage," or "collage," that style of communicating often thought suitable for the present time, when old myths, oppositions, and hierarchies are being overthrown (Schrift, 1990, p. 110). And I have looked for a way of speaking that might begin to constitute a common world for teachers and, indeed, many others. I do not intend to construct something I nominate to be the desired common world and ask readers to make it their own. Instead, I have set myself the task of arousing readers' imaginations, so that all of us can reach beyond the "illusory babels . . . odd intersections of meaning, strange corridors of history, unexpected echoes, unknown humors" (Smithson, 1979, p. 67) to some naming, some sense-making that brings us together in community.

Unless we make such an effort, it will be very difficult for us ever to decide what education ought to mean. We have associated it in the past with simple transmission, with communication, with initiation, with preparing the young "for the task of renewing a common world" (Arendt, 1961, p. 196). Now, with so many traditional narratives being rejected or disrupted, with so many new and contesting versions of what our common world should be, we cannot assume that there is any longer a consensus about what is valuable and useful and what ought to be taught, despite all the official definitions of necessary outcomes and desired goals.

One of the reasons I have come to concentrate on imagination as a means through which we can assemble a coherent world is that imagination is what, above all, makes empathy possible. It is what enables us to cross the empty spaces between ourselves and those we teachers have called "other" over the years. If those others are willing to give us clues, we can look in some manner through strangers' eyes and hear through their ears. That is because, of all our cognitive capacities, imagination is the one that permits us to give credence to alternative realities. It allows us to break with the taken for granted, to set aside familiar distinctions and definitions.

Recall that for generations people were unable to conceive of little children constructing meaningful worlds for themselves or, in fact, making meaning at all, even as they learned to speak. At best, children were thought of as incomplete adults foraging in a world that did not "make sense" to them. Today, we read children's poems and journals; we listen to their stories; we find ourselves actually entering into their realities by means not solely of our reasoning power but of our imagination. Similarly, but more shamefully, white people in Western countries were unable to credit those they called "Negroes" or "Africans" with ordinary intelligence or with the ability to read and write (Gates, 1992, pp. 52–62). Women, too, more often than not, were thought of by men as soft and relatively childlike, unable to think theoretically or rigorously. One of the advances of our time is a (sometimes grudging) recognition on the part of many of us that those we have long categorized as other for whatever reason (ethnicity, gender, religion, education, culture, mores, geographic location, physical condition) share in the human condition. Every one of us inhabits a humanly fabricated world, is mortal and can acknowledge that mortality, and can tell the story of what happens to him or her as he or she lives. Aware, then, on some level of the integrity and the coherence of what may seem to us to be a totally alien world in the person of another, we are called upon to use our imaginations to enter into that world, to discover how it looks and feels from the vantage point of the person whose world it is. That does not mean we approve it or even necessarily appreciate it. It does mean that we extend our experience sufficiently to grasp it as a human possibility.

Not always but oftentimes, the extent to which we grasp another's world depends on our existing ability to make poetic use of our imagination, to bring into being the "as if" worlds created by writers, painters, sculptors, filmmakers, choreographers, and composers, and to be in some manner a participant in artists' worlds reaching far back and ahead in time. It is the poetic imagination that enables us to enter into the social fabric and events of George Eliot's *Middlemarch* set in the English midlands, to journey in our country from the rural South to the lights and sounds of New York's Harlem in Toni Morrison's *Jazz,* to experience a frontier wedding through the body movement of Martha Graham's *Appalachian Spring,* to move from a pain-scarred self-portrait by a vibrant Frida Kahlo to a contemplative young Virgin by Murillo, to feel enlarged by the soaring melodic structures of Verdi's *Requiem.* I will say much about such encounters on the stages of this quest, as I connect the arts to discovering cultural diversity, to making community, to becoming wide-awake to the world. For me as for many others, the arts provide new perspectives on the lived world. As I view and feel them, informed encounters with works of art often lead to a startling defamiliarization of the ordinary. What I have habitually taken for granted—about human potential, for example, or gender differences or ecology or what is now called "ethnic identity" or the core curriculum—frequently reveals itself in unexpected ways because of a play I have seen, a painting I have looked at, a woodwind quintet I have heard. And now and then, when I am in the presence of a work from the border, let us say, from a place outside the reach of my experience until I came in contact with the work, I am plunged into all kinds of reconceiving and revisualizing. I find myself moving from discovery to discovery; I find myself revising, and now and then renewing, the terms of my life.

Even that is not all. We also have our social imagination: the capacity to invent visions of what should be and what might be in our deficient society, on the streets where we live, in our schools. As I write of social imagination, I am reminded of Jean-Paul Sartre's declaration that "it is on the day that we can conceive of a different state of affairs that a new light falls on our troubles and our suffering and that we *decide* that these are unbearable" (1956, pp. 434–435). That is, we acknowledge the harshness of situations only when we have in mind another state of affairs in which things would be better. Similarly, it may only be when we think of humane and liberating classrooms in which every learner is recognized and sustained in her or his struggle to learn how to learn that we can perceive the insufficiency of bureaucratized, uncaring schools. And it may be only then that we are moved to choose to repair or to renew.

What I am describing here is a mode of utopian thinking: thinking that refuses mere compliance, that looks down roads not yet taken to the shapes of a more fulfilling social order, to more vibrant ways of being in the world. This kind of reshaping imagination may be released through many sorts of dialogue: dialogue among the young who come from different cultures and different modes of life, dialogue among people who have come together to solve problems that seem worth solving to all of them, dialogue among people undertaking shared tasks, protesting injustices, avoiding or overcoming dependencies or illnesses. When such dialogue is activated in classrooms, even the young are stirred to reach out on their own initiatives. Apathy and indifference are likely to give way as images of what might be arise.

As my narrative in the making takes gradual and diversified shape, my concern for active learning in schools now in the process of reform will be apparent. I want to help us think in ways that move beyond schooling to the larger domains of education, where there are and must be all kinds of openings to possibility. To encourage this thinking, I have tapped certain human stories more than once, most particularly those that, like Virginia Woolf's story, speak of moving from entanglement in the "cotton wool of daily

life" to "moments of being" (1976, p. 72), to moments of awareness and intensified consciousness. I have laid out for us telling
memories and visions from childhood, such as the moment of
awakening recalled by the Lady in Brown in Ntozake Shange's
choreopoem, when a leap from the Children's Reading Room to
(against the rules) the Adult Reading Room led a little girl to the
story of Toussaint L'Ouverture and "the beginnin uv reality" for
her (1977, p. 26). I have presented repeated reminders of what it
signifies to move from the mechanical chain of routine behaviors
to moments, as Albert Camus wrote, when "the 'why' arises and
everything begins in that weariness tinged with amazement.
'Begins'—this is important. Weariness comes at the end of the acts
of a mechanical life, but at the same time it inaugurates the
impulse of consciousness" (1955, pp. 12–13). All depends upon a
breaking free, a leap, and then a question. I would like to claim
that this is how learning happens and that the educative task is to
create situations in which the young are moved to *begin* to ask, in
all the tones of voice there are, "Why?"

Moving from an account of school restructuring to a rendering of the shapes of literacy, this narrative in the making examines
and reexamines processes of human questioning, responses to
blank spaces in experience, resistances to meaninglessness. I place
the release of imagination with which I am so deeply concerned in
context in a variety of ways while discussing an emergent curriculum, the moral life, and justice in the public space. Because so
many of us are newcomers and strangers to one another, I particularly emphasize pluralism and heterogeneity, what is now often
called multiculturalism. I choose to do so in connection with the
arts and with a community always in the making—the community
that may someday be called a democracy.

Part One

Creating Possibilities

| Seeking Contexts

Standards, assessment, outcomes, and achievement: these concepts are the currency of educational discussion today. What ought sixteen-year-olds be expected to know, whoever they are, wherever they are? How can school achievement in this country be raised to world-class levels? What is required for national primacy in this postindustrial moment? How can we socialize diverse young people into a "cultural literacy" (Hirsch, 1987) that will counter both relativism and ignorance at once? What sort of curriculum can halt what has been called the "disuniting of America" (Schlesinger, 1992) by multicultural demands?

Discourse on such questions has given rise to what is generally conceived to be contemporary educational reality. On the lower frequencies of our conversations, there is still talk of "savage inequalities" (Kozol, 1991), family deterioration, neighborhood decline, and diminishing opportunity. Racism, joblessness, addictions, and rootlessness are mentioned. But when it comes to schools, the dominant voices are still those of the officials who assume the objective worth of certain kinds of knowledge, who take for granted that the schools' main mission is to meet national economic and technical needs. Traditional notions of ways to achieve efficiency feed into claims that schools can be manipulated from without to meet predetermined goals. The implication often is that for their own benefit, teachers and their students are to comply and to serve. How can teachers intervene and say how *they* believe things ought to be? What can they do to affect restructuring? What can they do to transform their classrooms?

Interested in shifting perspectives and different modes of seeing, I find myself turning to *Confessions of Felix Krull, Confidence Man* (1955), a novel by Thomas Mann. At the start, the young Felix asks himself whether it is better to see the world small or to see it big. On the one hand, he says, great men, leaders and generals, have to see things small and from a distance, or they would never be able to deal as they do with the lives and deaths of so many living beings. To see things big, on the other hand, is "to regard the world and mankind as something great, glorious, and significant, justifying every effort to attain some modicum of esteem and fame" (pp. 12–13). To see things or people small, one chooses to see from a detached point of view, to watch behaviors from the perspective of a system, to be concerned with trends and tendencies rather than the intentionality and concreteness of everyday life. To see things or people big, one must resist viewing other human beings as mere objects or chess pieces and view them in their integrity and particularity instead. One must see from the point of view of the participant in the midst of what is happening if one is to be privy to the plans people make, the initiatives they take, the uncertainties they face.

When applied to schooling, the vision that sees things big brings us in close contact with details and with particularities that cannot be reduced to statistics or even to the measurable. There are the worn-down, crowded urban classrooms and the contrasting clean-lined spaces in the suburbs. There are the bulletin boards crammed with notices and instructions, here and there interlaced with children's drawings or an outspoken poem. There are graffiti, paper cutouts, uniformed figures in the city schools; official voices blaring in and around; sudden shimmers when artists visit; circles of young people writing in journals and attending to stories. There are family groups telling one another what happened the night before, describing losses and disappearances, reaching for one another's hands. Clattering corridors are like the backstreets of ancient cities, filled with folks speaking multiple languages, holding their bodies distinctively, watching out for allies and for friends. There are shouts, greetings, threats, the thump of rap music, gold chains, flowered leotards, multicolored hair. Now and again there are the absorbed stares of youngsters at computer screens or the clink of glass and metal in school laboratories in front of wondering, puzzled eyes. There are textbooks with all their flaws, rows of desks, occasional round tables and paperbacks from which students can choose. For the one seeing things large, there are occasionally teachers who view every act as "a new beginning, a raid on the inarticulate/With shabby equipment always deteriorating/In the general mess of imprecision of feeling, undisciplined squads of emotion" (Eliot, [1943] 1958, p. 128). But there are also other kinds of teachers: those without a sense of agency, those who impose inarticulateness on students who seem alien and whose voices the teachers prefer not to hear. Yet the eager teachers do appear and reappear—teachers who provoke learners to pose their own questions, to teach themselves, to go at their own pace, to name their worlds. Young learners have to be noticed, it is now being realized; they have to be consulted; they have to question why.

The vision that sees things small looks at schooling through the lenses of a system—a vantage point of power or existing ideologies—taking a primarily technical point of view. Most frequently these days, it uses the lenses of benevolent policy making, with the underlying conviction that changes in schools can bring about progressive social change. As I have said, this may either be linked to national economic concerns or used to mask them. Whatever the precise vantage point, seeing schooling small is preoccupied with test scores, "time on task," management procedures, ethnic and racial percentages, and accountability measures, while it screens out the faces and gestures of individuals, of actual living persons. And indeed, it seems more equitable to many of those who take a general view to do their surveys and their measurements without consciousness of names and histories. They assume that existing social interests are identified with the value of what they are doing.

How is the teacher to cope with this? How is she or he to avoid feeling like a chess piece or a cog or even an accomplice of some kind? The challenge may be to learn how to move back and forth, to comprehend the domains of policy and long-term planning while also attending to particular children, situation-specific undertakings, the unmeasurable, and the unique. Surely, at least part of the challenge is to refuse artificial separations of the school from the surrounding environment, to refuse the decontextualizations that falsify so much. As part of this refusal, teachers can be moved to take account of connections and continuities that cannot always be neatly defined. That means attending to the impact of street life in all its multiplicity, danger, and mystery. It also means being somewhat aware of students' family life in its ease and unease. It means becoming conscious of the dramas played out on the playgrounds and front stoops, in the hospital emergency rooms and clinics, and in the welfare offices and shelters and social agencies that affect the lives of the young. Police stations, churches, drugdealers' corners, shaded places in nearby parks, libraries, and always the blinking light of television screens: all these are part of the educational reality seen large.

Teachers imaginative enough to be present to the heterogeneity of social life and to what has been called the "heteroglossia," or the multiple discourses, of the everyday (Bakhtin, 1981) may also have strong impulses to open pathways towards better ways of teaching and better ways of life. As did John Dewey, they may make efforts to identify the kinds of aims that give direction to their activities and to know more clearly what they are about (Dewey, 1916, p. 119). There is a significant restructuring movement underway today that does not require teachers to choose between seeing big and seeing small; nor does it require them to identify themselves as people concerned only with conditioned behavior or only with the conscious action that signifies a new beginning. Once granted the ability to reflect upon their practice within a complex context, teachers can be expected to make their choices out of their own situations and to open themselves to descriptions of the whole.

These emerging movements leave spaces for teachers to collaborate among themselves, with parents, and with teachers' colleges of various kinds. Networks are appearing of democratic schools, resurgent progressive schools, coalition schools, and magnet schools committed to renewal (Darling-Hammond, 1992; Elmore, 1990; Sizer, 1992; Wigginton, 1972). There is a general agreement among the educators involved that, as important as "caring communities" are, something more than such communities must be created. In the proposals coming from Howard Gardner at Harvard's Project Zero, Theodore Sizer, and others, "there is evidence of a very real concern that the curriculum be knowledgebased, interdisciplinary and capable of connecting with students" (Beyer and Liston, 1992, p. 391). Care, an end to violations, connectedness, and moral commitment: these too are talked about in increasing depth (Noddings, 1992; Martin, 1992).

In this aspect of the new reform efforts, there is considerable sensitivity to grasping a total picture. There is a clear recognition that young people will require a great range of habits of mind and a great number of complex skills if they are to have any meaningful job opportunities in a day of closing doors. The capacities needed to deal with catastrophes have to be nurtured. Young people may have to deal with ecological disasters, floods, pollution, and unprecedented storms; they may have to cope some day with chemotherapy and life support decisions. Literacy in more than one medium will be required if people are to deal critically and intelligently with demagogues, call-in shows, mystifying ads, and news programs blended with varying degrees of entertainment. The ability to perform adequate planning, which takes a good deal of organizational thinking and a knowledge of how to see things small, will be needed.

Another part of the total picture, however, is that teachers are also being asked to treat their students as potential active learners who can best learn if they are faced with real tasks and if they discover models of craftsmanship and honest work. Only when teachers can engage with learners as distinctive, questioning persons—persons in the process of defining themselves—can teachers develop what are called "authentic assessment" measures (Darling-Hammond and Ancess, 1993), the kinds of measures that lead to the construction of new curricula. Refusing externally provided multiple-choice tests and being willing to see things big when they encounter students, teachers can devise the modes of teaching that are appropriate for these persons, that can launch them in diverse ways into what we now understand as inquiry. As Donald Schön has said, a reflective teacher listens to her students. "She asks herself, for example, How is he thinking about this? What is the meaning of his confusion? What is it that he already knows how to do? If she really listens to a student, she entertains ideas for action that transcend the lesson plan" (1983, p. 332). Schön writes about the new meanings given accountability, evaluation, and supervision by teachers "willing to make independent, qualitative judgments and narrative accounts of experience and performance in learning and teaching" (pp. 333–334). These are the teachers now being asked to assess students by means of portfolios and exhibitions and by asking students to account for what they are saying and thinking as they try to become different and move beyond where they are.

Any encounter with actual human beings who are trying to learn how to learn requires imagination on the part of teachers— and on the part of those they teach. When I ponder the students I have met in schools and colleges, I think of a variety of quests. There is, for example, "the search" in Walker Percy's novel *The Moviegoer,* the quest that "anyone would undertake if he were not sunk in the everydayness of his own life. . . . To become aware of the possibility of the search is to be onto something. Not to be onto something is to be in despair" (1979, p. 13). Again, it takes imagination to become aware that a search is possible, and there are analogies here to the kind of learning we want to stimulate. It takes imagination to break with ordinary classifications and come in touch with actual young people in their variously lived situations. It takes imagination on the part of the young people to perceive openings through which they can move.

In many respects, teaching and learning are matters of breaking through barriers—of expectation, of boredom, of predefinition. To teach, at least in one dimension, is to provide persons with the knacks and know-how they need in order to teach themselves. No teacher, for example, can simply lecture youngsters on playing basketball or writing poetry or experimenting with metals in a chemistry lab and expect them to meet the requirements or standards she or he had in mind for that activity. Teachers must communicate modes of proceeding, ways of complying with rules and norms, and a variety of what have been called "open capacities" (Passmore, 1980, p. 42), so that learners can put into practice in their own fashion what they need to join a game, shape a sonnet, or devise a chemical test. Passmore writes that this involves the pupil in taking steps she or he has not been taught to take, "which in some measure surprise the instructor, not in the sense that no other pupil has ever done such a thing before . . . but in the sense that the teacher has not taught his pupil to take precisely that step and his taking it does not necessarily follow as an application of a principle in which the teacher has instructed him. The pupil in other words has come to be, in respect to some exercise of some capacity, inventive" (p. 42). I think of Mary Warnock speaking of the ways in which imagination enables us to realize that there is always more in experience than we can predict (1978, p. 202). I think of her explaining how children, when they begin to feel the significance of what they perceive, "will make their own attempts to interpret this significance." And how it will be "the emotional sense of the infinity or inexhaustibleness of things which will give point to their experience, not a body of doctrine which they might extract from it, if they were doctrinally inclined" (p. 206). I think of Wallace Stevens's "man with the blue guitar," the guitar that symbolizes imagination. The guitarist speaks of throwing away "the lights, the definitions" and challenges his listeners to "say of what you see in the dark" (Stevens, [1937], 1964, p. 183). These are the listeners who have been asking him to "play things as they are," because it is disruptive to look at things as if they could be otherwise. There is tension in this looking; there is a blank resistance for a while. But then resistance, imagination, open capacities, inventiveness, and surprise are shown to be joined somehow.

To approach teaching and learning in this fashion is to be concerned with action, not behavior. Action implies the taking of initiatives; it signifies moving into a future seen from the vantage point of actor or agent. That is what those now involved in school restructuring mean when they speak of active learning. They are interested in beginnings, not in endings. They are at odds with systematizations, with prescriptions, with assessments imposed from afar. Recall Dewey describing an aim as a way of being intelligent, of giving direction to our undertakings. He knew well that there are no guarantees; he was talking, as I am attempting to do, about openings, about possibilities, about moving in quest and in pursuit.

Dewey may well have been drawn, as I am drawn, by the lure of incompleteness to be explored, the promise inherent in any quest. In *Moby Dick,* Ishmael (skeptical of all systems, all classifications) says, "I promise nothing complete; because any human thing supposed to be complete must be for that very reason infallibly faulty" (Melville, [1851] 1981, p. 135). There are always vacancies: there are always roads not taken, vistas not acknowledged. The search must be ongoing; the end can never be quite known.

The chapters to come have to do with various kinds of searching in relation to teaching and learning and with unexpected discoveries teachers might make on the way. The silences of women and the marginalized have still to be overcome in our classrooms. The invisibility of too many students has somehow to be broken through. There are geographies and landscapes still to be explored by those of us hoping that we do not all have to be strangers to each other in our schools but that we can strive to interpret our new and many-faceted world. Some lines from one of Rainer Maria Rilke's verses ([1905] 1977, p. 3), capture the power for knowing others that resides in how we choose to see things and that I will be exploring:

> There's nothing so small but I love it and choose
> to paint it gold-groundly and great
> and hold it most precious and know not whose
> soul it may liberate. . . .

My interpretations are provisional. I have partaken in the post-modern rejection of inclusive rational frameworks in which all problems, all uncertainties can be resolved. All we can do, I believe, is cultivate multiple ways of seeing and multiple dialogues in a world where nothing stays the same. All I can do is to try to provoke my readers to come together in making pathways through that world with their students, leaving thumbprints as they pass. Our "fundamental anxiety," one writer has said (Schutz, 1967, p. 247) is that we will pass through the world and leave no mark; that anxiety is what induces us to devise projects for ourselves, to live among our fellow beings and reach out to them, to interpret life from our situated standpoints, to try—over and over again—to begin. In a sense, I have written *Releasing the Imagination* to remedy that anxiety. It grants a usefulness to the disinterest of seeing things small at the same time that it opens to and validates the passion for seeing things close up and large. For this passion is the doorway for imagination; here is the possibility of looking at things as if they could be otherwise. This possibility, for me, is what restructuring might signify. Looking at things large is what might move us on to reform.

Chapter Two

Imagination, Breakthroughs, and the Unexpected

Transformations, openings, possibilities: teachers and teacher educators must keep these themes audible as "Goals 2000: The Educate America Act" is debated and as we assess the practicality of the goals associated with it. This act has now been legislated into federal law. It sets forth national goals for education, intended to be achieved in five years. Five of them are generalized and unarguable: all children must be prepared when they enter school, graduation rates from high schools will be 90 percent, all Americans will become literate, the teaching force should be well educated, and parents should be involved in children's learning. The last two are more problematic: all students in the academic disciplines should meet world-class standards and rank "first in the world in science and math achievement," and a national assessment should be created to ensure that students can demonstrate competency over "challenging subject matter." This is presented as the new national agenda for education, and the presumption is that it is realizable, poverty and inequality notwithstanding. One problem has to do with the implication that standards and tests can simply be imposed; another has to do with the so far untapped diversity among American youth today—its still undefined talents and energies, its differentiated modes of expression. The familiar paradigms seem still to be in use; the need for alternative possibilities in the face of economic and demographic changes is repressed or ignored.

This chapter concerns the ways in which we and our students might come to use imagination in a search for openings without which our lives narrow and our pathways become cul-de-sacs. I also begin to seek out ways in which the arts, in particular, can release imagination to open new perspectives, to identify alternatives. The vistas that might open, the connections that might be made, are experiential phenomena; our encounters with the world become newly informed. When they do, they offer new lenses through which to look out at and interpret the educative acts that keep human beings and their cultures alive.

In many ways, school restructuring does, indeed, mean breaking with old quantitative models; but countering this break is an anxiety that is driving people into what John Dewey called "the quest for certainty" (1929). Present-day economic uncertainty has much to do with this anxiety as does the current challenge to traditional authorities. In response to school changes, many parents yearn not merely for the predictable but also for the assurances that used to accompany children's mastery of the basics. Talk of tapping hitherto untapped possibilities and exploring unexplored alternatives serves to intensify the unease of those who want perhaps most of all to recover the simpler world of a time long past. At the same time, parents and educators are becoming more and more aware of the changes in technology and communication that are making unprecedented demands where training and education are concerned. They are told by official spokespersons that material success can only be guaranteed for those able to master a whole range of novel and unfamiliar skills. There can be, it is suggested, no turning back to the days when elementary verbal literacy alone was a basic goal in itself, anymore than there can be a return to the fabricated world of the "Dick and Jane" basal reader. The contradictions continue to multiply between what it is said the schools must do and what parents understand education to be, especially for families feeling the powerlessness of impinging poverty and change in their own lives.

There is no question but that some students face fearful obstacles due to inequities in this country. The facts of race, class, and ethnic membership need to be taken into account along with the necessity of extensive social and economic restructuring. There are, as most of us have learned, objective as well as subjective realities to be considered; we cannot simply fantasize the disappearance of joblessness, homelessness, fatherlessness, disease. It may be, however, that a general inability to conceive a better order of things can give rise to a resignation that paralyzes and prevents people from acting to bring about change. An accompanying ebbing of the sense of personal and communal efficacy may submerge people in the given, in what appears impervious to protest and discontent. To call for imaginative capacity is to work for the ability to look at things as if they could be otherwise. To ask for intensified realization is to see that each person's reality must be understood to be interpreted experience—and that the mode of interpretation depends on his or her situation and location in the world. It depends as well on the number of vantage points a person is able or enabled to take—the number of perspectives that will disclose multiple aspects of a contingent (not a self-existent) world. To tap into imagination is to become able to break with what is supposedly fixed and finished, objectively and independently real. It is to see beyond what the imaginer has called normal or "common-sensible" and to carve out new orders in experience. Doing so, a person may become freed to glimpse what might be, to form notions of what should be and what is not yet. And the same person may, at the same time, remain in touch with what presumably *is*.

Recall Wallace Stevens's "Man with the Blue Guitar" once again.

> They said, "you have a blue guitar,
> You do not play things as they are."
> The man replied, "Things as they are
> Are changed upon the blue guitar."
> And they said then, "but play, you must,"
> A tune beyond us, yet ourselves,
> A tune upon the blue guitar
> Of things exactly as they are" [(1937), 1964, p. 165].

To play upon the blue guitar is to play upon the imagination, and the sound evokes listeners' ambivalence. Many want (yet do not want) a song that celebrates the ordinary and the comfortable. After a long poetic dialogue on whether the guitarist should or should not play "the rhapsody of things as they are," he tells his audience:

> Throw away the lights, the definitions,
> And say of what you see in the dark
> That it is this or that it is that,
> But do not use the rotted names.

He calls on them to look through their own eyes, to find their own voices, to avoid the formulations devised by official others. Do you, he asks the listeners, see

> You as you are? You are yourself.
> The blue guitar surprises you [p. 183].

Others determine "exactly" what "you are" and use fixed names. To be yourself is to be in process of creating a self, an identity. If it were not a process, there would be no surprise. The surprise comes along with becoming different—consciously different as one finds ways of acting on envisaged possibility. It comes along with hearing different words and music, seeing from unaccustomed angles, realizing that the world perceived from one place is not *the* world.

Moreover, to learn and to teach, one must have an awareness of leaving something behind while reaching toward something new, and this kind of awareness must be linked to imagination. As John Dewey saw it, for example, imagination is the "gateway" through which meanings derived from past experiences find their way into the present; it is "the conscious adjustment of the new and the old" (1934, p. 272). A reflective grasp of our life stories and of our ongoing quests, that reaches beyond where we have been, depends on our ability to remember things past. It is against the backdrop of those remembered things and the funded meanings to which they gave rise, that we grasp and understand what is now going on around us. Surely, for example, a woman makes sense of the professional or the political context differently than does a man, especially if she was brought up in a time when involvement in the public world was thought unwomanly, somehow wrong for her sex. A young person trying to become a ballet dancer is affected in her or his conception of a life in dance by the way those immediately around her or him in childhood talked about such a choice as worthy or impractical, as romantic or somehow suspect. Yet there is always a gap between what we are living through in our present and what survives from our past: "Because of this gap all conscious perception involves a risk; it is a venture into the unknown, for as it assimilates the present to the past it also brings about some reconstruction of that past" (Dewey, 1934, p. 272). Most of us can recall the enclave mentality of our early lives and their odd provincialism. We were probably convinced that normal people, "nice people," lived precisely as we did, observed the same rituals, and reacted to events in the same way. It took time before we became acquainted with—and were able to accept—the enormous variety of human lives, the multiplicity of faiths and ways of believing, and the amazing diversity of customs in the world. To come to terms with such additional realities always involves a risk, one many adults are still unwilling to take and to see their children take. If those children do have the imagination to adjust to what they gradually find out about the intersubjective world as they move further and further from the views of their original home, they are bound to reinterpret their early experiences, perhaps to see the course of their lives as carrying out the possible (among numerous possibilities) rather than the necessary.

It is this kind of realization, Dewey believed, that renders experience conscious and aware of itself. Without such realization, "there is only recurrence, complete uniformity; the resulting experience is routine and mechanical." Consciousness always has an imaginative phase, and imagination, more than any other capacity, breaks through the "inertia of habit" (1934, p. 272).

When nothing intervenes to overcome such inertia, it joins with the sense of repetitiveness and uniformity to discourage active learning. New beginnings become unlikely, yet it is only in the experience of a beginning that persons feel themselves to be the initiators, the authors of what they are doing or intending to do. Hannah Arendt writes that "it is in the nature of beginning that something new is started which cannot be expected from whatever may have happened before. This character of startling unexpectedness is inherent in all beginnings" (1961, p. 169). Her words hark back to what Stevens calls surprise and Dewey a venture into the unknown. She goes on to say that the new always happens "against the overwhelming odds of statistical laws and their probability, which, for all practical, everyday purposes amounts to certainty; the new therefore always appears in the guise of a miracle," something that could not be expected. And, indeed, when we look out at it from the vantage point of our old framework, the new always appears improbable. This is because the view from a bureaucratic or any other distance makes us see in terms of trends, tendencies, and theoretically predictable events. Whenever we are shown a report or a statistical account of what is happening within a school district or the system as a whole, this becomes evident. It is as if automatic processes were at work; it seems impossible to look at things as if they could be otherwise.

When, however, a person chooses to view herself or himself in the midst of things, as beginner or learner or explorer, and has the imagination to envisage new things emerging, more and more begins to seem possible. As Emily Dickinson puts it, "The Possible's slow fuse is lit/By the Imagination" ([1914] 1960, pp. 688–689). She knew, like Dewey, Stevens, and Arendt, that imagining things being otherwise may be a first step toward acting on the belief that they can be changed. And it would appear that a kindred imaginative ability is required if the becoming different that learning involves is actually to take place. A space of freedom opens before the person moved to choose in the light of possibility; she or he feels what it signifies to be an initiator and an agent, existing among others but with the power to choose for herself or himself.

Mary Warnock, as I have mentioned, speaks in the same vein when she emphasizes the importance of our believing that there is more in our experience of the world "than can possibly meet the unreflecting eye, that our experience is significant for us, and worth the attempt to understand it" (1978, p. 202). I connect this, for example, with the women who, after years of having their understandings dismissed, are now affirming that their experience is as significant as men's. Continuing to focus on how imagination breathes life into experience, Warnock goes on to speak of our imagination's intuition that "there is always *more* to experience and *more in* what we experience than we can predict. Without some such sense, even at the quite human level of there being something which deeply absorbs our interest, human life becomes perhaps not actually futile or pointless, but experienced as if it were. It becomes, that is to say, boring." For Warnock, it is a primary purpose of education to deny people the opportunity for feeling bored or for "succumbing to a feeling of futility, or to the belief that they have come to an end of what is worth having" (pp. 202–203). For Warnock, too, it is imagination—with its capacity to both make order out of chaos and open experience to the mysterious and the strange—that moves us to go in quest, to journey where we have never been.

In my view, the classroom situation most provocative of thoughtfulness and critical consciousness is the one in which teachers and learners find themselves conducting a kind of collaborative search, each from her or his lived situation. The search might begin with a deliberate attempt to break through "the cotton wool" of "nondescript" daily life, which Virginia Woolf thought marked by repetitions and banality. Each of us characterizes daily life in a distinctive way; Woolf's way was to emphasize activities "not lived consciously": "one walks, eats, sees things, deals with what has to be done; the broken vacuum cleaner; ordering dinner; writing orders to Mabel; washing; cooking dinner; bookbinding" (1976, p. 70). She associated all these with "non-being." Another person might associate such activities with the habitual, the taken-for-granted, the unquestioned. Young people might describe their daily round in terms of stuffy, crowded bedrooms, jangling noises in the halls, lines in public agencies or clinics, overcrowded swimming pools, and libraries closed before dark. Or an unquestioned day might be perceived in the light of the shopping mall culture: fast-food counters, clothing stores, fake plants, skating rinks, video games, and MTV. The point is not to posit an immorality in non-being or to say it is wrong to live unconsciously. My argument is simply that treating the world as predefined and given, as simply *there,* is quite separate and different from applying an initiating, constructing mind or consciousness to the world. When habit swathes everything, one day follows another identical day and predictability swallows any hint of an opening possibility. Only when the given or the taken-for-granted is subject to questioning, only when we take various, sometimes unfamiliar perspectives on it, does it show itself as what it is—contingent on many interpretations, many vantage points, unified (if at all) by conformity or by unexamined common sense. Once we can see our givens as contingencies, then we may have an opportunity to posit alternative ways of living and valuing and to make choices.

Albert Camus had much the same opportunity in mind when he

wrote of what it means when "the stage sets collapse" and everything we have taken for granted about our routines suddenly becomes questionable: "one day the 'why' arises and everything begins in that weariness tinged with amazement. 'Begins'—this is important. Weariness comes at the end of a mechanical life, but at the same time it inaugurates the impulse of consciousness" (1955, p. 13). If there is to be a beginning out of weariness—and consequently active learning initiated by those choosing to learn—there has to be an interrogation. There has to be a why, and I would add, in order to investigate this why, the capacity to imagine what is not yet.

Similar in mood is Walker Percy's work *The Moviegoer.* The narrator is desperately bored and submerged in the everyday until he gets the idea of the search that "is what anyone would undertake if he were not sunk in the everydayness of his own life." As I have mentioned, he describes it as feeling "as if I had come to myself on a strange island. And what does such a castaway do? Why he pokes around the neighborhood and he doesn't miss a trick. To become aware of the possibility of the search is to be onto something. Not to be onto something is to be in despair" (1979, p. 13). To see oneself on a strange island, clearly, is to imagine oneself in another space, looking at an unfamiliar world. To poke around is to investigate that world, to pay attention to it, to think about it.

The difficult task for the teacher is to devise situations in which the young will move from the habitual and the ordinary and consciously undertake a search.

We are becoming privy these days to the stories of persons so disabled by illiteracy that they can scarcely chart their paths through the world. The stuff of life seems formless and blank to those who are, in Paulo Freire's sense, "oppressed" (1970), who have to be aroused to a consciousness of how the real is constructed and who have to be challenged to "name" their lived worlds and, through the naming, to transform those worlds (p. 78). Freire also speaks of individuals' incompleteness, "from which they move out in constant search—a search which can only be carried out in communion with others." He finds that "hopelessness is a form of silence, of denying the world and fleeing from it. . . . Hope, however, does not consist in crossing one's arms and waiting. As long as I fight, I am moved by hope; and if I fight with hope, then I can wait" (p. 80). Dialogue, that is, cannot be carried on in a climate of hopelessness. People trying to be more fully human must not only engage in critical thinking but must be able to imagine something coming of their hopes; their silence must be overcome by their search.

There are, of course, many kinds of literacy. But as an object of hope and desire, any literacy will be associated with a yearning to make some sense and to leave that thumbprint on the world as Schutz said. Imagination will always come into play when becoming literate suggests an opening of spaces, an end to submergence, a consciousness of the right to ask why. I think of Alice Walker's novel *The Color Purple* and of Miss Celie writing halting, helpless letters to God: "I am fourteen years old. I have always been a good girl. Maybe you can give me a sign letting me know what is happening to me" (1982, p. 11). There is pathos in her cry for understanding, a tragic dimension in her inability to say, "I am." Through living and through finding a sister-teacher in blues singer Shug Avery, Celie finally begins to find a language she can use (her own "sign," perhaps). She can interpret what she sees; she can interrogate; she can imagine. When Shug tells her that everything—trees, flowers, people—wants to be loved, Celie says, "Well, us talk and talk bout God, but I'm still adrift. Trying to chase that old white man out of my head. I been so busy thinking bout him I never truly notice nothing God make. Not a blade of corn (how it do that?) not the color purple (where it come from?). Not the little wildflowers. Nothing. Now that my eyes opening, I feels like a fool" (p. 179). As Celie realizes what she did *not* know or even question, Shug advises her to imagine, to "conjure up flowers, wind, water, a big rock." Such conjuring is a struggle, not just in itself but because what is imagined is still partly shaped by past oppression, and Celie reports, "Every time I conjure up a rock, I throw it." Yet by finding her imagination, she has found a way out of oppression. She is beginning to look through her own eyes, name (in her own voice) her lived world.

The point of acquiring learning skills and the rudiments of academic disciplines, the tricks of the educational trade, is so that they may contribute to our seeing and the naming. Feeling the human connection, teachers can address themselves to the thinking and judging and, yes, imagining consciousness of their students. A person's *consciousness* is the way in which he or she thrusts into the world. It is not some interiority, some realm of awareness inside the brain. Rather, it must be understood as a reaching out, an intending, a grasping of the appearances of things. Acts of various kinds are involved: perceptual, cognitive, intuitive, emotional, and, yes again, imaginative. A perceptual act, for instance, enables a person to take a perspective on aspects of things in the sounding or appearing world. By attending, listening, gazing, a perceiver structures what presents itself. As Maurice Merleau-Ponty puts it, perceiving entails a return to the "there is" underlying the abstract conception, to the "object-in-general" or "to the site, the soil of the sensible and opened world such as it is in our life and for our body" (1964, p. 160). The way things are for our life and body allows us only a partial view of things, not the kind of total view we might gain if we were godlike, looking down from the sky. But we can only know as situated beings. We see aspects of objects and people around us; we all live in the kind of incompleteness that Freire identified and there is always more for us to see.

Once again, this is where imagination enters in, as the felt possibility of looking beyond the boundary where the backyard ends or the road narrows, diminishing out of sight. For a parallel, think of the way the lanes and roadways in Constable or Chardin landscapes evoke viewers' imaginative leaps. These paths are promises about where we might reach if we tried, if we kept, for instance, moving our pencils or tapping our word processor keys. Consciousness, I suggest, is in part defined by the way it always reaches beyond itself toward a fullness and a completeness that can never be attained. If it were attained, there would be a stoppage, a petrification. There would be no need for a quest.

If teaching can be thought of as an address to others' consciousness, it may be a summons on the part of one incomplete person to other incomplete persons to reach for wholeness. It may be a challenge to pose questions, to seek out explanations, to look for reasons, to construct meanings. It may be a provoking of dialogues within the classroom space: What has to be done to find out why Haiti has been under totalitarian control for so long? What can be done over time to document the phases of the moon? What kinds of studies are required to make sense of the immigration crisis today as compared with the crisis of 1900? How can we determine the validity of first-person accounts? What can be done to grasp a personal meaning while reading a novel like *The Scarlet Letter* and to make it significant in contemporary terms? How can we learn to listen to serial music or to look at abstract painting if we were brought up in reverence for traditional forms of music and painting?

Virginia Woolf writes about having felt powerless when unable to find explanations for fearful or particularly stirring phenomena in her life. When she found a reason for something "and was thus able to deal with the sensation, I was not powerless. I was conscious, if only at a distance, that I should in time explain it" (1976, p. 72). Woolf also finds that "as one gets older one has a greater power through reason to provide an explanation; and . . . this explanation blunts the sledgehammer force" of the blows one inevitably receives in the course of one's life. Yet she also finds value in these "sudden shocks," because the "shock is at once in my case followed by the desire to explain it. I feel that I have had a blow; but it is not, as I thought as a child, simply a blow from an enemy hidden behind the cotton wool of daily life; . . . it is a token of some real thing behind appearances, and I make it real by putting it into words. It is only by putting it into words that I make it whole, and this wholeness means that it has lost its power to hurt me; it gives me . . . a great delight to put the severed parts together." Without imagination, Woolf would have been unlikely to reach out for the delight of making the things behind the blows real; she might instead have submitted, as so many do, to the force of the blows that came upon her.

Acknowledging the difficulty of moving the young to bestir themselves to create their own projects or find their own voices, I nevertheless believe, as I argue in more detail later, that we must make the arts central in school curricula because encounters with the arts have a unique power to release imagination. Stories, poems, dance performances, concerts, paintings, films, plays—all have the potential to provide remarkable pleasure for those willing to move out toward them and engage with them. But that pleasurableness does not mean the arts are to be used simply to "balance" what is thought of as the cognitively rigorous, the analytical, the rational, and the serious. Nor should the arts be used as motivation. For one thing, participatory encounters with particular works may demand as much cognitive rigor and analysis as they do affective response. For another, works of art cannot be counted upon to have beneficent, consoling, or illuminating effects. Soul-chilling instances are multiple: we can all recall *Oedipus Rex,* the Japanese film *Ran,* Toni Morrison's *Beloved,* the play *Marat/Sade.* Images of horror and distortion still emerge if we summon up memories of paintings by Zurbarán, Velázquez, Goya, Géricault, Picasso. From the instances of heartless violence in *The Iliad* to the murder of the little princes in *Richard III* to the transgressive energies of Blake's challenge to Locke and Newton (indeed to anything measurable and "moral") to modern novelist Kathy Acker's sleek obscenities, the arts have not centered on depicting solely what is right and good. Awakening imagination, they have brought our bodies into play, excited our feelings, opened what have been called the doors of perception. Yes, there have been lovely moments marked by blooming daffodils or children's laughter or the shimmer of water, and yes, there has been and will be a sense of wonder at moments of consummation, moments when the last chord finds a resolution. But the role of imagination is not to resolve, not to point the way, not to improve. It is to awaken, to disclose the ordinarily unseen, unheard, and unexpected. The arts, as Denis Donoghue says, are on the margin, "and the margin is the place for those feelings and intuitions which daily life doesn't have a place for and mostly seems to suppress. . . . With the arts, people can make a space for themselves and fill it with intimations of freedom and presence" (1983, p. 129).

If it is indeed the case that the arts occupy the margin in relation to the conformist, the respectable, the moralistic, and the constrained, and if that marginality can be affirmed, the problems raised by multiculturalism may take a different form. Even mainstream art forms may then viewed as something other than carriers of messages from men in power and norms of the majority once we go below their surfaces and act for ourselves on those intimations of freedom and presence that we find. Art from other cultures—South Indian dance, Mayan creation myths, Chippewa weaving, Balinese puppets—may be given honored places on the margin, as individuals are gradually enabled to bring this art alive in their own experience, as they are gradually freed to let imagination do its work. In time, as many of us know, these works of art may radiate through our variously lived worlds, exposing the darks and the lights, the wounds and the scars and the healed places, the empty containers and the overflowing ones, the faces ordinarily lost in the crowds.

Imagination allows us to particularize, to see and hear things in their concreteness. There are so many examples that everyone will have her or her own preferences. Here is one of mine—Denise Levertov's poem "The Gaze Salutes Lyonel Feininger While Crossing the New Jersey Wastelands" (1984, p. 8). Feininger was an artist who, among other things, was a remarkable painter of New York City bridges, anchored simultaneously in the city and the New Jersey wastelands, which were for a long time stretches of swamp, garbage dumps, and abandoned machines. In her poem, Levertov's view of the real bridge and wasteland are colored by her knowledge of Feininger's painting:

> A certain delicacy in the desolation:
> olive-green the polluted
> stretches of grass and weeds, the small
> meres and sloughs dark with the darkness
> of smoked glass,
> gray air at intervals slashed with
> rust-red uprights,
> cranes or derricks;
> and at the horizon line,
> otherwise indeterminate,
> a spidery definition of viaducts and
> arched bridges,
> pale but clear in silverpoint.

The wasteland remains a wasteland; it is not in any sense redeemed, except by the language and its occasional metaphors. Reading the poem, however, whatever our situation, we see, and most probably we feel, something new about desolation, about nature, and about human making. Levertov's words summon up other paintings of the city—Joseph Stella's, Edward Hopper's, even (going backward in time) George Bellow's, John Sloan's, Georgia O'Keeffe's. We ourselves may now look at that horizon line from different angles; we may view those uprights, viaducts, and bridges as emergent from the polluted stretches, from the green and gray, and the image may become like music or like a drama of color and line. It is imagination that draws us on, that enables us to make new connections among parts of our experience, that suggests the contingency of the reality we are envisaging. Yes, Levertov is a modern Western poet and a woman; she writes here also as a city poet, gazing at the city from a distance but possessing it nevertheless. Of those who read the poem, some will be New York City dwellers who have never seen their city from the New Jersey side; others will be workers coming exhausted into the gray air, seeing the shapes before them only as markers on the way home; still others will be dwellers in other cities, perhaps without rivers, without bridges; still others will read through the defeated eyes of desolation.

When teaching, responding to the grasping consciousness of a young student in her or his distinctiveness, we can only continually combat life's anaesthetics, moving individuals to reach out toward that horizon line. The Levertov poem, if made accessible to the young, is one that may well function as Herbert Marcuse says art often functions: it "breaks open a dimension inaccessible to other experience, a dimension in which human beings, nature, and things no longer stand under the law of the established reality principle. . . . The encounter with the truth of art happens in the estranging language and images which make perceptible, visible, and audible that which is no longer, or not yet, perceived, said, and heard in everyday life" (1977, p. 72). In contradicting the established, or the given, art reaches beyond what is established and leads those who are willing to risk transformations to the shaping of a social vision.

Of course, this does not happen automatically or even naturally. Dewey, in *Art as Experience,* talks about how important it is for people to plunge into subject matter in order to steep themselves in it, and this is probably more true of works of art than other subject matters. There must be an answering activity if we are to perceive what presents itself to us; we must reach out toward the object or the text or the performance through an act of consciousness that grasps that which is presented. In our engagements with historical texts, too, with mathematical problems, scientific inquiries, and (not incidentally) the political and social realities we have constructed along with those around us, it is never enough simply to label, categorize, or recognize certain phenomena or events. There has to be a live, aware, reflective transaction if what presents itself to consciousness is to be realized.

Dewey asked for an abandonment of "conformity to norms of conventional admiration" in approaching art; he asked that we try to avoid "confused, even if genuine emotional excitation" (1934, p. 54). The beholder, the percipient, the learner must approach from the vantage point of her or his lived situation, that is, in accord with a distinctive point of view and interest. I would suggest again, however, that it may well be the imaginative capacity that allows us also to experience empathy with different points of view, even with interests apparently at odds with ours. Imagination may be a new way of decentering ourselves, of breaking out of the confinements of privatism and self-regard into a space where we can come face to face with others and call out, "Here we are."

Chapter Three

Imagination, Community, and the School

Those of us concerned for the young and for public schools today are more aware than ever before of the difficulty of reconciling the socioeconomic demands being made of those schools with the needs of children who are striving to survive in and to make sense of a not always hospitable world. When it comes to education, we hear constantly that we do not meet "world-class standards"—a commonly used fiction vaguely understood. We are not, we are reminded, teaching in the manner required if we are to ensure this nation's technological and military primacy. What, it is insistently implied, can be more important than being "number one" in the world? (Surely not the happiness and health of children, released to find their own ways of being children and of existing in the world.) And who dare deny that revised modes of assessment, increased rigor, and altered authority structures will guarantee success for us all? Given such a preoccupation, it follows that certain children are conceived of as human resources rather than persons. Much of the time, they are spoken of as if they were raw materials to be shaped to market demand. They belong, as it were, to a constructed category: beings who are to be shaped (benevolently and efficiently) for uses others will define. But there are other categories as well: those containing children labeled "poor" or "at risk" or lacking something needed by mainstream society. They are to be set aside if they cannot be used; they are to be made invisible. As Valerie Polakow puts it, "Poverty talk is always a discourse about *them*. . . . When we turn and look at *their children,* we feel concern about this future citizenry, this growing young population 'at risk,' whom we call 'at risk' less out of outrage and compassion than because their condition threatens our security and comfort, our children, our schools, our neighborhoods, our property values" (1993, p. 43). Nothing testifies more powerfully to the erosion of what Robert Reich calls the "benevolent community" in the United States. The "instruments of benevolence," he writes, "the programs we enact and fund—have come to have less to do with aid to the poor and more to do with redistribution among the relatively comfortable majority of Americans" (1987, p. 55).

What happens to that imaginative creation, the "American dream," in the face of this? In *The Great Gatsby*, Jay Gatsby's version of the dream is both individualistic and grandiose: "He was a son of God—a phrase which, if it means anything, means just that— and he must be about His Father's Business, the service of a vast, vulgar and meretricious beauty" (Fitzgerald, [1925] 1991, p. 104). Anyone worthy of such a father would, above all things, be devoted to the notion that material wealth determined a person's worth. He would possess the piteous credulousness of a Gatsby: a belief that money would assure him of membership in the upper class, a confidence that the "green light" at the end of the dock was actually attainable (pp. 167–168). There may be another imaging, the opposite extreme: that of Tom Joad in *Grapes of Wrath*, telling his mother that when he goes off, he will "be ever'where— wherever you look. Wherever they's a fight so hungry people can eat, I'll be there. . . . I'll be in the way guys yell when they're mad an'—and I'll be in the way kids laugh when they're hungry an' they know supper's ready" (Steinbeck, 1939, p. 572). In the case of Gatsby, the dreamer is the romantic loner, immoral in every ordinary sense except for one decent moment in his life when he takes the blame off Daisy for the fatal automobile accident. In Joad's case, the dreamer is the one who "ain't got a soul of his own, but on'y a piece of a big one" (p. 572).

To imagine a democratic community accessible to the young is to summon up the vision of the "conjoint experience," shared meanings, common interests and endeavors described by John Dewey ([1927] 1954, p. 153). Interconnectedness and communion, in contrast to Gatsby's self-sufficient image of himself, characterize such a community. A continuing search for intellectual freedom and freedom of articulation, in contrast to Tom Joad's immersion in the mass, give vibrancy and energy to the *possible* community. Envisaging what might be, educators cannot but work for a certain mastery of skills and an involvement with a range of literacies for young people who will grow up to participate in the democratic community. School people stress performance outcomes today, not discrete competencies; there are expectations that all young persons over time will develop the habits of mind that may enable them to take initiatives in the learning process, to become critical and self-reflective learners and ultimately practitioners. They are challenged to become active learners, not simply passive receivers of predigested information. They are asked, with increasing frequency, to tell their stories, to pose their own questions, to be present—from their own perspectives—to the common world.

It demands imaginative action many times for teachers to realize that youngsters who see different (who have been reared in poverty or come from distant places) have something to say about the way things might be if they were otherwise. Once again today, we are confronting assertions of genetic determinism, the purported inherent inferiority of certain groups. The controversies surrounding *The Bell Curve* by Charles Murray and Richard J. Herrnstein (1994) have harped on the impropriety of using social science to argue political points of view. But in reflecting the fearsome fatalism the book arouses—the doomed prospects of poor people, suffering people, excluded people—they also reveal the great importance of imaginative thinking about alternative social arrangements and possibilities of things being otherwise.

Remembering the man-as-machine metaphors of Elmer Rice's play *The Adding Machine* or Charlie Chaplin's film *Modern Times* may cause us to grope for images similarly appropriate for this particular moment and the immediate future. Hal, the computer in *2001: A Space Odyssey*, beckons toward an information highway, with the continuing danger of our losing control of the cybernetic world. *Robocop* and *The Terminator* and even the Power Rangers suggest new automatized images of human beings, imprisoned in armor, defending against an ambiguous world. There will be enormous differences from what we have been used to; there will be instability, what some call ephemerality. There will be emphases on process, on shifts and tangents in individual lives. We will be less and less likely to rely on stable norms and presences. Yet, paradoxically, increasing numbers of people will be assigned to work-stations where automatic responses are called for, where the consciousness of agency is denied. The relatively few individuals anticipating work in the professions already recognize changes taking place in unprecedented ways. The only safe generalization that can be made is that none of the women and men emerging from our schools in the next decade should expect to lead to purely mechanical, conforming, robotic lives. They must not be resigned to thoughtlessness, passivity, or lassitude if they are to find pathways through the nettles, the swamps, the jungles of our time. Nor can they be left to the realm of separateness and privacy that makes community so difficult to achieve and alienates the fortunate from those who remain tragically in need.

Again, it may be the recovery of imagination that lessens the social paralysis we see around us and restores the sense that something can be done in the name of what is decent and humane. I am reaching toward an idea of imagination that brings an ethical concern to the fore, a concern that, again, has to do with the community that ought to be in the making and the values that give it color and significance. My attention turns back to the importance of wide-awakeness, of awareness of what it is to be in the world. I am moved to recall the existential experience shared by so many and the associated longing to overcome somnolence and apathy in order to choose, to reach beyond. Mary Warnock, among others, speaks of the moral function of imagination in this regard. Referring to Wordsworth and to Mill, Warnock writes of the importance of teaching young people to look and listen in such a fashion that "the imaginative emotion follows" (1978, p. 207). Meanings spring up all around, she reminds us, as soon as we are conscious, and it is the obligation of teachers to heighten the consciousness of whoever they teach by urging them to read and look and make their own interpretations of what they see. We must use our imagination, she writes, to apply concepts to things. "This is the way we render the world familiar and therefore manageable. At a different level, and sporadically, we may also use it to render our experience unfamiliar and mysterious. If, below the level of consciousness, our imagination is at work tidying up the chaos of sense experience, at a different level it may, as it were, untidy it again. It may suggest that there are vast, unexplored areas, huge spaces of which we may get only an occasional awe-inspiring glimpse, questions raised by experience about whose answers we can only with hesitation speculate" (pp. 207–208).

Later, I will take more heed of the promise of art experiences to open perspectives and move the young to look and listen, to overcome the taken-for-granted and the routine. But think here just for a moment about what poetry and dance can do and the magic done by painting and poetry writing. I think, for example, of John Cage's enabling us to hear sounds somehow silenced by the habitual and excluded by what we ordinarily name as music, of his offering us an instance of what it means to open up a world. And then I think again of how infrequently poor children and at-risk children are exposed to live dance performances or museum exhibitions. I think of how often, even in this day of "whole language" and "writing across the curriculum," such children are condemned to basal readers and phonics instead of being offered actual works of literature.

We must not allow the enthusiasm for and the publicity about changed methods of reading instruction to obscure the facts of exclusion and neglect. Too rarely do we have poor children in mind when we think of the way imagination enlarges experience. Focusing on remediation for these children, we overlook the ways in which imagination opens windows in the actual, discloses new perspectives, sheds a kind of light. The same "sudden shocks" of awareness that Virginia Woolf found released her from "non-being" may well awaken troubled or unhappy children to glimpses of possibility. Woolf, as we have seen, found that a shock was always followed by her "desire to explain it," and she felt she lost the powerlessness she associated with an inability to understand such things as her brother's striking out at her without reason or a family friend's suicide when she became conscious that "in time" she would be able to "explain it" (1976, pp. 70–72). And what can be more important for us than helping those called at risk overcome their powerlessness?

Imagination is as important in the lives of teachers as it is in the lives of their students, in part because teachers incapable of thinking imaginatively or of releasing students to encounter works of literature and other forms of art are probably also unable to communicate to the young what the use of imagination signifies. If it is the case that imagination feeds one's capacity to feel one's way into another's vantage point, these teachers may also be lacking in empathy. Cynthia Ozick writes of a metaphorical concentration by means of which "those [doctors] who have no pain can imagine those who suffer. Those at the center can imagine what it is to be outside. The strong can imagine the weak. Illuminated lives can imagine the dark. Poets in their twilight can imagine the borders of stellar fire. We strangers can imagine the familiar heart of strangers" (1989, p. 283). Is it not imagination that allows us to encounter the other as disclosed through the image of that other's face? And is this face not only that of the hurricane survivor or the Somalian child or the homeless woman sitting on the corner but also of the silent or the fidgety or the hopeless child in the classroom, be that child girl or boy?

Imagination can cross many lines including gender lines. The cry of "They just don't get it!" that greeted the handling of Anita Hill's testimony at the Senate confirmation hearings for Clarence Thomas's appointment to the U.S. Supreme Court, signaled that the male senators' inability to grasp what was happening was due not only to their amused indifference but was also to a failure of imagination, and this failure should be instructive for teachers. Without the ability to imagine how it was for Anita Hill, or for anyone they conceived as other, the senators showed how lack of imagination results in an incapacity to create or even participate in what might be called community. This may be the case on the part of the oppressed as much as it is on the part of the oppressor, particularly when those who suffer deprivations thrust all who appear as members of the majority into one category. Most poignant, of course, is the plight of the person of a different culture, the kind of person that the majority was so long encouraged to submerge in a category labeled "minority." Ralph Ellison's narrator in *Invisible Man* is entirely right in saying that his invisibility "occurs because of a peculiar disposition of the eyes of those with whom I come in contact. A matter of the construction of their *inner* eyes, those eyes with which they look through their physical eyes upon reality" (1952, p. 7). It must be granted that these particular inner eyes are constructed through a number of factors, some economic and social and some simply racist. But at root they are constructed by an absence of imagination—the absence of an ability to see the narrator as a living human being, a man, like all other men, at once "the paragon of animals" and "this quintessence of dust" as Hamlet tells us (II.ii.307–308). It is not only those who can look right through individuals like Ellison's narrator who are seriously afflicted; the individuals themselves, as the narrator has learned, come to doubt if they exist:

> You wonder whether you aren't simply a phantom in other people's minds. Say a figure in a nightmare which a sleeper tries with all his strength to destroy. It's when you feel like this, out of resentment, you begin to bump people back. And, let me confess, you feel that way most of the time. You ache with the need to convince yourself that you do exist in the real world, that you're a part of all the sound and anguish, and you strike out with your fists, you curse and you swear to make them recognize you. Alas, it's seldom successful [pp. 7–8].

Think of what it would mean, in our increasingly multicultural classrooms, if all teachers were enabled by Ellison's art to imagine what it signifies to be invisible and to realize that the invisible person, too, is kin to them. Think what it would mean if they remembered the effort a character in Toni Morrison's *Beloved* makes to describe how he felt about a particular woman: "She is a friend of my mind. She gather me, man. The pieces I am, she gather them and give them back to me all in the right order. It's good, you know, when you got a woman who is a friend of your mind" (1987, pp. 272–273). This is another way to imagine imagining: it is becoming a friend of someone else's mind, with the wonderful power to return to that person a sense of wholeness. Often, imagination *can* bring severed parts together, can integrate into the right order, can create wholes.

If we can link imagination to our sense of possibility and our ability to respond to other human beings, can we link it to the making of community as well? Can we encourage the ability of young persons to interpret their experiences in a world they come together to name? G. B. Madison, writing about the centrality of the imagination, says that "it is through imagination, the realm of pure possibility that we freely make ourselves to be who or what we are, that we creatively and imaginatively become who we are, while in the process preserving the freedom and possibility to be yet otherwise than what we have become and merely are" (1988, p. 191).

I believe that the kind of becoming Madison describes is in a large degree dependent on membership in a community of regard. Those who are labeled as deficient, fixed in that category as firmly as flies in amber, have little chance to feel they can be yet otherwise than what they have become. Marginalized, they are left to the experience of powerlessness unless (usually with support) they are enabled to explain their "shocks" and reach beyond.

How are we to comprehend the kind of community that offers the opportunity to be otherwise? Democracy, we realize, means a community that is always in the making. Marked by an emerging solidarity, a sharing of certain beliefs, and a dialogue about others, it must remain open to newcomers, those too long thrust aside. This can happen even in the local spaces of classrooms, particularly when students are encouraged to find their voices and their images. Hannah Arendt once wrote about the importance of diverse persons speaking to one another as "who" and not "what" they are and, in so doing, creating an "in-between" among themselves (1958, p. 182). The creation of an in-between among different people is a concept I will expand on in a later chapter, but many of us have seen an in-between arise when children inscribe ideas and feelings in journals that can be read by the other children around them or when children draw or paint delight or pain on sheets of paper and hang them up for others to see.

In thinking of community, we need to emphasize the process words: making, creating, weaving, saying, and the like. Community cannot be produced simply through rational formulation nor through edict. Like freedom, it has to be achieved by persons offered the space in which to discover what they recognize together and appreciate in common; they have to find ways to make intersubjective sense. Again, it ought to be a space infused by the kind of imaginative awareness that enables those involved to imagine alternative possibilities for their own becoming and their group's becoming. Community is not a question of which social contracts are the most reasonable for individuals to enter. It is a question of what might contribute to the pursuit of shared goods: what ways of being together, of attaining mutuality, of reaching toward some common world.

As I described in Chapter Two, people need a continuing consciousness of new beginnings if they are to avoid the sense of being fixed by someone else's categorization or inner eye, of being caught up in trends and tendencies, of behaving not acting, since acting means the taking of initiatives. Think of the Reverend Martin Luther King, Jr., addressing himself to individuals in a church, moving them in their diversity to envisage possibility—renewed possibility for them as individuals but also as members of a gathering concerned with civil rights. As they came awake to a dimension of lived life they could scarcely have predicted for themselves, they came to feel a transcendence that came from their being together in a particular way. The transcendence was often deeply personal, but through experiencing it, they came together in a revitalized community. In that sense, they were a community of *beginners,* moved to imagine what *might* be if they took action together. Numbers of them were children, despised by many in the surrounding white world. Regard, responsibility, imagination, yes, and a love for them as worthy human beings: these are what moved them beyond themselves and changed their very lives.

Moments like that in the civil rights movement, and later in movements supporting homosexuals or working on behalf of the homeless, seem to mark the need for an active reciprocity among different people before community can arise. There are instances of high school students deciding to rehabilitate old buildings for their homeless classmates, instances of assistance to people with AIDS, instances of garden-planting and tutoring: all of these "interrupt," as Arendt wrote, the "automatic processes" of the apparently banal, uneventful, or sensation-seeking ordinariness of young lives (1961, p. 169). Incarcerated for his political views and experiencing the desperate boredom and hopelessness of prison life, Vaclav Hável nevertheless expressed hope in human communality in letters to his wife. A better outlook for such communality, he wrote to her, does not lie in new programs or projects necessarily, but in "a renaissance of elementary human relationships. . . . Love, charity, sympathy, tolerance, self-control, solidarity, friendship, feelings of belonging, the acceptance of concrete responsibility for those close to one, these are, I think, expressions of the new 'interexistentiality' that alone can breathe new meaning into the social formations . . . that shape the fate of the world" (1983, p. 372). Hável recognized the need for reflectiveness and dialogue if inauthenticity or utilitarianism was to be avoided and if choices were to be made on behalf of what was life-giving. He remained (improbably) open to hope, kept alive by imaginatively partaking "in movements of youth in revolt, in genuine peace movements, in varied activities in defense of human rights . . . in short, in all the constantly recurring attempts to create authentic and meaningful communities that rebel against a world in crisis, not merely to escape from it, but to devote their full efforts—with the clear-sighted deliberation and humility that always go with genuine faith—to assume responsibility for the state of the world" (p. 372).

And responsibility for the state of the children, we should add, children whose identities are contingent on the existence of humane communities. Individual identity takes form in the contexts of relationship and dialogue; our concern must be to create the kinds of contexts that nurture—for all children—the sense of worthiness and agency. The stigma of "disabled" or "low I.Q." or "lower socioeconomic class" too frequently forces young persons to become the recipients of "treatment" or "training," sometimes from the most benevolent motives on the part of those hoping to "help." Far too seldom are such young people looked upon as beings capable of imagining, of choosing, and of acting from their own vantage points on perceived possibility. Instead, they are subjected to outside pressures, manipulations, and predictions. The supporting structures that exist are not used to sustain a sense of agency among those they shelter; instead, they legitimate treatment, remediation, control—anything but difference and release.

This is one of the reasons we should argue strenuously for the presence of the arts in classrooms. We are finding out how storytelling helps, how drawing helps; but we need to go further to create situations in which something new can be added each day to a learner's life. Postmodern thinking does not conceive the human subject as either predetermined or finally defined. It thinks of persons in process, in pursuit of themselves and, it is to be hoped, of possibilities for themselves. Some people have begun to speak of bringing to bear limited resistance to the workings of power in local spaces, rather than trying to fight against it in huge arenas. It may now be possible to consider (as we could not before) what it might signify to break the hold of some specific fixities and constructed categories, to let (as it were) specific children go. Attending concretely to these children in their difference and their connectedness, feeling called on truly to attend—to read the child's word, to look at the child's sketch—teachers may find themselves responding imaginatively and, at length, ethically to these children. To respond to those once called at risk, once carelessly marginalized, as living beings capable of choosing for themselves is, I believe, to be principled. Attending that way, we may be more likely to initiate normative communities, illuminated by principle and informed by responsibility and care.

Lending their lives, young readers expand and deepen experience, ordered on these occasions in unfamiliar ways. Through this expansion, the readers discover ordinarily unseen and unknown dimensions of their own experiences. Not only may there be a pull toward new relationships, toward community, but such readers may be moved also to new modes of self-definition, new beginnings arising from an emerging awareness of both difference and possibility. Links may be discovered between familiar reader selves and the self of Pecola or the railroad worker or the mambo player; and as imagination is set free, windows open in the actual, and all sorts of new alternatives for living become clear.

Of course, it is difficult to affirm the values of plurality and difference while working to build a community of persons who have a feeling of agency, who are ready to speak for themselves. Yet, once the distinctiveness of the many voices in a classroom is attended to, the importance of identifying shared beliefs will be heightened. Again, these beliefs can only emerge out of dialogue and regard for others in their freedom, in their possibility. Through proffering experiences of the arts and storytelling, teachers can keep seeking connection points among their personal histories and the histories of those they teach. Students can be offered more and more time for telling their stories, or dancing or singing them. Students can be provoked to imaginatively transmute some of their stories into media that can be shared in such a fashion that friends can begin looking together and moving together in a forever expanding space in their little world. Given their expanding sense of diversity, their storytelling and their joining together may be informed now and then by outrage too—outrage at injustices and reifications and violations. Not only do teachers and learners together need to tell and choose; they have to look toward untapped possibility—to light the fuse, to explore what it might mean to transform that possibility.

As teachers, we cannot predict the common world that may be in the making; nor can we finally justify one kind of community more than another. We can bring warmth into places where young persons come together, however; we can bring in the dialogues and laughter that threaten monologues and rigidity. And surely we can affirm and reaffirm the principles that center around belief in justice and freedom and respect for human rights, since without these, we cannot even call for the decency of welcoming and inclusion for everyone, no matter how at risk. Only if more and more persons in their coming together learn to incarnate such principles and choose to live and speak in accord with them, are we likely to bring a community into being. All we can do is to speak with others as passionately and eloquently as we can; all we can do is to look into each other's eyes and urge each other on to new beginnings. Our classrooms ought to be nurturing and thoughtful and just all at once; they ought to pulsate with multiple conceptions of what it is to be human and alive. They ought to resound with the voices of articulate young people in dialogues always incomplete because there is always more to be discovered and more to be said. We must want our students to achieve friendship as each one stirs to wide-awakeness, to imaginative action, and to renewed consciousness of possibility.

Chapter Four

Discovering a Pedagogy

These are what Hannah Arendt (borrowing from Brecht) once called "dark times." She meant times when the light that should arise from the public realm is "extinguished by 'credibility gaps' and 'invisible government,' by speech that does not disclose what is but sweeps it under the carpet, by exhortations, moral and otherwise, that under the pretext of upholding old truths degrade all truth to meaningless triviality" (1968, p. viii). The same conditions, she said, were described in Sartre's *Nausea,* where everything there is "exists in an opaque, meaningless thereness." And she pointed to signs of similar experiences in Heidegger's *Being and Time,* particularly when the power of "mere talk" is described, mere talk that assaults the authentic and the real (1962). What does this view of dark times signify for pedagogy in the present day? How can the authentic be secured? How can meaning be restored? How can the extinguished light be lit again so that teachers and learners can appear before one another and show, in speech and action, who they are and what they can do?

In this chapter, I begin a search for some answers with images, with some notions of what is possible, and with some cautionary words. The images are drawn from works of imaginative literature, largely because literature, unlike documentary material, resonates. That is, the words mean more than they denote, evoking in those willing to pay heed other images, memories, things desired, things lost, things never entirely grasped or understood. With these images, I want to recall to you aspects of an intersubjective world, a dangerous and endangered world about which we need to choose to teach. We have somehow to understand this world and provoke others to understand it if we are in some fashion to transform it. The first image I offer is of a "noxious cloud." This particular cloud appears in Don DeLillo's novel *White Noise* (1985), and it is invisible, created by the escape of a deadly chemical from a railroad car in an ordinary midwestern college town in the midst of normal life. Alluding to the "cloud," adolescent Heinrich comments, "The real issue is the kind of radiation that surrounds us every day. Your radio, your TV, your microwave oven, your power lines just outside the door, your radar speed-trap on the highway. For years they told us these low doses weren't dangerous" (p. 174). What do people do in relation to the nameless, the odorless, the ubiquitous? What do they do under a weight they can neither interpret nor understand? As DeLillo imagines it, they go shopping in supermarkets, hunt pills that will stave off the fear of death, or take refuge in Hitler studies in a preoccupation with what is technicized, computerized, and depersonalized. At the novel's end, we read, "And this is where we wait together, regardless of age, our carts stocked with brightly colored goods. A slowly moving line, satisfying, giving us time to glance at the tabloids in the racks. The tales of the supernatural and the extraterrestrial. The miracle vitamins, the cure for cancer, the remedies for obesity. The cults of the famous and the dead" (p. 326).

Yes, some people attempt to make sense of the cloud—literal sense, technical sense, even semiotic sense—at least in relation to popular culture. But how can one grasp a toxic cloud, described on the radio as a "feathery plume?" How does one grasp a technician's explanation that a "massive data-base tally" has determined one is dead (and that one is therefore "the sum-total" of one's data), even though this tally does not necessarily mean that anything is going to happen "to you as such, at least not today or tomorrow"? How does one integrate the constant presence of men in Mylex suits with German shepherds trained to sniff out toxic stuff hidden in the cracks? The men wear masks with hoses attached; one cannot see their faces or read their expressions or know what they know.

The thought of knowledge concealed in various ways summons up another image, that of the labyrinthine library in Umberto Eco's *Name of the Rose* (1983), a library that is part of a medieval monastery, where monks are being murdered to seal their lips, where windows and manuscripts and cryptograms and sculptures and mirrors and ordinary household objects compose a shifting reality of signs and symbols that can only be deciphered by the liberated mind. The books in the library and the knowledge they contain are possessed, controlled, and kept secret. The "hoard of learning" (p. 195) there is not to be put at others' disposal. William, an English monk ostensibly sent to solve various crimes, finds a "lust for knowledge" (p. 395) characterizing the guardians of the library labyrinths, a lust he associates it with onanism (p. 396) because the knowledge is sought for its own sake. However, we may also choose to see the monks' self-serving guardianship of knowledge as a metaphor for current mystifications. There are, most probably, no hexagonal rooms in official agencies today, no carved doorways, no stained glass renderings of sealed books and mythological monsters. But in what Jürgen Habermas calls the "distortions" of context-free communication (1971, p. 164), in the language of costs and benefits, and in the language of instrumental reason by which phenomena are "explained," there exists among many purveyors of information a deceptive if not simply indecipherable reality of signs and symbols. The knowledge they present is not knowledge for its own sake, but it is secret knowledge nonetheless and often dangerous in its implications. Those who guard it and possess it are in their own fashion lustful, and there is no way of challenging them if we do not know how to read with great awareness.

And who are "they," the anonymous ones who have established themselves in control? That question suggests another image, one I have mentioned before. When Marlow, Joseph Conrad's storyteller in *Heart of Darkness* ([1902] 1967) tells the three nameless officials—the Director of Companies, the Lawyer, and the Accountant—about "the dark places" on the earth, about what it is like to confront the wilderness, to live in the midst of the incomprehensible where "the truth is hidden—luckily," he is trying to explain what conquerors are like, to say something intelligible about the fascination of greed and brute force, "the powerless disgust, the surrender, the hate." Yet he also realizes the unlikelihood of their understanding him, and he tells them (ironically, bitterly), "mind, none of us would feel exactly like this. What saves us is efficiency— the devotion to efficiency" (p. 214). Immersed in their own roles in the power structure, frozen in natural attitudes, the three auditors are incapable of understanding what he is saying; indeed, they try to stop him at various moments as he tells of search for Kurtz, one who conquered but then stayed in his dark place. "You can't understand," cries Marlow. "How could you? With solid pavement under your feet, surrounded by kind neighbors ready to cheer you or to fall on you, stepping delicately between the butcher and the policeman." There are, Marlow says, people who are too dull to notice assaults by the "powers of darkness," or so "thunderingly exalted" as to be deaf and blind "to anything but heavenly sights and sounds." But for most of us, he asserts, "the earth is a place to live in, where we must put up with sights, with sounds, with smells, too, by Jove!—breathe dead hippo, so to speak, and not be contaminated" (p. 261).

Marlow draws attention to the living world that the attitude of his listeners (like that of the "dull" and the "exalted") obscures, but such a world, it must be clear, is not explicable in terms of cause-and-effect connections; no quantitative measurements can account for what happens. At best, it can become variously and provisionally meaningful from the perspectives of those who inhabit it. Marlow's living world is inhabited by ivory hunters; managers; riverboat pilots; black helmsmen; "native" women; a girl who believes forever in Kurtz's "greatness—his generous mind"; and Kurtz himself, who cries out, "The horror! The horror!" before he dies (p. 289). Of course, "the truth is hidden"; but there remains the possibility of meaning—and the choice need not be contaminated as we go down the rivers of our lived worlds.

Let me further apply these images—the cloud, the secret knowledge, and the desire not to know reality—to our current situation. When we "do" the human sciences—phenomenology of childhood, hermeneutics, semiotics, literary criticism—we have to relate ourselves somehow to a social world that is polluted by something invisible and odorless, overhung by a sort of motionless cloud. It is the cloud of givenness, of what is considered "natural" by those caught in the taken-for-granted, in the everydayness of things. I also think we have to hold in mind that the modern world is an administered world structured by all sorts of official languages. More often than not, they are the languages of domination, entitlement, and power; and there are terrible silences where ordinary human speech ought to be audible, silences our pedagogies ought somehow to repair. The modern world is, as well, a world where what we conceive to be our tradition is petrified, located in private enclaves, or surrounded by auras that distance it from lived experience, from the landscapes of our lives.

Too few individuals are being enabled to crack the codes, to uncover that in which they are embedded, to appropriate visions and perspectives legitimately theirs. I am sure we all believe that our efforts to understand the young and recover our own landscapes must be linked to notions of pedagogical praxis and that the pedagogies we devise ought to provoke a heightened sense of agency in those we teach, empower them to pursue their freedom and, perhaps, transform to some degree their lived worlds. We may have to reflect more deeply than we have, however, about how we can cherish the integrity of the meanings children make and the intuitions they share, while intentionally educating them—or learning along with them—to interpret and to cope with the mystified, endangered world. We have to take seriously the critiques of those who take certain radical social and political views, even as we try to break with the frames that falsify children's lives. We all want to explore and recover what have been called the secret places, but we ought also to link the secret places to public spaces, acting in the name of what Paulo Freire calls "humanization" (1970, pp. 27ff.) and what Hannah Arendt calls the "common world" (1961, p. 196).

Can we decide to act in a certain manner, choose a better order of things, and thereby bring values into being, as Sartre suggests? What is the possibility, the "different state of affairs" that we might conceive so that a "new light falls on our troubles and our suffering" and helps us "*decide* that these are unbearable." What might we begin imagining for our pedagogies, using the "education and reflection" required to move us toward what is not yet (Sartre, 1956, p. 435).

There are no specific blueprints for a better society or even a better school system. But we might well begin to shape our imagining by exploring more images from literature. As I offer these images, I ask readers to look for themselves beyond the actual, to play with untapped possibilities.

An initial image that comes to mind is the one of men, women, and children in a sunlit garden rendered by Alice Walker at the end of *The Color Purple* (1982): "Why us always have family reunion on July 4th, say Henrietta. . . . White people busy celebrating they independence from England July 4th, say Harpo, so most black folks don't have to work. Us can spend the day celebrating each other" (p. 250). Another, that I have mentioned before, comes from Ntozake Shange's *For Colored Girls Who Have Considered Suicide, When the Rainbow Is Enuf* (1977). It is the recollection of the lady in brown of the time she ran into the Adult Reading Room when she was not supposed to and "came across" Toussaint L'Ouverture, the "beginnin uv reality for me" (p. 26). The first is an image of connectedness and family love; the second, of transcendence, of a leap beyond by a child who knew that "pioneer girls & magic rabbits & big city white boys" were keeping her in an unbearable place (p. 26).

A third image is also set in a library: it is Virginia Woolf's description of looking for books by women in the library of the British Museum and then reading Trevelyan's *History of England* to find out what he said about women. When she finishes, she concludes, "Indeed, if woman had no existence save in the fiction written by men, one would imagine her a person of the utmost importance; very various; heroic and mean; splendid and sordid; infinitely beautiful and hideous in the extreme; as great as a man, some think even greater. But this is woman in fiction. In fact, as Professor Trevelyan points out, she was locked up, beaten, and flung around the room" ([1929] 1957, p. 45). Might it not have been at this moment that Virginia Woolf decided this reality was unendurable and moved on to her demand that one should have "a room of one's own"? She read; she reflected; she refused. Sartre would have said that she became educated.

The fourth and last image has to do with the reflective too and also deals more overtly with the ethical, with the refusal of someone who has indeed lived in the world to be contaminated. I have in mind Tarrou and Dr. Rieux as they take an hour out for friendship from their struggle against an epidemic of both body and mind in Albert Camus's novel *The Plague* (1948). Speaking both pragmatically and metaphorically about the reasons why people ought to keep "endless watch on themselves," Tarrou explains that no one is free from plague, and in a careless moment, anyone is likely to breathe it into someone else's face and transmit the microbe. The good man, who "hardly infects anyone," is the one who has "the fewest lapses of attention." Telling the story of his life to Rieux, Tarrou says, "You see, I'd heard such quantities of argument, which very nearly turned my head, and turned other people's heads enough to make them approve of murder; and I'd come to realize that all our troubles spring from our failure to use plain, clean-cut language. So I resolved always to speak—and to act—quite clearly, as this was the only way of setting myself on the right track. That's why I say there are pestilences and there are victims, no more than that. . . . That's why I decided to take, in every predicament, the victims' side, so as to reduce the damage done" (p. 230). Taking the "path of sympathy," he wants to be "a saint without God." Although it may not be the case that most of our troubles spring from a failure to speak clearly, choosing to link clarity to compassion in a world of doctrines and denials opens a vision of one type of possibility. When "the plague" signifies, among other things, indifference, abstractness, and complicity (approving murder, approving humiliations), vigilance is indeed required to combat it. And this may be the vigilance—and care—our pedagogies ought to release.

Before moving on from these images to a sketch of the pedagogies they suggest, I have a few cautionary words. Michel Foucault has reminded us that many of us who teach share in a widespread cultural consciousness distinctive of Western intellectuals and that we cannot help but be in some manner "agents for this system of power" (1977, p. 207). Our very idea of bearing responsibility for "consciousness" and discourse, he said, forms part of the system. Power inheres in our very language, emancipatory though it may appear to be. Look, for example, at the dissonances between what some of us hope to do in the schools in the way of teaching critical thinking and imaginative futuring and the demands of conservative community. Foucault believed that any mode of discourse is bound to raise resistances (even though many may be small ones), and when I think of resistances by fundamentalists and other conservatives (frightened and uninformed though they may be) to new pedagogies, I am thrust into perplexity. It seems evident that this resistance is something teachers and teacher educators will have to confront and take into account.

Another cautionary word has to do with the social structures that stand in the way of the free play of energies, the wide-awakeness, the authenticity, and the moral sensitivity I, at least, would like to see in our classrooms. We cannot ignore or set aside the inequities, the indecencies, and the pressures of ideology. Nor can we ignore the unequal transmitting of knowledge, the tracking of children, the demeaning of poor and immigrant people's experience, the proposing of one-dimensional reforms, all of which are functions of existing social structures and tendencies. This is not to suggest, deterministically, that our schools inevitably reflect what is happening in the culture outside. I do suggest, though, that meanings that emerge from the transactions between schools and the existing socioeconomic order tend to have more to do with channeling than with opening opportunities, with constraining than with emancipating, with prescribing than with setting persons free. I am not sanguine that teachers can resist these meanings, given the nature of bureaucracies and their administration. Nor am I comfortable with the thought of career ladders and the identification of "master teachers" in the days to come. A new taken-for-granted attitude in respect to meritocracies, hierarchies, and ladders demands new kinds of critical interpretation, new ways of questioning lived worlds, and it is difficult to predict if a human science orientation will be strong enough to withstand such an attitude.

My last cautionary word has to do with the human condition itself, with the experiences of absurdity we live through when our deepest existential questions are met with blank silences. It has to do with mortality, randomness, absences, and the emptiness of the sky. I think again of Alfred Schutz pointing to the "fundamental anxiety" that he associated with the feeling that our lives may be essentially meaningless, that we may walk across the earth and leave no sign that we have ever been alive (1967, p. 247). Yet out of such anxiety come ideas for projects and plans of action. By means of making such plans, anticipating what they involve, and acting consciously upon them, we create our identities in the situations of our lives. Specific human acts, as Sartre put it, cut across the social milieu even as they take its determinations into account; and they transform the world to a degree, not in spite of but on the basis of given conditions. Therefore, our transformative pedagogies must relate both to existing conditions and to something we are trying to bring into being, something that goes beyond a present situation. As Sartre said, this going beyond is what characterizes a person fundamentally, that and what that person succeeds in making out of what he or she has been made (1963, pp. 92–93). In some sense, this kind of action is a response to what Freud called "civilization and its discontents" (1953), for who can deny that to be "civilized" is to be to a degree "schooled"? Who can deny that to be civilized means, to a degree, giving up the simple pursuit of pleasure and repressing certain desires while sublimating others? One of teachers' shared interests ought to be in finding alternatives to templates and schemata that overwhelm primordial landscapes. Another ought to be in creating a civilization that can tolerate the potency of desire, the thrust of diverse energies, the vitality of play, and the intention to transform.

We who are teachers have to strive against limits, *consciously* strive. The alternatives are not to be found in a rediscovery of untrammelled subjectivity or in acceptance of total determinism. A dialectical relation marks every human situation: it may be the relation between individual and the environment, self and society, or living consciousness and object-world. Each such relation presupposes a mediation and a tension between the reflective and material dimensions of lived situations. Because both dimensions are equally significant, the tension cannot be overcome by a triumph of subjectivity or objectivity; the dialectic cannot be finally be resolved.

Moreover, there are always survivals from the past; there are always pressures; there is always a certain *weight* in the lived situation—a weight due to the environment, to traumas from the past, or to experience with exclusion or poverty or the impacts of ideology. We achieve freedom through confrontation with and partial surpassing of such weight or determinacy. We seek this freedom, however, only when what presses down (or conditions or limits) is perceived as an obstacle. Where oppression or exploitation or pollution or even pestilence is perceived as natural, as a given, there can be no freedom. Where people cannot name alternatives or imagine a better state of things, they are likely to remain anchored or submerged.

If we teachers are to develop a humane and liberating pedagogy, we must feel ourselves to be engaged in a dialectical relation. We are more likely to uncover or be able to interpret what we are experiencing if we can at times recapture some of our own lost spontaneity and some awareness of our own backgrounds, either through communication with children, psychotherapy, or engagement with works of art (I discuss this recapturing further in Chapter Six). Any such engagement may provoke us to recall that rationality itself is grounded in something prerational, prereflective—perhaps in a primordial, perceived landscape. When I read Wordsworth,

Melville, Elizabeth Bishop, and Toni Morrison, when I look at paintings by Cézanne and van Gogh, I am convinced that this is true. Maurice Merleau-Ponty wrote that "perception is a nascent *logos* . . . it teaches us, outside of dogmatism, the true conditions of objectivity itself . . . it summons us to the tasks of knowledge and action" (1964, p. 25). The conditions of objectivity, of course, have to do with the vantage points of the embodied consciousness, moving, seeing, touching, hearing in the midst of things. Merleau-Ponty does not reduce knowledge to sensation but tries to recover "the consciousness of rationality," by showing how rationality begins in the perspectives of situated consciousness, in the lived experiences to which the cogito always refers.

As the young move into the life of language, Merleau-Ponty believed, as they begin thematizing and symbolizing their experiences, horizons are breached; the landscape is transformed; experiences are clarified. The prereflective, that is, what we perceive before we reflect upon it, becomes the launching place of rationality. And, indeed, our presentness to ourselves depends to a large degree upon our capacity to remain in touch with the perceived world in its completeness and openness, to *think* that world while also keeping our consciousness open to the common culture our ideas cannot but express.

It seems clear, for example, that the three officials in *Heart of Darkness* are no longer capable (if they ever were) of being present to themselves in such a fashion. Nor is the contemptible Kurtz, with his talk of "My Intended, my station, my career, my ideas"; his greed for "lying fame, sham distinction . . . all the appearances of success and power" (Conrad, [1902] 1967, p. 282). Nor are those who are plague-stricken. Nor are those who think they can possess knowledge and presume it to be complete. That is why my images of possibility have so much to do with color and shape and motion; it is why they extend to renderings of connection, compassion, and care. That is why incompleteness seems so important, along with the refusal of false finalities and total *systems* of thought, of what is sometimes called "commensurability" (Rorty, 1979, pp. 315ff.).

We need only go back to children. We know that their perceiving is our initial mode of configuring the experience of external events, of orienting the self to the surround. Like imagination, which organizes the imaginary (ranging all the way from elves and unicorns to the adult world not yet seen and adventures not yet lived), their perception is the primordial operation that underlies the relation between the knowing subject and the object that is known. Such initial modes of ordering lived reality, along with the feelings associated with family and other relationships, have much to do with children's language learning and their intellectual elaboration of experience. This insight surely points to the importance of our freeing children to tell their stories, not only so that we can hear them but so that they can make meaningful the birth of their own rationality. It may remind us, too, of the importance of affirming the validity of many kinds of experience, even those that seem incompatible with our own interpretations of the world.

Radical critics speak often of the demeaning effects of atmospheres that exclude the lived lives of children who are seen as strangers or that impose overlays of information that seem to falsify what such children live and know. Indeed, we teachers are all too familiar with the feeling that many of those we believe we are teaching are simply accommodating us by imitating our languages, memorizing our terminology. Their distancing themselves is not ordinarily a resistance, although it may sometimes seem that way. It is often an expression of childhood alienation or a split in consciousness. The need to deal with such alienation is one of the many reasons why we need to try harder than we usually do to attend to these children as we develop our particular projects and struggle to move beyond. We can learn from those who have already learned to listen to children, paying heed to what they say and write. We can consciously do more to place children in speech and free writing situations in which they can find out what they think and why and what they see and how as they talk about it, write about it, and bring meaning into their worlds.

Merleau-Ponty spoke of "lived" decentering and of the gradual achievement of reciprocity within the vital order as parts of a process by which children can affect, renew, and continually restore their relations with one another and with others around them. For Merleau-Ponty, this vital order is an equilibrium attained with respect to virtual, not existing, conditions. Individuals bring virtual conditions into existence by going beyond ordinarily accepted limits in order to shape a proper milieu for themselves (Merleau-Ponty, 1967, pp. 145–146). This, it will be recalled, is what Shange's lady in brown did as a child when she moved on into the Adult Reading Room. Then, said Merleau-Ponty, individuals move

beyond the vital order to a "human order," which involves the production of new conditions and structures. He believed (as I think
most teachers do) that what defined the embodied consciousness
of the living human being was "the capacity of going beyond created structures in order to create others" ([1962] 1967, p. 175). This
has everything to do with the capacity to choose and to create varying points of view—beyond the computers and the tabloids and
the tales of extraterrestrials. It has to do with perceptual consciousness, with the emergence for the individual of a signified and
signifying world.

To recognize that things, truths, and values are constituted by
all human beings, including children, as they orient themselves to
aspects of their lived worlds, is to begin to ground what we do in
classroom. To enable children to have a signified and signifying
world is among the crucial concerns of a humane and critical pedagogy. Merleau-Ponty's idea that the *logos* has to be brought to birth
suggests to me that our students (like us when we were young),
perceiving profiles and incompleteness all around, live in a world
of constantly shifting perspectives and horizons. Imagining what it
is like where the road turns, where their fathers and mothers go in
the early mornings, what the indistinct voices are really saying, what
the darkness holds, they become gradually conscious of what it
means to make connections in experience. They become aware of
finding and sedimenting the meanings they accumulate; they find
out something about *reading* the flickering and multiform world.
And yes, since theirs is also a dialectical experience, they may feel
themselves struggling against the restraints of dependency and
given structures, against facticity itself.

Individuals' modes of understanding perceived landscapes are
not limited to remembering, imaginative engagement, and reflection
of course. As we develop our pedagogies, we ought not to exclude
what structural and semiotic approaches can tell us. Nor ought we to
overlook the kinds of thought that Hans-Georg Gadamer, for one,
expresses when he describes "the idolatry of scientific method and
of the anonymous authority of the sciences" as "the peculiar false-
hood of modern consciousness." Gadamer calls for a concern with
understanding rather than a preoccupation with method and a vin-
dication of the "noblest task of the citizen—decision-making according to one's own responsibility—instead of conceding that task to the
expert" (1975, p. 316).

This brings me back to my argument that we teachers must make an intensified effort to break through the frames of custom and to touch the consciousness of those we teach. It is an argument stemming from a concern about noxious invisible clouds and cover-ups and false consciousness and helplessness. It has to do as well with our need to empower the young to deal with the threat and fear of holocaust, to know and understand enough to make significant choices as they grow. Surely, education today must be conceived as a mode of opening the world to critical judgments by the young and to their imaginative projections and, in time, to their transformative actions. There are those among us who oppose what they see in this of an adult-centered approach, who find it hopelessly permeated with the desire for power of which Foucault spoke. They view the approach as oppressive and would sometimes choose to leave children be. Like those who appear to put their faith in the ability of the untrammelled "natural" creature to act in some ideal fashion once freed from the weight of hegemony, such thinkers seem to believe that the young will be able to constitute better and fresher worlds only out of their untaught innocence and creativity. Such views ignore the reality of the human condition and the challenges of this age of nuclear threat and of accident, torture, and inequities. We must acknowledge the fixities and corruptions of our consumer-based and technicized culture. We must take into account the languages of technology and violence, even as we do the miseducation in much that is done in schools. They are, after all, largely hierarchical, bureaucratic institutions with their own internal demands for self-perpetuation and equilibrium. By their very nature, they make it extraordinarily difficult for openings to be explored and critical thinking to take place.

But all of us know that interstices can be found in the structures; communities can be created; desires can be released. We must learn how to enable the diverse young to join the continually emergent culture's ongoing conversation. I think we in education have a particular responsibility to bring renewal to that conversation, to do what we can to include within it the voices of the long silent or unheard in this country: women's voices, newcomers' voices, Hispanic and Oriental and African and Arab and Indian voices. It may be a matter of opening work in the sciences and humanities as possibilities for individual children and young people and opening the children themselves to discoveries that lead to new perspectives on their and our common world. We are all familiar with the problem of what has been called "cultural reproduction" and what Pierre Bourdieu has called "the conversion of economic into symbolic capital" (1977, p. 196). We know the degree to which process of transmitting culture can be used to screen out and even deny the contradictions and negations associated with the economy. But that problem should spur us to work for the reappropriation of cultural forms by all the diverse students in our classes—through our emphasis on interpretive and critical approaches, through our continuing efforts to break through enclaves and make all sorts of forms accessible to new and unexpected readings. Recognizing that meanings are not simply given or unearthed but are to be variously achieved, we ought to be able to find new modes of initiating the young into "provinces of meaning" (Schutz, 1967, p. 231.) that allow for many ways of directing attention to the world. To understand how children themselves reach out for meanings, go beyond conventional limits (once the doors are ajar), seek coherence and explanations is to be better able to provoke and release rather than to impose and control.

Young persons have the capacity to construct multiple realities once they have begun to name their worlds. And that naming is a function of a growing acquaintance with conceptual networks and symbol systems characteristic of the culture's way of making sense. The young can be empowered to view themselves as conscious, reflective namers and speakers if their particular standpoints are acknowledged, if interpretive dialogues are encouraged, if interrogation is kept alive. Idiomatic understandings are always likely, but the construction cannot but be in terms of the culture to which the young belong or intend to belong. It becomes all the more important that they tap the full range of human intelligence and that as part of our pedagogy, we enable them to have a number of languages to hand and not verbal or mathematical languages alone. Some children may find articulation through imagery; others, through body movement; still others, through musical sound. Mastery of a range of languages is necessary if communication is to take place beyond small enclosures within the culture; without multiple languages, it is extremely difficult to chart the lived landscape, thematizing experience over time. Speaking with others, working with others, playing with others, and making things with others, the young may attain some reciprocity of perspectives as they try to create networks of relationships within and among themselves. I am not talking about moving them into what was once called the "house of intellect." I am not speaking of an attempt to induct them into the social system of intellectuals in a way that separates them from the lived and the shared. Even those who go on to become specialists—physicists, literary critics, anthropologists—need not lose touch with their own vantage points, their landscapes, their intersubjectively lived worlds.

Nor need they ever overlook the fact that reality must be understood as interpreted experience, and that there can be multiple perspectives and interpretations within a given context and according to acknowledged norms. Only through a recognition of this, I think, will their and often our stunned sense of domination by "white noise" be lessened and the screen of distorted communication be pulled aside. For this to happen, teachers themselves must maintain an open and interpretive approach, not merely to subject matter but to the texts of children's and young people's lives and to the meanings the young achieve as they find out how others, "across the sea or down the corridor, organize their significative world" (Geertz, 1983, p. 154). Perhaps, with this in mind, we should think of children as others who are capable of ordering and accumulating meanings. There is much to consider about "how meaning gets moved, or does not, reasonably intact from one sort of discourse to the text," about intersubjectivity and how separate individuals come or do not come to conceive "reasonably similar things," and "about how thought frames change" and "thought norms are maintained, thought models acquired" (p. 154). Meaning is for the subject. We know that. And meanings are always identified in a field. The "heteroglossia" of a culture (Bakhtin, 1981, p. 273) are cognitive meanings and commonsense meanings but also street-fair meanings, theatrical meanings, intimate meanings, folksayings, anecdotes, and the rest. Somehow teachers and inquirers might try, with the help of the young, to tap into such heteroglossia as they try to read the world through a multiplicity of consciousnesses, theirs and those they are trying to reach.

It is not enough to emancipate individuals or to enable them to disclose their lived worlds for their enlightenment and our own.

Lived worlds themselves must be open to reflection and transformation. The culture and its traditions compose part of the context—so do the languages of the present and the noxious clouds, hoarded books, and socioeconomic phenomena of the world. I hope we can ponder the opening of wider and wider spaces of dialogue, in which diverse students and teachers, empowered to speak in their own voices, reflect together as they try to bring into being an in-between. Not only may they weave what Hannah Arendt called a "web of relations" (1958, p. 184) among themselves as embodied consciousnesses. They may through their coming together constitute a newly human world, one worthy enough and responsive enough to be both durable and open to continual renewal. Of course, this has to begin in local places, in schoolrooms and schoolyards and neighborhood centers; it has to begin where people know each others' names. But it can reach beyond, toward an enlarging public space where more and more common interests are articulated. It can radiate to inform the "conversation" and to empower individuals to open themselves to what they are making in common. Once they are open, once they are informed, once they are engaged in speech and action from their many vantage points, they may be able to identify a better state of things— and go on to transform. Sometimes, I believe it is our only hope.

> And so each venture
> Is a new beginning, a raid on the inarticulate
> ·
> There is only the fight to recover what has been lost
> And found again and lost again and again; and now, under conditions
> That seem unpropitious. But perhaps neither gain nor loss.
> For us, there is only the trying [Eliot, (1943) 1958, p. 128].

Trying, yes, and the pursuit of freedom and critical understanding and a transformation (if we are lucky) of lived worlds.

Chapter Five

Social Vision
and the Dance of Life

With traditional rationality now in question, more and more people have come to view philosophy as a mode of social critique. That is, philosophy is seen as a way of posing questions about inequities and brutalities that offend against shared norms. It involves as well an unmasking of the ways in which communication is distorted by technicizing and by confusing types of inquiry useful in the social as opposed to the natural sciences. Frequently, philosophical critique takes us into examination of ideologies and their coercive effects on thinking. It may move people to consider as well how their preoccupation with artificial constructs and the "object-in-general" alienates them from lived life and connection, from values and the particularities of things. As Merleau-Ponty's essay "Eye and Mind" reminds us, it is important that we insist on what we know through our own situations and that we return to the "there is" that underlies scientific and cybernetic thinking, "to the site, the soil of the sensible and opened world such as it is in our life and for our body—not that possible body which we may legitimately think of as an information machine but that actual body I call mine, this sentinel standing quietly at the command of my words and acts. Further, associated bodies must be brought forward along with *my* body" (1964, pp. 160–161).

A similar emphasis of the grounding of perspective in lived life can be found in the work of Paulo Freire (1970). Concerned with the ways in which certain situations are perceived as hopelessly limiting and obstructive, he talked of the need to move from abstract formulations to concrete renderings of the situations in which individuals actually find themselves. When this happens, he wrote, "individuals begin to behave differently with regard to objective reality, once that reality has ceased to look like a blind alley and has taken on its true aspect: a challenge men must meet" (p. 96). What John Dewey called "the practical character of reality" is relevant here as well. Calling for a philosophy that starts afresh from the most active tendencies of its day and gives a large place to the "practical and personal," Dewey also talked about knowledge as making a difference in and to things, of knowing as "a change in reality" (1931, p. 54).

Social critique, from these points of view then, entails an ongoing effort to overcome false consciousness by rejecting an absolute and static view of reality and its resulting subject-object separation. At the same time, it involves the creation of new interpretive orders as human beings come together not only to "name" but to change or to transform their intersubjective worlds. And for all this to occur, the act of critiquing requires an authentic self-reflectiveness, a thoughtfulness that informs knowing in the many contexts of everyday life. Once open to its limitations and perspectives and to novel possibilities, this attitude of mind strains toward the normative, toward what might be, what ought to be. At that point, it becomes a search for a social vision of a more humane, more fully pluralist, more just, and more joyful community.

For those of us in education, it seems peculiarly important that both the critique and the vision of education be developed within and not outside what we conceive to be our learning community. I am sure that many of us are familiar with the belief that somehow individuals can "see" better and more clearly when they are not submerged in their own taken-for-granted conventional life. Indeed, when we take a Marxist, neo-Marxist, Freudian, Frankfurt School, or postmodern vantage point, we often feel we can recognize and resist more effectively the hegemonies, for example, of television or popular culture or evangelism or consumerism, the false promises and comforts of American society today. Acknowledging a cultural invasion of the land by those who, say, read the tabloids, listen assiduously to talk shows, or buy lottery tickets, we nonetheless feel justified in bringing, as we often think, a "higher consciousness" to those who come to us to improve their skills. We hope we enable them to widen their perspectives on their lives.

However, Michael Walzer, writing of the ways outsiders derive critical authority from their very detachment or marginality (1987, p. 37), also makes the point that certain kinds of disconnected critics press practitioners toward manipulation and compulsion. They may intervene from without in accord with standards that seem better than (or higher than) those prevailing in the society at hand; they may coerce and even demean. Some of us have learned from the late Myles Horton (of the Highlander Folk School) and the few like him how necessary it is (and how hard it is) to guard against the temptation to intervene prematurely; others of us will remember learning the same lesson from the civil rights or the welfare rights movement or from forays into activist voluntarism in the days of the War on Poverty. Thus Walzer draws attention to critics who are "already inside" a community and see no advantage in radical detachment, and he calls for "collective reflection, criticism from within" on the part of these critics (p. 64).

I like to think of this "criticism from within" taking place within a context of solidarity, a context of shared human stories within a changing human community. Recalling Henri Matisse's wonderful depiction of human solidarity and abandonment in the painting he called "Dance," I call the action of critiquing within a shared context "the dance of life." Not only does Matisse's work present an authentic human involvement with others and the natural world; it somehow draws us into the dancers' movement and suggests the vital networks in which we live or ought to live our lives. Nietzsche wrote that the value of what we read or hear depends a great deal on whether the writer or composer can walk or dance, because if he or she cannot, he or she more than likely composes under closeted conditions. We ought to dance to our own pipes, even if we move ponderously. "What does it matter that you are failures? How much is still possible! So *learn* to laugh away over yourselves! Lift up your hearts, you good dancers. . . . And do not forget good laughter" ([1883–1892] 1958, p. 407). Laughter, or the very idea of laughter, connotes what Marcuse thought of as the "claim of the biologically embodied individual to gratification and happiness" (1968, pp. 96–97); and I must say I agree that, in a defensible social vision, happiness is as important as clarity and consensus, love (as others have said) as important as logic.

The idea of being engaged in the dance of life as we examine life also sends me back to the critic Bakhtin's description of the "carnivalesque" (1981, p. 273) and the role it and its rogues and clowns play in our reality and our language and literature. Bakhtin writes, for example, about the two lives of medieval man: "one official, monolithically serious and somber; beholden to strict hierarchical order; filled with fear, dogmatism, devotion and piety; the other, of carnival and the public place, free; full of ambivalent laughter, sacrileges, profanations of all things sacred, disparagement and unseemly behavior, familiar contact with everybody and everything" (1984, pp. 129–130). It is not only that the carnival is the expression of popular culture. Just as importantly, it challenges the pompous and the authoritative; it reduces the grandiose to size; it makes holes in empty pieties. Jesse Helms, rendered aghast by a photographic exhibition, provided a recent example of what can happen when pretenses of purity and righteousness are challenged.

Obviously, I am not saying it is sufficient simply to dance or to laugh. I am saying that it seems to me important to release the kind of energy that will permit "familiar contact with everybody and anything"—custodians, caretakers, bureaucrats, managers. At the very least, such energy may lay down a ground for critique *within* the community. As I shall describe in more detail later, the value of such energy connects greatly with an argument for including the arts and humanities in our pedagogical programs, whatever our ends in view.

I have long been fascinated by the relation between philosophy and the enactments of release and experiences of emancipation. Many persons seem to have been provoked to engage on philosophical quests because they were so outraged by the thought of confinement, by the tamping down of energies, by living beings trapped and immobile in the dark. Not surprisingly, the themes of repression, confinement, or alienation have also intensely engaged writers and poets since almost the beginning of human history. Who of us cannot recall that moment in Plato's *Republic* when a prisoner released from the cave moves haltingly up the incline into the light of the sun? Or Francis Bacon as he tries arouse his readers to take heed of the "idols" that obscure their vision and distort their rational capacities? Or David Hume as he rages against sophistries and illusions? I am convinced that it was Karl Marx's inability to tolerate the sight of pallid children slaving in the dark

factory halls and his fury at the worker's sinking "to the level of a
. . . most miserable commodity" that prodded him to study political economy and, at length, philosophy. Even today, I am stirred
by the paean to the energy, yes, to the bourgeois energy that "made
everything solid melt away," that we find in *The Communist Manifesto* ([1848] 1935, p. 26), a declaration that also describes the constriction of human possibility as market values absorb energy and
as everything nonmarketable gets repressed. Recall William James
refusing fixity and determinism and affirming contingency and
what he called "a sea of possibilities" ([1897] 1912, p. 150); W.E.B.
Du Bois holding up visions of a free and intelligent civilization
([1903] 1982); Dewey, as we have seen, struggling against mere
habit, routine, deadening fixity; William Blake perceiving the existence of "mind-forg'd manacles" ([1793] 1958, p. 52), a perception that is ancestor to our realization that coercion today is not to
be found, at least for most of us, in the whips and iron doors and
bars that marked a more explicitly brutal time. We confront, rather,
a constriction of consciousness, a deformation of thinking and feeling, a distancing, and a privatism not often directly experienced as
coercive.

Multiple motivations move people into lifelong learning. Some
have to do with breaking through the limits of lived situations or,
more generally speaking, achieving greater fulfillment. No teacher
can condemn the effort to reach further, to become different, to
surpass. At the same time, we cannot but be aware of the narrowing of the public space today, the erosion of communication, the
silences in the place of dialogue. Efficiency, competence, and sal-
ability used as standards seem to have eaten away the ideal of citizenship. Indeed, as I described earlier, the demands being made
of education today have far more to do with "world-class" technical achievement than with creating a community of citizens.

It is not long since the sight of East Germans clambering fences,
of the triumph of Solidarity in Poland, of a "velvet revolution" in
Czechoslovakia fastened our attention on the intensity with which
others were pursuing democracy. They sacrificed so much and
thought the democratic utopia was worth dying for. Meanwhile, in
our own wealthy country, appalled as we often are by its inequalities and violations, many of us are becoming increasingly cynical.
We lose our hopes for what is now scornfully called liberalism. We

spend little time thinking seriously or hopefully about the traditions of democracy, of the ways in which they took root in the American experience a little more than two centuries ago. Now, even as we ponder critique, emancipatory thinking, reflective practice, and the distinctive pedagogies required for significant change, we may think too seldom about what is problematic in equality and freedom. Indeed, preoccupied as we are, and must be, with the range of important literacies students must gain, we may think too seldom about the connections in a democracy between freedom and relationship, literacy and the public dialogue, happiness and social concern.

Since the days of de Tocqueville, we have realized in this country that material success and even equality do not ensure human happiness. De Tocqueville talked about the passions of people living in democratic times and how those passions converged in a pursuit of wealth that made people increasingly like one another and imparted a fundamental monotony to their lives ([1835] 1945, pp. 48–56). Nearly a century later, Dewey wrote about the "social pathology which works powerfully against effective inquiry into social institutions and conditions. It manifests itself in a thousand ways, in querulousness, in impotent drifting, in uneasy snatching at distractions, in idealization of the long established, in a facile optimism assumed as a cloak, in riotous glorification of things 'as they are,' in intimidation of all dissenters—ways which depress and dissipate thought all the more effectually because they operate with subtle and unconscious pervasiveness" ([1927] 1954, p. 170). Individuals in this society may have only begun to understand that pathology and to develop critiques that deal with it. That is why we teachers must so emphasize the importance of persons becoming reflective enough to think about their own thinking and become conscious of their own consciousness. People must become aware of the ways they construct their realities as they live together—how they grasp the appearances of things, how and when they interrogate their lived worlds, how they acknowledge the multiple perspectives that exist for making sense of the commonsense world.

Confronted as we are with the depredations and violations of an uncaring society, we teachers know that therapeutic education is not enough. Pondering the scope of drug addiction in this country (and the absence of drug treatment centers for the poor); the fearful expansion of the AIDS epidemic; the numbers of abused babies, abandoned babies, and homeless people; the racism; the school drop-outs; and the violence—knowing this is part of the society which we inhabit—we have to find ways of creating situations in which persons will choose to engage in cooperative or collective action in order to bring about societal repairs. Perhaps we can do so in the light of norms and principles derived from whatever networks of concern currently exist or from what standards were traditionally considered to constitute a rational framework of norms: justice, regard for human rights, freedom, respect for others. These are standards that every intelligent individual in the community ought to be expected to heed, or so many of us believe.

Dewey found that democracy is an ideal in the sense that it is always reaching towards some end that can never finally be achieved. Like community itself, it has to be always in the making. For Dewey, community involves collaborative activity whose consequences are appreciated as good by the individuals who participate. The good is realized in such a way and shared by so many that people desire to maintain it. When this happens, there is community. And the clear consciousness of a communal life constitutes the idea of democracy ([1927] 1954, p. 148).

It follows that the principles of equality, justice, freedom, and so on that we associate with democracy cannot be decontextualized if they are to be significant. They have to be understood and realized within the transactions and interchanges of community life. Moreover, they have to be *chosen* by living individuals in the light of the individuals' shared life with others. Therefore, an important dimension of all education must be the intentional bringing into being of norm-governed situations, situations in which students discover what it is to experience a sense of obligation and responsibility, whether they derive that sense from their own experiences of caring and being cared for or from their intuitions and conceptions of justice and equity.

What recurring shapes does the absence of care and concern take? There are many images in American literature that suggest shapes that have recurred and continue to recur in American life. There is, for example, the overwhelming image of Melville's Captain Ahab, alone, fearfully autonomous, consumed with forcing a shipload of isolates to pursue his own manic quest, the death of the white whale who had torn off his leg. He will coerce the members of his crew by mystifying them, dangling before them whatever reward each one dreams of, muttering "Cash! Ay, cash!" ([1851] 1981, p. 216). There is Henry James's Gilbert Osmond, in *The Portrait of a Lady,* who lives in total indifference to those he considers despicable, whose fundamental concern is to be wealthy enough to live according to the empty forms of tradition, wholly above the hot struggles of the poor. His wife, Isabel, once she realizes this, associates his beliefs with mold and decay, and discovers that—for all the hopes, curiosity, and awareness of liberation she had had, he had made for her "a house of darkness, . . . of dumbness . . . a house of suffocation" ([1881] 1984, p. 478). And then there is the fearful description in *The Great Gatsby* after Gatsby has been killed: "It was all very careless and confused. They were careless people, Tom and Daisy—they smashed up things and creatures and then retreated back into their money or their vast carelessness or whatever it was that kept them together, and let other people clean up the mess they had made" (Fitzgerald, [1925] 1991, pp. 187–188).

I present these images not so much to indicate that the students we have are all so privatist and selfish and indifferent they have somehow to be redeemed. I present them to suggest that there is always a shadow side in American culture—an uncaring, separatist aspect too many associate with freedom—and I believe we must take the shadow into account when we educate and when we think of reform. The Italian novelist Ignazio Silone has thought about both this shadow side and the need for internal criticism. Examining how radical criticism often begins when people take seriously the principles taught to them by their teachers, he observes that "these principles are proclaimed to be the foundations of present-day society, but if one takes them seriously and uses them as a standard to test society as it is organized . . . today, it becomes evident that there is a radical contradiction between the two. Our society in practice ignores these principles . . . But for us they are a serious and sacred thing . . . the foundation of our inner life. The way society butchers them, using them as a mask and a tool to cheat and fool the people, fills us with anger and indignation" (1937, pp. 157–158). Once again, we are confronted with the indignation, the outrage in the face of confinement and constriction out of which so much philosophy begins, but this time we see teachers supplying part of the knowledge that lets individuals see their confinement. We should think of education as opening public spaces in which students, speaking in their own voices and acting on their own initiatives, can identify themselves and choose themselves in relation to such principles as freedom, equality, justice, and concern for others. We can hope to communicate the recognition that persons become more fully themselves and open to the world if they can be aware of themselves appearing before others, speaking in their own voices, and trying as they do so to bring into being a common world. This common world may make real those serious and sacred norms of which news seems to have reached the other side of the world. In part, it will be created by story, by giving voice to personal perspectives, listening to others' stories, seeking agreement, enlarging on it, and trying to expand the referent of what is shared.

My concern is to find out what we can do to open such spaces where persons speaking together and being together can discover what it signifies to incarnate and act upon values far too often taken for granted. We well know that defining this society in terms of the American Dream or in the light of life, liberty, and the pursuit of happiness means nothing if the people in this society do not feel called upon to act upon such ideals and so realize them. We must intensify attentiveness to the concrete world around in all its ambiguity, with its dead ends and its open possibilities. And attending, as Dewey and Freire have helped us see, is not merely contemplating. It is to come to know in ways that might bring about change. What sort of change? What is the vision? I suggest that we think in the light of "local knowledge" at first. That we have what Clifford Geertz calls "a feeling for immediacies" (1983, p. 167). That means the immediacies of our own institution; neighborhood; surrounding streets, doors, and windows; and people on the street. Beginning there, we and our students can move from the close to the distant, the particular to the general without the risk of losing ourselves in the large abstractions that are so often confused with certainties or of acquiescing in the global definitions that so often breed global crises. Where education is concerned, large-scale solutions hold little relevance for situation-specific undertakings. Local knowledge and local coming together ought to counter the tendency toward abstraction, as should a conscious concern for the particular, the everyday, the concrete. (Introducing works of literature and art into teacher education can help teachers develop this conscious concern. Literature deals with particularities, seduces persons to see and to feel, to imagine, to lend their lives to another's perspective.)

To move, then, from the particularities to wider and wider graspings is, in part, a matter of looking through more and more particularities, to discover in others' questions and visions more and more ways of transcending one-dimensional grasping. As the dialogue expands, it allows, on the one hand, for the gradual constitution of an in-between; on the other hand, it allows the gradual coming into being of a norm-governed common world. And perhaps, if that world is lived by those who experience friendship with one another, whose mode of relationship is out in the open and grounded in mutual regard, more and more people will find pleasure in looking differently at the shared world, varying perspectives while feeling their own ultimate understanding enlarged.

Of course, questions may be raised about the principles we choose to identify as those defining a democratic space. Are they objective? Are they universal? Referring back to Richard Rorty, I suggest that the best we can do is to describe the familiar procedures of justification in our society rather than reaching for some fixed truth. Like Rorty's pragmatist, I would suggest that we not seek out a theory of truth but affirm an ethical base for our accounts of the value of cooperative human inquiry. All we can do is articulate as clearly as possible what we believe and what we share (1991).

Many of us found ourselves saying after the terrible events in Tiananmen Square that such a massacre was simply not permitted in the modern world, that we believed it was categorically and objectively wrong. Yet even as we chose ourselves as the kind of people who would act on our belief of wrongness if given an opportunity, we nonetheless knew on some level that the wrongness of it was not, after all, objectively given. Certainly the aged leaders of China did not recognize what they did as wrong, anymore than their predecessors had recognized previous massacres as wrong. That sense of absolute wrongness was not unlike the way certain of us felt at the time of the death sentence handed down on Salman Rushdie, or, further back, the way some people (although certainly not all people) felt at the time of the Holocaust or later at the trial of Adolf Eichmann. Yes, it is painful not to be able to identify ourselves with some Truth or Good that rests above and beyond us. But what we can do is turn to the articulation and grounding of what we share, affirming that the roots of what we share are in a lived life and hoping, continually hoping, that the plurality can be enlarged, that more people will become willing to choose as absolute the right of human beings to act in their freedom.

Hannah Arendt, in a beautiful account of the weaving of a "web of human relationships" (1958, p. 183), describes how people's action and speech is often primarily concerned with their worldly and objective interests. These interests—the planning of a meeting, the setting up of a caring group for people with AIDS, the launching of a basic literacy program—lie between people and therefore can relate and bind them together. Most of our action and speech has to do with this kind of "in-between," and thus most words and deeds are about some worldly reality (grocery lists, car repairs, business profits and losses, university admissions, theater experiences, shared religious faith) in addition to being disclosures of the acting, speaking agents involved. Arendt says that, although this disclosure of the agent, this subjective in-between that originates when people act and speak directly to each other, is integral to the most objective intercourse, it then overgrows that objective interest. This subjective in-between is not tangible; it will not leave behind it a meeting in session, a café for the aged, an AIDS counseling center. "But for all its intangibility, this in-between is no less real than the world of things we visible have in common. We call this reality the 'web of human relationships,' indicating by the metaphor its intangible quality" (1958, p. 183).

Arendt's idea that we disclose ourselves as subjects, as unique and distinct persons when we come together, seems to me to be of the utmost importance, so important that we must find ways of integrating it into our notions of community and collaborative action. It is an essential idea too when we think of making principles, norms incarnate, and when we choose to live according to these principles and try to persuade others to do the same. Only a *subject*, after all, can choose—can decide to break from anchorage and insert himself or herself into the world with a particular kind of identity and responsibility, a particular mode of valuing what lies around and of straining toward what ought to be. The straining and the imagining ought to be part of the dance of life, part of the capacity unleashed in us when we join in or watch a dance, hear Mahler or Mozart or Stravinsky, read a poem or a novel, or listen to a story. The arts have given me many imaginative experiences that I am sure are not mine alone. One occurred in reading Toni Morrison's *Beloved,* that remarkable novel about slavery and escape from slavery and the loss of children. There is no woman who has been a mother who will not discover a quite new aspect of mothering, of mother-loving, when she reads, for example, how Baby Suggs felt having her children sold away from her.

> [He was] the last of her children, whom she barely glanced at when he was born because it wasn't worth the trouble to learn features you would never see change into adulthood anyway. Seven times she had done that: held a little foot; examined the fat fingertips with her own—fingers she never saw become the male or female hands a mother would recognize anywhere. She didn't know to this day what their permanent teeth looked like; or how they held their heads when they wailed. Did Patty lose her lisp? What color did Famous' skin finally take? Was that a cleft in Johnny's chin or just a dimple that would disappear soon's his jawbone changed? Four girls, and the last time she saw them there was no hair under their arms. Does Ardelia still love the burned bottom of bread? All seven were gone or dead [1987, p. 139].

Grasping those details in Morrison's created world, we move from the well-remembered and the deeply cherished to what would be for most of us unthinkable. We are likely to find what we have always considered natural cruelly subverted. How could any human being take responsibility for selling children, for depriving a mother of seven to whom she had given birth, and feel justified because of customs, codes, internalized images, and a taken-for-grantedness people were not willing to question? Memories of what it is like to fondle and raise little ones are likely to surge up, along with recollections of a deeply repressed dread of losing them. And this may be when outrage may flood in, authentic outrage—retroactively with regard to children sold into slavery, presently with regard to children abused or lost. We may, after the outrage and passion, also feel a longing for resolution and repair.

This is some of what can come from the presence of a subject standing in the public space—the space where visions should take shape, where at odd times and spontaneously, people feel themselves part of the dance of life.

Chapter Six

The Shapes of Childhood Recalled

We are first cast into the world as embodied beings trying to understand. From particular situated locations, we open ourselves to fields of perception. Doing so, we begin to inhabit varied and always incomplete multiverses of forms, contours, structures, colors, and shadows. We become present to them as consciousnesses in the midst of them, not as outside observers; and so we see aspects and profiles but never totalities. We reach out into the world—touching, listening, watching what presents itself to us from our prereflective landscapes, primordial landscapes. We strain toward horizons: horizons of what might be, horizons of what was. Because we have the capacity to configure what lies around us, we bring patterns and structures into existence in the landscape. Before we enter into the life of language, before we thematize and know, we have already begun to organize our lived experiences perceptually and imaginatively. We inform our encounters by means of activities later obscured by the sediments of rationality.

Clearly, we cannot return to the landscapes of those prereflective days. We can only become present to them by reflecting on them. Yet even so, if we do make the effort to reflect upon them we become far more present to our enmeshed and open-ended selves. In this context, Merleau-Ponty speaks of the "primacy of perception," that is, of giving perception a "primacy" in our lives, because "perception is our presence at the moment when things, truths, values are constituted for us." And, as mentioned earlier, he also sees perception as "a nascent *logos*: . . . it teaches us, outside all dogmatism, the true conditions of objectivity itself; . . . it summons us to the tasks of knowledge and action" (1964, p. 25). In other words, he suggests that our knowledge and our conceptualizations are grounded in what William James described as "vividness or pungency, the vital factor in reality" ([1890] 1950, p. 301).

Moreover, since perception always takes place from a particular vantage point in the lived world—since our efforts to grasp reality must, therefore, always be incomplete projects—we feel ourselves summoned to take the kinds of initiatives that relate perspectives into a more or less coherent, even if unfinished whole. It is, I am suggesting, incompleteness—the open question, perhaps—that summons us to the tasks of knowledge and action. Recall Virginia Woolf putting a "shock" into words in order to "make it whole" (1976, pp. 70–71). What seems crucial is the noticing, the active insertion of one's perception into the lived world. Only after that does a project come to be, putting an explanation into words, fighting a plague, seeking homes for the homeless, restructuring inhumane schools. To ponder this is to become convinced that much of education as we know it is an education in forgetfulness. Distracting the young from the their own perceived landscapes and shapes, we teachers insist on the givenness of predetermined explanatory frames. We loosen the connections between the young and the objects, images, articulations, and other people with which they have been enmeshed, that is, "the true conditions of objectivity itself."

I have learned from such women writers as Belenky, Clinchy, Goldberger, and Tarule (1986) that the search for narrative has indeed imparted a shape to my childhood, perhaps a kind of worthwhileness to my experience I might never have known before. In this chapter, I illustrate the notion of recalling the shapes of childhood with reference to a life story. I cannot truly say "*my* life story." That would imply that, spiderlike, I have somehow spun a web solely from the stuff of my own being, when, in fact, I cannot exclude the contexts of my gender, sibling and maternal relationships, political and professional phenomena, and even aging and decline from "my self." I am not so "individual" that I can claim to be free from the shaping influence of contexts. Nor can I forget that, conscious as I have tried to be, I have lived inside a whole variety of ideologies and discursive practices, in spite of trying—through resistance and critique—to liberate myself. When I return to my "site, the soil of [my] sensible and opened world," associated bodies must be brought forward along with my own, "the 'others' along *with* whom I haunt a single, present, and actual Being" (Merleau-Ponty, 1964, p. 168). On the original landscape where an individual is grounded, where her or his life began, there is always a sense of consciousness being opened to the common. When we are in the midst of things, we experience objects and other people's actions corporeally and concretely. And despite the distancing and symbolizing that come later, the narratives we shape out of the materials of our lived lives must somehow take account of our original landscapes if we are to be truly present to ourselves and to partake in an authentic relationship with the young. As I view it, it is on that primordial ground that we recognize each other, that ground on which we are in direct touch with things and not separated from them by the conceptual lenses of constructs and theories.

It is appropriate here to examine more closely the idea of the search, or quest, that I referred to earlier. Like Charles Taylor and others, I find the very effort to shape the materials of lived experience into narrative to be a source of meaning making. It is because we are reflecting back when we tell our stories, that we may be able to recapture the nascent *logos*—our mind just before it emerged from the perceived and vivid and began abstracting. If we cannot "but orient ourselves to the good," as we invent our narratives, "and thus determine our place relative to it and hence determine the direction of our lives," then we must also "inescapably understand our lives in narrative form, as a 'quest'" (Taylor, 1989, pp. 51–52). Seeing our lives as quests opens the way to our also seeing them in terms of process and possibilities, in terms of "a route, an experience which gradually clarifies itself, which gradually rectifies itself and proceeds by dialogue with itself and with others" (Merleau-Ponty, 1964, p. 21). I think of Frost writing, "Two roads diverged from where I stood." They disappear, you recall, in the distance; we choose one knowing that its reality is contingent on our perception at the moment, on the way the road presents itself to us. To take one road, surely, is to embark upon a quest—and, perhaps, to choose the one that seems to us "less traveled by" may (or may not) make all the difference. There is nothing objectively certain about either road. All we can say is that from the vantage point of a situated consciousness, perspectives are opening, vistas are appearing, shapes—yes, and shadows too—are making themselves visible. This is the kind of moment I hope we can keep alive, even though (as Frost reminds us) there is no "going back" ([1916] 1972, p. 51).

One of the ways of beginning the reflection that may enable us to create a narrative and to start understanding imagination in our lives is through the recovery of literary experiences that have been significant at various times in our lives. The reading of literature may nurture all kinds of understanding of lived structures of meaning, although not chronologically necessarily, not in any particular logical order. But imagination may be released through the reading, and when it is, meanings derived from previous experiences often find their way through the gateway of imagination (as Dewey saw it) to interact with present-day experiences. When aspects of the present are infused by materials originating in the past, there is always a re-viewing of the past, even as the new experience (enriched now) comes to consciousness. Always interested in the need to resist the inertia of habit that could prevent this consciousness from happening, Dewey turned to the artistic aesthetic, to what he called "art as experience." Active engagements with diverse works, active attempts to realize them as objects of experience, might, he thought, counteract the *an*aesthetic, the humdrum, the banal, the routine. When it came to the meeting of past experiences with present ones, he emphasized the ways in which the formed matter of an aesthetic experience could directly express meanings also evoked when imagination begins to work (1934, p. 272).

Everyone, of course, has her or his own association with such an experience. For me, the description in *Moby Dick* of Ishmael's depression, the suicidal sadness that made him decide to go to sea, as "a damp, drizzly November in my soul" (Melville, [1851] 1981, p. 2) recalls to me innumerable Novembers in my own past life and innumerable moments of hopelessness and melancholy, some of which feed in various ways into my present. It is not only of importance that Melville found a powerful metaphor that is recognizable to most people in the Northern Hemisphere and, yes, the Western tradition. It is also important that he found a way to release specific recollections for individuals. Some meanings released for me, for example, by that figure of speech include watergazing in New

York harbor, the pulsating sailing ships anchored there, the ocean extending to the horizon, and the sense of reaching out, reaching beyond, straining toward what is not yet. The sadnesses of the past somehow alter, as the present experience is transmuted and enlarged. The drizzly November becomes a beginning, a breaking with anchorage, a choice of quest, of what might be. Looking back, I find myself seeing past experiences in new ways—and I realize what it means to say that I have lived one possible life among many—and that there are openings even today to untapped possibilities. Recall that Jean-Paul Sartre reminded readers that, when confronted with a fiction, they have to create what is disclosed when they read—they have to give it life (1949). Ishmael's deciding is then our deciding after all; we lend him our life as we read. Cathy's passion for Heathcliff in *Wuthering Heights* is *our* passion; Joe's murderous love for Dorcas in Toni Morrison's *Jazz* is our own epiphany—we lend it its taste and flame.

Writer and reader both are responsible for the universe brought into being through the act of reading. For Sartre, that means a universe supported by the joint effort of two freedoms—the reader's and the writer's. Both are breaking with the mundane, with fixity; they are futuring, choosing them in the face of possibility. The book becomes a kind of gift, largely because it is addressed to human freedom—the capacity to move beyond what is, to create identity in the light of what might be (1949, pp. 62–63). Addressed in such a fashion, a reader—as Ronald Barthes has said—can rewrite the text of what she or he reads in the texts of her or his life. For Barthes, we can rewrite our lives as well in the light of such texts (1975, p. 62).

It is that kind of rewriting that I will do here, as an example, using some of the texts that have been important to me in the making of a narrative and the search for shapes of childhood. This is not, I want to stress, a memory game. This kind of search is intended to restore a visibility to the shapes of a primordial, perceived landscape; and I have discovered that literature (for me) has the potential of making visible what has sunk out of sight, of restoring a lost vision and a lost spontaneity. If I can make present the shapes and structures of a perceived world, even though they have been layered over with many rational meanings over time, I believe my own past will appear in altered ways and that my presently lived life—and, I would like to say, teaching—will become more grounded, more pungent, and less susceptible to logical rationalization, not to speak of rational instrumentality. I realize that recollection of literary experiences cannot but be affected by critical and other cognitive judgments (my own and others). Still, such judgments can be bracketed out, put in abeyance while we reach for the prereflective experiences that art can make accessible if we attend. And surely, even remembered literary encounters can open pathways in one's mind and experience that no other articulations can open in the same way.

An example of what I am reaching for can be found in Elizabeth Bishop's poem "In the Waiting Room." It has do with a young Elizabeth sitting in a dentist's waiting room while her Aunt Consuelo is being treated. She reads a *National Geographic* magazine and studies the photographs—embarrassing to her—of African peoples and the bare breasts of "women with necks wound round and round with wire like the necks of light bulbs." She hears her aunt's voice in a cry of pain and realizes to her surprise that she too has uttered a cry. She looks around at the people waiting with their grey knees and boots, and she thinks of the war going on (since it is February 1918) and there are night and slush and cold in Worcester, Massachusetts.

> I said to myself: three days
> and you'll be seven years old.
> I was saying it to stop
> the sensation of falling off
> the round, turning world
> into cold, blue-black space.
> But I felt: you are an *I,*
> you are an *Elizabeth* . . . [(1975) 1983, p. 159].

The value to me of my encounter with this poem is not a matter of my remembering back to a waiting room on a similar slushy day. Nor it is a matter of my tracing the origins of my fear of dentists. Instead, it is the resonance for me of that image, the shape of someone falling off or on the verge of falling off the turning world. In one dimension, it is the fear of falling; in many others, it is a shock of awareness that accompanies many falls—from Eden, from the Maypole dance, from innocence; or into chimneys, like Blake's chimney sweeper, into pits, into the void. The image has the cold bite of becoming vulnerable in an unexpectedly bitter way, as seven-year-old Elizabeth goes on to think with ambivalent fear of becoming like the adults in the room, becoming "one of them." When I read it, something comes through the gateway mediated by imagination. There may be other things trying to thrust through at the same time, but the one I can grasp now comes with the sound of lightning striking the roof in a mountain cottage and my running from leaning paperdolls against a wall with a friend to find my mother. My friend found hers rapidly and in no time took refuge in her mother's lap along with her baby brother. But my mother's lap was full because there were baby twins in my family, and I felt as if there were no place to hide, no place to be safe. I felt as if she had rejected me, thrust me into the world of grown-ups suddenly. Now, reading that poem and thinking back, the experience is enlarged. The shape of childhood of the child falling off the blue-black world begins to inform my memory of lightning crash, frail little paper dolls against a bedroom wall, my mother's arms full of babies, my clinging to the hem of her skirt, afraid and scornful at once, wanting to let go, be on my own.

And then I recall something else I have read about a different kind of falling that is also absolutely familiar to me. In *Childhood*, Nathalie Sarraute relates having to recite a poem when she was a little girl, feeling, "I've let myself in for it, I didn't dare resist when they picked me up under my arms and stood me on that chair so they could see me better." She talks about the people looking at her, waiting, and then about the affected babyish tone of voice she finds herself adopting. "I have been pushed, I have fallen, into this voice, this tone, I can't retreat, I have to advance, masquerading under this disguise of a baby." She follows the event through, thinks of it as submission, as renunciation of what she really is. Recalling that after they lift her off the chair, "of my own accord I make the little curtsey of the well-brought up, good little girl and run off to hide . . . in whose lap? . . . what was I doing there? . . . who had taken me there? . . . to the approving laughs, the amused, sympathetic exclamations, the loud clapping . . ." (1984, p. 52).

My father made me do exactly that—stand up (in my case, on the radiator cover) and recite (sometimes, to my horror, a poem I had written myself). It was, I knew, as much to show off a new dress with smocking as to show me off, to show that the investment was worthwhile. I hated it and loved it, and that is the point I see now. Among colliding shapes and images, dissonant colors, and uncertain meanings, Thomas Mann's *Tonio Kröger* returns to me; and I am not at all surprised that the image of a green wagon recurs and recurs. There is something in my memory about my father pulling me in little wooden wagon. I see him very tall against the sky, and I hear myself repressing my protest at the bumpy, dangerous ride on the hillside, wanting to please, wanting to go home. Yes, it was different in Mann's story; but the memory had a huge effect on me when I was young, and I realize now how much what the story evoked had to do with the patterns I was constructing as a child, the horizons toward which I was extending my hands.

Tonio is a writer-to-be, with a disciplined, respectable father and a black-haired mother who plays the piano and mandolin, and is totally indifferent to her son's vagaries and his school failures. He thinks: "It is true enough that I am what I am and will not and cannot alter: heedless, self-willed, with my mind on things nobody else thinks of. And so it is right they should scold and punish me and not smother things all up with kisses and music. After all, we are not gypsies living in a green wagon; we're respectable people, the family of Consul Kröger" (Mann, [1903] 1950, p. 9). Yet Tonio admires the conventional people, the solid majority, even as he knows he is different—a stranger among them. Later, he yearns after the blonde, graceful Ingeborg, while seeing himself as fated to dance only with the girl who always falls down in the quadrille. As I see the shape of that wagon now—my wagon/gypsy wagon— summon up the movement of the quadrille, realize what it is to be marginal, to look from without and to suffer, and to *want* to be without, I shape the materials of my own story dialectically. And now I realize, as I did not when this part of my story was happening, how much of it was affected by gender considerations. You are a good girl if you conform, if you hang on the hem of the skirt, if you recite for your father, if you stifle your own desire, if you accede. And you are also an unhappy girl, an unpleasant one, many would say an ugly one, because you do not look like your sister, dress like your sister. You are the stubborn Antigone rather than her gentle, ladylike sister Ismene. You are Dorothea Brooke in *Middlemarch* rather than her sweet young sister Celia. Looking back from *Antigone* now, I feel I recognize the drama somehow because of the rigid, unbending shapes marking the field opened to me and because of the flexibility of other shapes responding and flowing away and around. While Dorothea, who wanted to be Saint Theresa but, given the hindrances of the age, was foundress of nothing, makes me think back to perceptions of doorways, winding hallways, networks, textures, and someone reaching, trying to break free (Eliot, [1871–1872] 1964, p. 26). At the end of *Middlemarch,* George Eliot writes that the determining acts of Dorothea's life were not ideally beautiful but "were the mixed result of a young and noble impulse struggling amidst the conditions of an imperfect social state, in which great feelings will often take the aspect of error, and great faith the aspect of illusion" (p. 896). And my narrative, too, seems to be one of struggling for something—for expression, for a less imperfect social state—and I see it now as I read these others. I see myself moving out and then curtseying, daring to write and falling down in the dance, and wanting, yearning to be blonde like Ingeborg, outside and in the midst of life.

Then I associate to Tillie Olsen's "I Stand Here Ironing," that story of a mother forced to account for her daughter—"a child of her age, of depression, of war, of fear." She was "thin and dark and foreign-looking at a time when every little girl was supposed to look or thought she should look a chubby blonde replica of Shirley Temple" (1961, p. 15). At the end of the story, the mother says: "Let her be. So all that is in her will not bloom—but in how many does it? There is still enough left to live by. Only help her to know—help make it so there is cause for her to know—that she is more than this dress on the ironing board, helpless before the iron" (p. 21). For me, that iron becomes the very emblem of determinism—of a force, heavy and unfeeling, pressing down, flattening, silencing.

There was a time when I connected feelings and events like that with custodians, caretakers, guards, and (in time) bureaucracy, or "rule by Nobody" as Hannah Arendt says, the worst kind of dominion ever known (1972, p. 137). Later on in my life, the fearful specters of Fascism accompanied the news filtering out of Europe during and after the Second World War. There was Elie Wiesel's film *Night and Fog;* there were the recurrent images of barbed wire, boots, belts, guns, and whips. For me and many others, these were enmeshed with other images in our landscapes—authoritative faces, empty eyes, things bearing down. Words like "nobodyness" and metaphors like "invisibility" were invented by black writers like James Baldwin and Ralph Ellison to describe their existence—helpless and unseen under the iron, an iron often moved back and forth by righteous women and men. I am not suggesting that I could claim a kindred suffering, but at the same time, because of *Invisible Man* and *Native Son* and *The Bluest Eye* and *The Color Purple* and *The Women of Brewster Place* and *My Eyes Are Watching God* and *Beloved,* new meanings have fed into my own past shudderings and fears, and my present encounters with power, with force, with irrational pieties, with irons are extended somehow, and they are grounded in my lived world, my first landscapes, my "rememory." Reflecting back, I attend not only to and not first to principle. I attend to my grounded self, haunted by others around. There have been moments when Ralph Ellison's narrator's words of emerging visibility and selfhood seemed a response: "In going underground, I whipped it all except the mind, the *mind*. And the mind that has conceived a plan of living must never lose sight of the chaos against which that pattern was conceived" (1952, p. 502). It was the idea of pattern that moved me, a provisional pattern but not from nowhere, from a situated point of view. "Who knows?" the narrator asks later. "I may speak for you." No one of us can see the whole or sing the whole. Since I was a little child, I have known that all perspectives are contingent that no one's picture is complete.

The discovery that there were different kinds of breakfasts, that people saw differently even around our dining room table, that my sister with her Dutch bangs liked different music than I—and insisted that her music was absolutely the "best"—it all gave me an introduction to ways of seeing. It had something to do with my collecting words when I was young; and it had to do with my wanting desperately to find out how to put them together into stories, into poems, so that I could *show*, could make myself visible and capture the looks of things the people around me seemed never to see. Looking back, I realize that I yearned for finalities. I wanted to be among people who understood me so well (and whom I understood so well) that we could speak in a common language to one another. First, I suppose, I wanted, like the little girl in *The Member of the Wedding,* to belong and to be connected; and then, as time went on and I heard more about the war world and the worlds of suffering and separation, I wanted to be part of something linked to a cause. For a long time, I was haunted by André Malraux's novel *Man's Fate,* based on the Shanghai Revolution of 1927, when Chiang Kai-shek betrayed his Communist allies. Everything about it—from the shifting prisms through which the reader is asked to look at particular characters, to the fog on the river, to the glancing lights in the gambling rooms, to the sounds of the voices in the record shop—meshed and merged more visually for me than conceptually. Engaged, lost in the narrative, I was back in my prereflective world. At once, desires that had been accumulating to resist the pressure of the iron, to free people, and to act on what echoed in my head from Camus in *The Plague* about taking the side of the victims in times of pestilence and trying to become a healer came back when I read Malraux's novel. In the story, after the rebels' defeat, hundreds of wounded men are in a prison shed awaiting execution—they are to be thrown into the firebox of a locomotive. Kyo, the intellectual dissident, thinks about the fact that he has fought "for what in his time was charged with the deepest meaning and the greatest hope; he was dying among those with whom he would have wanted to live; he was dying, like each of these men, because he had given a meaning to his life. What would have been the value of a life for which he would not have been willing to die? It is easy to die when one does not die alone. A death saturated with this brotherly quavering, an assembly of the vanquished in which multitudes would recognize their martyrs" (1936, p. 323). Soon after Kyo's pondering, Katov, a Bolshevik existentialist, gives away the cyanide he has carried in order to be able to commit suicide in just such a situation of imminent torture. He gives it to someone who needs it more and walks to his execution through the darkness of the vast hall with the sound of breathing all around, with silent men watching him go. I know. I know. What does that have to do with the narrative of a comfortable Brooklyn adolescent—at once abhorring banality, fighting off boredom, believing nothing was intrinsically worthwhile, and confident she could speak to multitudes and lead a revolution if only she could learn enough, know enough? Grandiosity, romanticism? Of course. But even today, there is something about Kyo's monologue that expands my experience when I ponder teaching, ponder emancipation, ponder possibility in a drab, contaminated social world.

It was necessary first for me to realize, of course, that what appealed to me so was a man's, or perhaps a boy's, heroic dream and that no women were expected to become apostles of dignity like Kyo and Katov. It took me a while to realize that, although Malraux's original title was *La Condition Humaine* ("the *human* condition"), not *Man's Fate,* the novel showed *man's* fate indeed. This is just one example of how an engagement with literature can summon to visibility experiences and perceptions never noted before—significant as they must have been on that first unreflective ground. But surely, if past experiences with, for example, inferiority and sex-typing can move through the gateway of imagination, present experiences can be fed by the new recognitions and, yes, the new possibilities can become larger and more complicated.

I needed, as I got older, to struggle toward some new integrations of my perception of being alive as an American woman with my desires to commit myself to make things change and to live out that commitment. Yes, there were emergent possibilities in my world and in literature. There was Virginia Woolf refusing the idea of merging with a male society and speaking of a "society of outsiders" as she objects to signing a male manifesto in favor of disinterested culture and intellectual liberty. How disinterested can a military, male-dominated culture be, she asks? She is addressing herself, she says, to the daughters of educated men who have enough to live on "not to commit intellectual adultery." These women ought not "dream dreams about ideal worlds behind the stars" but consider facts in the actual world ([1938] 1966, p. 93). Reading this, reaching back and forward, I ask myself about the connection between the need to merge and the need to be outside. I think of marches—civil rights marches, peace marches, Norman Mailer's *Armies of the Night,* Alice Walker's *Meridian,* and my own wanting and needing to be myself, to be on my own. And then I find Woolf writing that, given typewriters and other tools, women are free to speak their minds at last and in their own fashion. Confronted by women who think that involvement with the mass, the public, will belittle them, she declares that the public "is very like us; it lives in rooms; it walks in streets; and is said moreover to be tired of sausage. Fling leaflets down basements; expose them on stalls; trundle them along streets on barrows to be sold for a penny or given away. Find out new ways of approaching 'the public'; single it into separate people instead of massing it into one monster, grown in body, feeble in mind." She charges women with the obligation to tell the truth to artists and writers who offend, to put their own opinions into practice and refuse to read or look at what is warlike, what is wrong. In time, they may break the vicious circle, "the dance round and round the mulberry tree, the poison tree of intellectual harlotry" ([1938] 1966, p. 98).

Reading that, looking both ways, I felt my notions of what I could do as a woman expanding; but I also found myself somehow excluded by what felt like a kind of elite sisterhood of "the daughters of educated men." Moreover, it did not take children very much into account—except to the extent that Woolf proposed using photographs of dead children and ruined houses rather than analysis in arguing against war. I found myself going back to Tillie Olsen and her ambivalent perspectives on childhood. I also went to Grace Paley again and was startled by a return to one of my beginnings: the idea of a fall. Paley's story about Ruth and Edie's friendship as children made me resonate in many ways. Later, when they are grown up, they have arguments about children, and they wonder how much torture they would resist if they were mothers of the very young. When Ruth's grandchild, Letty, talks about remembering and asks in vain for her aunt, she begins to "squirm out of Ruth's arms." Ruth is holding her tightly, and Letty calls, "Mommy, . . . Gramma is squeezing. But it seemed to Ruth that she'd better hold her even closer, because, though no one else seemed to notice—Letty, rosy and soft-cheeked as ever, was falling, already falling, falling out of her brand-new hammock of world-inventing words onto the hard floor of man-made time" (1986, p. 126).

The feeling of falling, the touch and the sounds of childhood, the desire to reach out from them for a being in the public world: these are arranged in my experience in a manner that has little to do with my texts' interconnections or even with their contexts in the world. In some strange way, by grasping them, by making them objects of my experience, I have imposed my own order, my own context, as I have pursued my own adventures into meaning. The narratives I have encountered in my journey have made it possible for me to conceive patterns of being as my life among others has expanded: to look through others' eyes more than I would have and to imagine being something more than I have come to be.

Part Two

Illuminations and Epiphanies

Chapter Seven

The Continuing Search for Curriculum

Since the founding of the common school, discussions of curriculum have focused on knowledge (or what would come to be called cognitive skills) and the uses of knowledge in the contexts of "real life." Inevitably, the very idea of curriculum changed in response to cultural and economic changes. The skills required for success and upward mobility became increasingly complex; and as factory or menial jobs decreased, the predicaments of poor children or immigrant children or troubled children became more and more difficult. Hard choices had to be made if the vast numbers of young people were to be treated equally. The content of curriculum could no longer remain fixed; nor could its structures. Adaptations had to be made; "top-down" teaching and supervision had to be questioned; integrated and interdisciplinary curricula had to be explored. Moreover, the ordering of knowledge, beliefs, and values that might be equated with curriculum had to be left open to the unexpected as society became increasingly technologized and the economy began shifting from the production of goods to the provision of services. How would it be possible to educate for the sake of an expanding technology and at the same time for the emergence of what Dewey called an "articulate public" ([1927] 1954, p. 184)? How would it be possible to counter the dullness and banality of many service jobs by enabling the young to find fulfillments outside of the world of work? What of curriculum as itself a search for meaning?

For most educators over the years, curriculum has had to do with cultural reproduction, the transmission of knowledge, and, at least to some degree, the life of the mind. As such, it always involved a process of enabling the young to make sense of their lived lives, to make connections, to construct meanings. Inevitably, curriculum has had to deal with ambiguities, with relationships; it has often opened the way to transformations and unexpected change. I wish to make the point in this chapter that the arts in particular can bring to curriculum inquiry visions of perspectives and untapped possibilities. I choose to make this concrete by describing the personal curriculum I found in and through the arts as I grew up and relate it to curriculum exigencies today.

I have already mentioned Wallace Stevens's man with the blue guitar who refuses to play things as they are and who asks us to destroy the "crust of shape," of fixity, and to abandon "rotted names" in favor of seeing anew through our imaginations ([1937] 1964, p. 183). As we see anew, we share perspectives offered by knowledge and understanding. Elizabeth Bishop, in "At the Fish-houses," compares knowledge with the cold water of the sea, "icily free above the stones."

> If you should dip your hand in,
> your wrist would ache immediately,
> your bones would begin to ache and your hand would burn
> as if the water were a transmutation of fire
> that feeds on stones and burns with a dark gray flame.
> If you tasted it, it would first taste bitter,
> then briny, then surely burn your tongue.
> It is like what we imagine knowledge to be:
> dark, salt, clear, moving, utterly free,
> drawn from the cold hard mouth
> of the world, derived from the rocky breasts
> forever, flowing and drawn, and since
> our knowledge is historical, flowing, and flown [(1955)
>   1983, pp. 65–66].

It struck me early in my life that the languages of imaginative literature disclosed alternative ways of being in and thinking about the world. I read not only the fairy stories, but Charles Kingsley's *Water Babies* (which I did not originally realize was the work of some-one outraged by the mistreatment of child laborers), and Kenneth Grahame's *Wind in the Willows*. Before I entered into Lewis Carroll's

Alice in Wonderland and *Through the Looking Glass,* James Barrie's *Peter Pan* was a climactic discovery for me. The metaphor of flight through an open window toward Never-Never Land gave me some hint of what imagination could do before I ever learned the word. I believe I found William Blake's *Songs of Innocence* in those days as well and began to suspect something about the ways in which organized authority and power slammed shut open windows, cast shadows on the "Ecchoing Green" ([1789] 1958).

Then, however, there was Louisa May Alcott's *Little Women,* and like countless other girls, I found a role model in Jo March. She concocted a gothic melodrama for a bleak family Christmas during the Civil War. Breaking with Victorian exemplars, she invented open spaces for herself and even a kind of swashbuckling language. She managed to do all that while remaining loyal and loving, bravely responsible for those around, as she chose herself to be reader and writer, to be someone who *demanded* to be free. More challenging, more perplexing than Jo, of course, was Nathaniel Hawthorne's Hester Prynne in *The Scarlet Letter,* to which I was introduced some time later and which I have kept rediscovering ever since. It was not so much Hester's adultery that fascinated me, or even that extravagant letter *A.* It was her emancipated thinking after she was ostracized and living on the outskirts of town. Having "habituated herself to such latitude of speculation," she looked from an "estranged point of view at human institutions, and whatever priests or legislators had established; criticizing all with hardly more reverence than the Indian would feel for the clerical band, the judicial robe, the pillory, the gallows, the fireside, or the church" ([1850] 1969, p. 217). She began also to question the condition of women in her time. "Was existence worth accepting, even to the happiest among them?" she asked herself, in the conviction that it was not and would never be (p. 184). Hawthorne, of course, made the point that her life turned from passion and feeling to thought in her terrible solitude, as if she could not be womanly and speculative at one and the same moment. It took me a while to realize that she did achieve a reconciliation when she returned to New England at the end and spent the rest of her life comforting and counseling women suffering "wounded, wasted, wronged, misplaced, or erring and sinful passion" (p. 275) and wondering who would be the prophetess of the new order to come. Slowly, I came to realize (experiencing the "bitter" taste of knowledge) that the novel presented an insoluble problem and that its author had not chosen a "side." On the one hand, there was the necessity on the part of a free, thoughtful, sexually alive woman to break with the rigid forms of theocracy and to challenge everything the elders took for granted. On the other hand, there was the importance of membership for her, even in an inhuman community. The recognition that there was no clear answer, that there could be no final resolution of the tensions involved, made me begin to understand the ways in which engagement with literature feeds into interrogation. Reading, working to achieve works of fiction as meaningful within my own experience, I found that the questions remained forever open. I could never, never be sure.

The "as if," that is, my imaginative vision, launched me then— and continues to launch me—on quests I hope will never cease. I am constantly reminded of two works I have mentioned before: Walker Percy's *Moviegoer,* in which the narrator discovers that to be without awareness of "the possibility of the search" is to be "in despair" (1979, p. 13); and Mary Warnock's argument that "it is the main purpose of education to give people the opportunity of not ever being . . . bored," in the sense "of not ever succumbing to . . . the belief that they have come to an end of what is worth having" (1978, p. 203). The despair Walker Percy's narrator talks about is surely linked to this feeling of boredom and futility. The search takes away the opportunity for boredom by instilling a consciousness of what is not yet, of what might, unpredictably, still be experienced.

Percy's narrator also sees himself as a new "castaway" poking around his "strange island." And that image of being a stranger is one that also suggests how imagination is aroused. Becoming aware of the ways in which particular works of literature defamiliarized my experience, I came to see that the taking of odd or unaccustomed perspectives can indeed make a person a stranger and able to "see" as never before. I think of the voyages of Ishmael in Herman Melville's *Moby Dick* and of Marlow in Conrad's *Heart of Darkness* and of how they enabled me to select out certain aspects of my existence I felt but could not name. To confront "the whiteness of the whale" in *Moby Dick* (Melville, [1851] 1981) was to be able to identify a number of figures against the ground of my lived life. What, after all, do I have in common with someone who, having felt a "damp, drizzly November" in his "soul" (p. 2), decides to go to sea as a sailor? And what in common with someone who links whiteness with "a dumb blankness, full of meaning—a colorless, all-color of atheism from which we shrink" (p. 198)? What do I have in common with someone who has lived in the midst of the "incomprehensible" and the barbaric yet is moved to say sardonically to his interlocutors that they are saved from this by "the devotion to efficiency" (Conrad, [1902] 1967, p. 214)? And what in common with that same man as he explains how he had to look out on his voyage into darkness for dead wood in the river that might have ripped apart his steamboat, how "when you have to attend to things of that sort, to the mere incidents of the surface, the reality—the reality—I tell you—fades. The inner truth is hidden—luckily, luckily. But I felt it all the same; I felt often its mysterious stillness watching me at my monkey tricks, just as it watches you fellows performing on your respective tightropes for—what is it? half-a-crown a tumble" (pp. 244–245). Male views or not, they made me *see* in the sense Conrad explained when he wrote, in a preface that is now famous, that it is the writer's task "by the power of the written word to make you hear, to make you feel—it is, before all, to make you see. That—and no more, and it is everything. If I succeed, you shall find there according to your deserts: encouragement, consolation, fear, charm—all you demand—and, perhaps, also that glimpse of truth for which you have forgotten to ask." Moreover, the writer may also convey a vision "that might awaken in the hearts of the beholders that feeling of unavoidable solidarity; of the solidarity in mysterious origin, in toil, in joy, in hope, in uncertain fate," which binds human beings to one another and "to the visible world" ([1898] 1967, pp. ix–x).

I think that fictions like these revealed to me my stake in the human condition, helping me reach the ground of my being—which is also the ground of learning, of reaching beyond where one is. It took some time for me to confront what it signified that as a woman I was excluded, on some level, from the steamboats and sailing ships I imagined myself aboard. It took the perceptions gained from Charlotte Perkins Gilman in "The Yellow Wallpaper," Kate Chopin in *The Awakening*, and Virginia Woolf in *Three Guineas* and *A Room of One's Own* to move me into concrete confrontations with exclusion, indifference, and contempt. I needed that mad vision of the women creeping out of the wallpaper in Gilman's work as I needed my own indignation at Edna's shortsightedness in *The Awakening* and my ambivalent indignation at her suicide. I, after all, was lending these people my life; I was, through my reading, allowing them to emerge in my consciousness and, by so doing, to transform it, as social scientific accounts or even psychological ones would never do. Tillie Olsen came later and Maya Angelou and Marge Peircy and Margaret Atwood and Toni Morrison; and I began, for the first time, seeing through many women's diverse eyes.

I wanted to see through as many eyes and from as many angles as possible, and for a long time, I believe I deliberately sought visions that might enable me to look from the other side of the looking glass, to begin to feel those "multiple realities" or "provinces of meaning" that mark lived experience in the world and to learn that "it is the meaning of our experiences and not the ontological structure of the objects which constitutes reality" (Schutz, 1967, p. 231). We have begun only recently to recognize the constriction of our interpretations due to gender and ethnic exclusions, to our denial of the dialogical "heteroglossia" that deepens "as long as language is alive and developing" and that is more evident in literature than anywhere else (Bakhtin, 1981, p. 272). To hear the languages of *The Brothers Karamazov,* the indeterminacies, the openness, is to break with "the hegemony of language over the perception and conceptualization of reality" (p. 369) and open the way to all kinds of changes. To read William Faulkner's *Sound and the Fury* and to move from Benjy's idiot voice to the voices of Candace, Jason, Quentin, or Dilsey is to recognize the inconceivability of a stable "objective" world. Benjy loves three things "the pasture, . . . his sister Candace, firelight" (1946, p. 19) and largely in their absence. Yet his interpretation too, like the interpretations of those who laugh and take a "carnivalesque" view (Bakhtin, 1981, p. 273), must be taken into account as what is called reality is variously achieved.

Ralph Ellison shocked me into a new awareness of this when I read *Invisible Man.* Yet, I saw before very long that the "construction of [people's] *inner* eyes" that rendered the narrator invisible was a function of and a response to a racist society and that an education for reflectiveness might play a part in altering such "a peculiar disposition of the eyes" (1952, p. 7). This alteration cannot be achieved by emphasizing categories, abstract formulations, or prescriptions of any kind. The particularities of the world revealed by Ellison—public arenas, offices, bars, tenement stoops, Sambo dolls, light bulbs, paint cans, an oily piece of filed steel (with "a heap of signifying wrapped up in it," p. 336), a manhole cover, the arch of a bridge, an underground room—offer the reader a context in which interpretations can be made and significations read as they cannot be read in contextless abstractions.

"Ambiguous and unpredictable, details undermine ideology," declared the writer of *The New Yorker*'s "Talk of the Town" column (1989):

> They are connective. They hook your interest in a way that ideas never can. If you let in the details of some aspect of life, you almost have to allow that aspect to be what it really is rather than what you want or need it to be. And yet details are also mysteriously universal. If fiction is news, it's largely news about the details of other lives, but if fiction has a vital interest for people, it's because in those details they somehow get news of themselves. The readiness to be interested in the details of lives unlike one's own is a profound measure of trust. Resisting details is usually an expression of xenophobia, of some insecurity of shyness, of a need to keep safely to oneself.

Without some knowledge of connective details, it is extraordinarily difficult to overcome abstraction in dealing with other people. A fearful oversimplification takes over: in the blankness, we see only "Russia," "student movement," "ethnic minorities." We are likely to chart things in terms of good/bad, white/black, either/or. We become pawns in a Manichaean allegory of good and evil. Primo Levi, the late chronicler of Holocaust experiences, once reminded us that popular history and the history taught in schools are influenced by this Manichaean tendency "which shuns half-tints and complexities; it is prone to reduce the river of human occurrences to conflicts, and the conflicts to duels—we and they, . . . winners and losers, . . . the good guys and the bad guys, respectively, because the good must prevail, otherwise the world would be subverted" (1988, pp. 36–37). For Levi, it is altogether important for people to realize that no person exists in an entirely different zone of ethics than the people responsible for the Holocaust or any other violation of humankind. To think otherwise is to impose a false clarity on history by ridding ourselves of ambiguities and paradoxes. Yet this is what is done, more often than not, when the past is unrolled for children to see. Our forebears emerge as untainted by greed or the lust for power; our victorious generals appear untouched by battlefield brutality, by suffering or betrayal; our democratic representatives appear untarnished by prejudice or deceit. "We" (those on "our side") are good in a manner that is unqualified; "they" are evil in the total void of good.

Whether Shakespeare's Lear, George Eliot's Dorothea Brooke, or Henry James's Isabel Archer, no figure in serious imaginative literature is free from "half-tints and complexities"; each has a multiplicity of voices contesting within; each, even those at Lear's advanced age, is in the making. Literature, therefore, always has the potential to subvert dualism and reductionism, to make abstract generalizations questionable. Moreover, it has the capacity continually to frustrate readers' expectation of some final harmony or coherence. Wolfgang Iser, in *The Act of Reading,* speaks of the ways in which people cling to classic paradigms where reading is concerned: they seek out hidden meanings; they yearn for revelations of a symmetrical, unified, complete totality (1980, pp. 13–15). At the same time, they recognize that the traditional paradigms no longer hold and that we can no longer posit an objective system to which our ideas and fictions ought to "correspond."

When Iser and other exponents of "reader reception" theory speak of the aesthetic experiences reading can make possible, they illuminate one relationship of the arts to curriculum inquiry. As did Jean-Paul Sartre (1949, pp. 43–45) and John Dewey (1934, pp. 52–54), Iser and others emphasize the exploratory and productive *action* required of the reader or percipient in the arts. If we regard curriculum as an undertaking involving continuous interpretation and a conscious search for meanings, we come to see many connections between the grasping of a text or artwork and the gaining of multiple perspectives by means of the disciplines.

For Iser, readers grasp texts by engaging with sentences as those sentences are situated within particular perspectives at various moments of reading. If the text at hand is Virginia Woolf's *To the Lighthouse,* for example, the reading viewpoint wanders between

Mrs. Ramsey's perspective and Mr. Ramsey's, between young James's perspective and Lily Briscoe's, between the student Charles Tansley's point of view and the background point of view, between the fragmented vision in the section "Time Passes" and the vision of those outsiders who have chosen to read the book. These perspectives continually challenge and modify one another. Foregrounds interchange with backgrounds; associations accumulate to produce new experiences. Among these shifts and changes, readers work to achieve the work as at once meaningful and aesthetic. Iser, in Deweyan mode, describes transactions between readers' presence to the text and their habitual experiences as the aesthetic experience somehow transcends that past experience. Discrepancies readers find as they make the effort to create patterns become significant. Lily Briscoe, unmarried woman painter, sees the sea-surrounded Hebrides world quite differently than does the analytical Professor Ramsay. Both viewpoints are at odds with those of the various children, the aged poet, or the lighthouse keeper. When the characters are seen to view things differently, this phenomenon may make readers conscious of the inadequacy of some of the patterns or interpretations they themselves have produced along the way. They may become self-reflective. Iser writes:

> The ability to perceive oneself during the process of participation is an essential part of the aesthetic experience; the observer finds himself in a strange, halfway position: he is involved, and he watches himself being involved. . . . The resultant restructuring or stored experiences makes the reader aware not only of the experience but also of the means by which it develops. Only the controlled observation of that which is instigated by the text makes it possible for the reader to formulate a reference for what he is restructuring. Herein lies the practical relevance of the aesthetic experience: it induces this observation, which takes the place of codes that otherwise would be essential for the success of communication" [1980, p. 134].

This approach to reading strongly suggests how we might come to conceive of our curriculum and of learning itself. The approach challenges subject-object separations. Not only is there no presumption of an objectively existent world to be uncovered but once the reader becomes entangled with the characters' thoughts and perceptions, she or he finds herself or himself conscious of questions and concerns buried in her or his ordinary experience. Something is brought into the foreground then, and it in some way alters the background consciousness against which the themes of the text are pursued and its meanings gradually achieved. Take, for example, the well-known dinner party scene at the heart of *To the Lighthouse*. Mrs. Ramsey has arranged the dinner to satisfy her own needs for order, stability, and (perhaps) control. Conversation has been going on, and twilight has given way to darkness outside.

> Now all the candles were lit, and the faces on both sides of the table were brought nearer by the candle light, and composed, as they had not been in the twilight, into a party round a table, for the night was now shut out by panes of glass, which, far from giving any accurate view of the outside world, rippled it so strangely that here, inside the room, seemed to be order and dry land; there, outside, a reflection in which things wavered and vanished, waterily.
>
> Some change at once went through them all, as if this had really happened, and they were all conscious of making a party together in a hollow, on an island; had their common cause against that fluidity out there [Woolf, (1927) 1962, p. 114].

For me and some other, perhaps many other, readers, the idea that social life and even civilization are human creations in the face of nothingness may have been buried in our ordinary experience of the world and never quite confronted. To confront the idea here, in the midst of a rendering of a cultivated British family's dinner party in the country, is to come upon something unexpected and at the same time shattering. In the context of the novel, the passage partly prepares the way for the intermediate section called "Time Passes," a period of the Second World War, of death in childbirth and death on the battlefield, of "the chaos and tumult of night, with the trees standing there, and the flowers standing there, looking before them, looking up, yet beholding nothing, eyeless, and thus terrible" (p. 156). It is not that I learned anything altogether new; moreover, I was made to *see* what I had not particularly wanted to see. But once seen, it moved me to summon energies as never before to create meanings, to effect connections, to bring some vital order into existence—if only for a time. It made me recall Maurice Merleau-Ponty's statements that "because we are in the world, we are condemned to meaning" and that "we witness every minute the miracle of related experiences, and yet nobody knows better than we do how this miracle is worked, for we are ourselves this network of relationships. . . . True philosophy consists in relearning how to look at the world" ([1962] 1967, pp. xix–xx).

It was in large measure because of insights like these that I included works of literature in my classes in the history and philosophy of education, as well (more or less recently) in aesthetics. The importance of imagination increased for me as I saw that it is a capacity not solely for reaching beyond to the "as if" or the "not yet" or to the "might be." Imagination, just as Virginia Woolf says, "brings the severed parts together" (1976, p. 72); it breaks with the humdrum and the repetitive; it brings integral wholes into being in the midst of multiplicity. Not insignificantly, it makes metaphor possible. Earlier I quoted Cynthia Ozick describing how doctors could imagine the sufferings of their patients. She had been asked to address an assembly of physicians who, like many doctors, were said not to have seen the connection between a patient's vulnerability and their own unacknowledged susceptibility. Associating imagination with "inspiration," for which they had no use, the doctors were irritated and demanded "plain speech." As a writer, "an imaginer by trade," Ozick knew that she could "suggest a course of connecting, of entering into the tremulous spirit of the helpless, the fearful, the apart." She could "demonstrate the contagion of passion and compassion that is known in medicine as 'empathy', and in art as insight" (1989, p. 266). Ozick, pondering the connections between poetry and inspiration, and metaphor and inspiration, says, "I mean to persuade the doctors that metaphor belongs less to inspiration than it does to memory and pity. I want to argue that metaphor is one of the chief agents of our moral nature, and that the more serious we are in life, the less we can do without it" (p. 270). This is reminiscent of Conrad's words about solidarity; both insights have to do with relationality, reciprocity, and mutuality.

It is difficult for me to teach educational history or philosophy to teachers-to-be without engaging them in the domain of imagination and metaphor. How else are they to make meaning out of the discrepant things they learn? How else are they to see themselves as practitioners, working to choose, working to teach in an often indecipherable world?

An ability to take a fresh look at the taken for granted seems equally important; without that ability, most of us, along with our students, would remain submerged in the habitual. We and they would scarcely notice, much less question, what has appeared perfectly "natural" throughout our life histories. We and they would, therefore, be almost incapable of reflective critique. Although it may be the case that certain newspaper and television disclosures, public events like assassinations, and things whispered in corridors and on street corners can shock people into a kind of awakeness, the arts have a power distinctive from that of these random messages. As Arthur Danto reminds us, literature may be viewed as

> a kind of mirror, not simply in the sense of rendering up an external reality, but as giving me to myself for each self peering into it, showing each of us something inaccessible without mirrors, namely that each has an external aspect and what that external aspect is. Each work of literature shows in this sense an aspect we would not know were ours without benefit of that mirror: each discovers . . . an unguessed dimension of the self. It is a mirror less in passively returning an image than in transforming the self-consciousness of the reader who in virtue of identifying with the image recognizes what he is. Literature is in this sense transfigurative [1985, p. 79].

To realize that works of literature were deliberately created to communicate multiple but particular perceptions of dimensions of the human reality is come in touch with what has been called the "conversation" going on "both in public and within each of ourselves (Oakeshott, 1962, p. 199). Today, many of us think of this exchange as a contextualized conversation or dialogue, open to increasing numbers of voices. Moreover, having learned about the significance of chance and discontinuity in the history of thought (Foucault, 1972, p. 231), and choosing contingency over the false clarity the arts help us combat, we want to release persons for a transfigurative initiation through our curricula and to become more likely, also, to discover transformative dimensions in what we ourselves do.

There are numerous examples of adventures into meaning that might provoke learners to learn for the sake of repairing deficiencies in their social world as well as of becoming different in their personal lives. I have always been struck by Sartre's point in *Being and Nothingness* about what it takes to move people to transformative action, the education and intelligence it requires to decide that certain failures and lacks are "unbearable" (1956, p. 435). Doctrinaire or explicitly revolutionary literature is not needed when literary works of art have the capacity to move readers to imagine alternative ways of being alive. For Sartre, a work of art can become both a gift and a demand. If, through art, "I am given this world with its injustices, it is not so that I might contemplate them coldly, but that I might animate them with my indignation, that I might disclose them and create them with their nature as injustices, that is, as abuses to be suppressed." That indignation, he insisted, was a "promise to change" (1949, p. 62). Think of works like Toni Morrison's *Beloved,* which talks in particular and searing terms about slave children sold away from their mothers but that raises our indignation about any violation of children and ought to lead to a promise to change. Think of antiwar writings present and past; of Nadine Gordimer's *Burger's Daughter* and other renderings of apartheid; of the *Diary of Anne Frank,* the novels of Elie Wiesel, and the stories and essays of Primo Levi surrounding the Holocaust; of novel after novel that exposes discrimination against women or minorities in this country. If these works are attended to as created worlds and are achieved by readers in the ways described, the experiences they open to informed awareness cannot be self-enclosed and cannot miseducate. Instead, as Marcuse put it, awareness itself may be "intensified to the breaking point," especially when the created world is one of slavery, imprisonment in Auschwitz, of responsibility for wounded children after the Soweto uprising in South Africa. As Marcuse said, the world can be "demystified" and "the intensification of perception can go as far as to distort things so that the unspeakable is spoken, the otherwise invisible becomes visible, and the unbearable explodes. Thus the aesthetic transformation turns into indictment—but also into a celebration of that which resists injustice and terror, and of that which can still be saved" (1977, p. 45).

Similar experiences occur with certain theatrical works and films as they render worlds that are entered only when imagination is released and beholders are ready to lend these worlds their lives. Film art, particularly, may be of special relevance today because of the importance of the visual in our lives and people's growing familiarity with the language of visual images. A recent instance of the power of film and the richness and complexity of the world it can make visible is Spike Lee's *Do the Right Thing*. What with the renewed upsurge of racism in America's cities and with the ubiquity of "explanations" and diagnoses, a film of this order can be a living argument for what a work of art can do compared to discursive or descriptive talk. Set in the Brooklyn ghetto, populated by a diversity of distinctive personalities (including an Italian pizza store owner and a Korean couple who run a grocery store), the film presents both a range of vital yet deprived lives and a range of perspectives on how those lives are experienced and what ought to be done. It ends, as it must, with no resolution—simply one quotation from Martin Luther King and one from Malcolm X displayed upon the screen. Viewers are left with disrupted categories, with numerous particularities in their eyes and minds, with unresolved tensions, with relentless ambiguities. If they are informed at all about what it signifies to engage with film, to perceive it as something other than photographed reality, they are left with huge and provocative questions. They are the kinds of questions that can be refined only by sensitive inquiry, by dialogue, by connectedness, and by reformulation within the framework of what Dewey called social inquiry ([1927] 1954, p. 184). At once, and strangely, viewers are left with an expanded vision, with a consciousness of wonder and the pleasure only attainable when living beings lend their lives to works of art and bring the works into being in their own experience.

Clearly, the languages and symbols systems of the various arts differ measurably from one another and cannot, as Nelson Goodman made so clear, be translated into one another. However, in a special sense, we "read" all of the arts, "we have to read the painting as well as the poem, and that aesthetic experience is dynamic rather than static. It involves making delicate discrimination and discerning subtle relationships, identifying symbol systems and characters within these systems and what these characters denote and exemplify, interpreting works and reorganizing the world in terms of works and works in terms of the world" (1976, p. 241). For Goodman too, we do not engage with artworks to find copies of an objectively existent world but to experience the artworks' capacity to enable us to see more, to discover nuances and shapes and sounds inaccessible without them.

In my changing encounters with the visual arts over time, I found particularly important the recognition that paintings ordinarily emerge after a long dialectical struggle between a painter and his medium. John Gilmour, for one, has made startlingly clear (in part through reminding us of Henri Matisse's *Red Studio*) how enlightening it can be to realize that paintings emerge in a context of meanings and that the "artist's concern with the subject of his painting parallels the philosopher's quest for self-understanding" (1986, p. 16). Struggling for significant responses to problems arising in his or her own life and work, the artist's attempts "to make sense of the world through the created pictures reflects a *cultured* vision" (p. 18). To realize this, to understand that meanings here develop in cultural contexts as they enable us to view the world *in accord with* what is presented by Picasso or Matisse or any other pictorial artist, is to open ourselves to new disclosures. Also, it is to be moved to make new interpretations of the paintings, the world, and of ourselves. The meaning of what any artist is going to say "does not exist anywhere—not in things, which as yet have no meaning, nor in the artist himself, in his unformulated life. It summons one away from the already constituted reason in which 'cultured men' are content to shut themselves, toward a reason which contains its own origins" (Merleau-Ponty, [1948] 1964, p. 19). This can only mean an originally perceived "landscape" or ground and a background of sedimented, changing meanings. When pictures are met *as paintings* and not as illustrations or representations, the search we hope to be engaged in can be urged to go on. The meaning, not solely for the artist, but for the beholder as well, lies ahead.

Coupled with any contextualized quest for meanings in the domains of painting ought to be the consciousness that "seeing comes before words. It is seeing which establishes our place in the surrounding world; we explain that world with words, but words can never undo the fact that we are surrounded by it. The relation between what we see and what we know is never settled" (Berger, 1984, p. 7). Beyond thinking about seeing, there is a need for critique of paintings, especially those used to mystify and those treated as holy relics, beyond the reach of ordinary persons. For John Berger, if we were to learn more about using the language of images, we would be able "to define our experiences more precisely in areas where words are inadequate. . . . [These areas are] not only personal experience, but also the essential historical experience of our relation to the past: that is to say the experience of seeking to give meaning to our lives, of trying to understand the history of which we can become the active agents" (p. 33).

That idea seems to me to feed directly into what is important about curriculum inquiry and, in some manner, to sum up much of what is important about the arts in relation to curriculum. Not only can teachers feel the importance of releasing students to be personally present to what they see and hear and read; they can also be reminded of the need for students to develop a sense of agency and participation and to do so in collaboration with one another. I am reminded of Alfred Schutz's consideration of "making music together" as a paradigm for social intercourse. He spoke of a "simultaneity" created by the flux of the musical process, a coming together of the composer's stream of consciousness with the listener's. This sharing of another's flux of experiences in inner time, he wrote, "this living through a vivid present in common, constitutes . . . the mutual tuning-in relationship, the experience of the 'We', which is at the foundation of all possible communication" (1964, p. 173).

To conceive the arts in relation to curriculum is to think of a deepening and expanding mode of tuning-in. There have to be disciplines, yes, and a growing acquaintance with the structures of knowledge, but at the same time, there have to be the kinds of grounded interpretations possible only to those willing to abandon already constituted reason, willing to feel and to imagine, to open the windows and go in search. The search—sometimes rigorous, sometimes gay—ought to be accompanied by the sound of a blue guitar.

Chapter Eight

Writing to Learn

The National Writing Project in California is one of several programs around the country that focus on the encouragement of "freewriting" and the relationships between reflective reading and being motivated to write. These programs have led to the encouragement of journal writing by teachers as well as their students. Poetry, stories, and anecdotes by young people appear daily in a variety of bindings and portfolio presentations. This chapter is based on a piece requested by the editors of the quarterly published by the National Writing Project. The writer was asked to provide a more or less autobiographical account of how learning to write may lead to learning in other domains. It was treated as an instance of what is called qualitative research.

When you tell, as most teachers know by now, you are making connections, creating patterns, making sense of what seems devoid of meaning. As a child, I was always reading. I was shamed by being called a "bookworm," but reading itself was never enough; nor was recounting stories about what I read to my sister when the lights were out. It was essential for me to make my own sense of what I read, to incarnate it, to *learn* what it had to tell me.

Like Eudora Welty's family (Welty, 1984, p. 6), mine proudly owned *The Book of Knowledge.* Rather like Sartre's autodidact, or "Self-Taught Man," in *Nausea,* I was intent on reading right through the volumes of *The Book of Knowledge,* moving alphabetically through all there was to know. I am not sure how I happened on the "M" section so soon, but it was certainly under the heading "Mexico" that I read what prompted me to begin a novel in a black and white notebook to give to my father as a birthday present. The account that started me off had to do with Mexican peasants shanghaied and taken from their villages to work in the mines, and it told about seven-year-old Ramona going in search of her abducted father. (*I* was seven, and it made considerable sense.) I decided that Ramona lived near the city of Guadalajara, and that meant I had to figure out the geography of that part of Mexico so I could decide on my wanderer's route. Because I needed to know it, I not only learned a great deal about that area's topography and geography, I also developed quite some expertise on the Mexican mining industry early in the century. I am sure that Ramona's search was inconclusive, but I did give it to my father as a present, although it took some years before I discovered how much I had learned about my and my father's relationship through the choices of symbols and metaphors I had made in the course of my writing (without any suspicion that there was a Sigmund Freud anywhere in the world). Lately, writing something else, responding in part to Elizabeth Bishop's poem "In the Waiting Room," I learned still more about what it was to be seen and what it was to make meaning through writing. Earlier, I quoted part of this poem, describing the sudden sensation of the nearly seven-year-old Elizabeth, in response to several dislocating events, little shocks, in a dentist's waiting room, that she is

> . . . falling off
> the round, turning world
> into cold, blue-black space.
> But I felt: you are an *I*,
> You are an *Elizabeth* . . . [(1975) 1983, p. 159].

I have learned, presently and retrospectively, how much writing has to do with that recognition of an "I," who is also (as the poet goes on to say) "one of *them*."

Some years after my childhood effort, immediately after I graduated from Barnard College with a major in American history, I decided to write an American historical novel. Seven hundred pages it was, and it dealt with the turbulent years before the election of Jefferson to the presidency. I did research on the Democratic Societies, the people who were imprisoned under the Alien and Sedition Acts, the sympathizers with the French Revolution, and the rest. The hero (naturally!) was modeled on the Revolutionary poet Philip Freneau, but *my* character was a folksinger (prematurely, I grant) writing protest songs against the establishment of the time.

I never sold the novel; but I learned about a period in American history as I never had in all my years of specialization at Barnard. Again, I was incarnating the material I read for my own symbolic and affective purposes. Something very important happened for me in mediating great events through a single consciousness, viewing the personal in relation to the public, the public from a private point of view. I was beginning to recognize the importance of vantage point when it came to the dialogue that is history. As time went on and I came closer to discovering my own "voice," meaning my woman's voice, through the writing I was doing, I learned much more about vantage point and more about history.

It was her "shock-receiving capacity" that Virginia Woolf thought made her a writer (1976, p. 72). I have already mentioned how she felt that "a shock is in my case followed by the desire to explain it." Finding a reason, she said, made her feel less passive, less victimized. Few of us are likely to become artists like Virginia Woolf; but we can still attend to the smothering and silencing consequences of our submergence in the "cotton wool" of "non-being" or the taken-for-granted. In my life, it has been extraordinarily important to identify myself in what I think of as a dialectic relation with the forces around that determine and condition and (now and then) manipulate. Some of those forces have to do with my history and my gender; some of them inhere in the social and political environment. It is when I experience those forces as inhibiting, demeaning, and interfering with my freedom, that I am moved very often to *tell* about them. The shocks I receive are very often those that come when I feel the spaces of my choosing (and my acting) narrowing. It is by writing that I often manage to name alternatives and to open myself to possibilities. This is what I think learning ought to be.

The philosopher Merleau-Ponty writes: "The world is not what I think, but what I live through. I am open to the world, I have no doubt that I am in communication with it, but I do not possess it; it is inexhaustible" ([1962] 1967, pp. xvi–xvii). The very notion of the inexhaustibility of the world suggests that the search for ways of articulation or sense-making will be ongoing. Surely, that is what happens when we write, at whatever age; we undertake a search that anyone would undertake "if he were not sunk in the everydayness of his own life" (Percy, 1979, p. 13).

Yes, I believe the National Writing Project can work against despair. I also believe we need to make it possible for writers to name not only the shapes and byways of their lived worlds but the problems and the predicaments that have stopped and silenced them. Somehow, we have to enable them to transmute these problems into shocks to be explained and to develop the shock-receiving capacity in each one. The alternative may be submergence in the everyday or even in despair. I recall Tillie Olsen writing about "the *hidden* silences; work aborted, deferred, denied—hidden by the work which does not come to fruition" (1978, p. 8). And then I think (and may be learning it better by writing this chapter) how inattentive so many teachers have been to hidden silences in students and how these silences can be overcome if we can free students to write.

It is not an accident, it seems to me, that the upsurge of interest in writing, in instituting Eliot's "raid on the inarticulate" is accompanied by a philosophic concern with life as narrative. Alaisdair MacIntyre connects the very conception of personal identity with the idea of narrative. He writes that the narrative of any one life "is part of an interlocking set of narratives," while the unity of a human life is "the unity of a narrative quest" (1981, p. 203). More recently, as we have seen, Charles Taylor relates that same quest to an orientation to the good as we try to determine our places and our life direction relative to the good (1989, p. 52). But one could perhaps start from another point: because we have to determine our place in relation to the good, therefore we cannot be without an orientation to it, and hence must see our life in story.

Taylor, like many of us teachers, is interested in the problem of human *agency* in a time when there is so much powerlessness and disengagement, when we are caught in technicizations of so many kinds. He and MacIntyre are not part of any writing projects; but their concern (part of a swelling philosophical concern) for language, dialogue, conversation, narrative, story, and quest connects with our quest for self-creation among individuals in worlds of potentially shared experience. Learning to write is a matter of learning to shatter the silences, of making meaning, of learning to learn.

Chapter Nine

| Teaching for Openings

Risking a charge of hubris, I choose to start this chapter with a quotation from Michel Foucault's *Discourse on Language:* "I would really like to have slipped imperceptibly into this lecture. . . . I would have preferred to be enveloped in words, borne way beyond all possible beginnings. At the moment of speaking, I would like to have perceived a nameless voice, long preceding me, leading me merely to enmesh myself in it, taking up its cadence, and to lodge myself, when no one else was looking, in its interstices as if it had paused an instant, in suspense to beckon to me. There would have been no beginnings; instead, speech would proceed from me" (1972, p. 215).

I am tempted, you see, to remain within what Foucault elsewhere calls "the established order of things"—pedagogical things, liberal education things (1973, p. xxi). I am drawn to affirm the timelessness of what I have come to love over the years, of what I choose to think of as the very sources of my self. Allowing myself to be carried along by the great conversation initiated by others (and, indeed, maintained by others), I would not have to disrupt. I would not have to begin anything; I would need only be swept along by what the great ones have said and remain partially submerged in them.

But then I think of how much beginnings have to do with freedom, how much disruption has to do with consciousness and the awareness of possibility that has so much to do with teaching other human beings. And I think that if I and other teachers truly want to provoke our students to break through the limits of the conventional and the taken for granted, we ourselves have to experience breaks with what has been established in our own lives; we have to keep arousing ourselves to begin again. I recall Merleau-Ponty writing that "choice and action alone cut us loose from anchorage" ([1962] 1967, p. 456). And always in my mind there is Woolf, writing about the shock-receiving capacity that probably made her a writer. Both of them move me to reach into my own story, into the ambivalence of my own choosing to act in such a way that I break loose from anchorage and that I stir others to break loose along with me, so that we all become different, that we all engage in a dialectic to reach beyond where we are.

I must recognize, however, how hard it has been to confront the controls, the principles of exclusion and denial that have allowed me a certain range of utterances and prevented others. I have not easily come to terms with the ways in which education, too often following the lines of class, gender, and race, permits and forbids the expression of different people's experiences. Think of performance artist Karen Finley talking about the fear of naming and what doesn't get talked about, of the children Michelle Fine discovered who expressed a "terror of words" (1987, p. 159)], and of what Mina Shaughnessy called the "trap" set by academic writing for entering students at the City University of New York (1977, p. 71). I say the words but find it hard not to evade the implications of what most of us acknowledge by now: that "every educational system is a political means of maintaining or of modifying the appropriation of discourse, with the knowledge and powers it carries with it" (Foucault, 1972, p. 227).

When we teachers have wanted to believe that education has been a means of giving every living person access to any sort of discourse that person might prefer, when we have wanted to believe that literacy is a personal achievement, a door to personal meaning, it takes an effort for us to realize how deeply literacy is involved in relations of power and how it must be understood in context and in relation to a social world. It is evident enough that people are born into a culturally defined literacy, which some acquire in the course of growing up and which some never fully grasp. They many not grasp it because their families are poor, remote from institutional efforts to socialize people into productive participation in society. They may not grasp it because they are out of the mainstream for any number of reasons, including immigrant or minority status. Many of the alienated or marginalized are made to feel distrustful of their own voices, their own ways of making sense, yet they are not provided alternatives that allow them to tell their stories or shape their narratives or ground new learning in what they already know. The favored ones, in contrast, seldom question the language of dominance or efficiency or efficacy in which they were reared, although they may seek out discourses more appropriate for a shared young culture or for moments of rebellion or adolescent discontent. Seldom do we see actual participation in the shaping of literacy. Seldom do we see a questioning of the context—of technical language, for instance—or of purely linear or analytical discourse or discourse that presumes the objective existence of what is taken to be the "normal" world.

This chapter has to do with teaching that provokes critical questions around the many modes of literacy, the preferred languages, the diversity of languages, and the relation of all of these to the greater cultural context. Prevailing literacies and discourse should be taken as occasions for study and expression, for the sake of disclosing more materials in lived experiences—the multiplicity of lived experiences that mark our society today. People who lack access to the language of power, who are inarticulate even about their lived lives, are unlikely to "surmount the boundaries in which all customary views are confined, and to reach a more open territory" (Heidegger, 1968, p. 13). Yes, becoming literate is also a matter of transcending the given, of entering a field of possibles. We are moved to do that, however, only when we become aware of rifts, gaps in what we think of as reality. We have to be articulate enough and able to exert ourselves to *name* what we see around us—the hunger, the passivity, the homelessness, the "silences." These may be thought of as deficiencies in need of repair. It requires imagination to be conscious of them, to find our own lived worlds lacking because of them. Recall Dr. Rieux's voice, at the end of Camus's *Plague,* speaking of those "unable to be saints but refusing to bow down to pestilences," who "strive their utmost to be healers" (1948, p. 278). No great heroism or self-sacrifice is asked of us who view ourselves as ordinary people. But we do have the capacity to refuse and to strive in this way and to do so by seeing clearly through our own eyes and speaking clearly in our own voices as Rieux does in his.

In my own case, immersed as I was for so long and immersed as I wanted to be, it took years before I realized that the great tradition—what Harold Bloom has called the "Western canon, the books and schools of the ages" (1994)—required that I look through the eyes of others and master what was at the time the authoritative way of articulating the world. It came as a shock to realize that what I had believed was universal, transcending gender and class and race, was a set of points of view. I had considered it a kind of beneficence for someone like me to be initiated into a traditional dimension of the culture's conversation, even if only into a rivulet of those unnamed voices that had been made faintly available to those who did not quite belong. Now, in the midst of remembered delights and still-beckoning desires in my field, I found myself directly challenged to think about both my own thinking and speaking and the discourses in which I had been submerged.

This meant singling out determining factors in my life—the seductions as well as the controls. I had consciously to resist certain prohibitions, certain pieties, guilts, embarrassments, fears. Only by means of such resistance, I discovered, can we widen the spaces in which we hope to choose ourselves. To meet a wall or a barrier in our way and simply take another path is to acquiesce, not to resist. To speak of a dialectic is to speak of forces in contest: the factors that hold us in place, that stand in the way of our growing, and the factors that provoke us to act on our desires, to break through the obstacles, to become different, to *be*. Not to recognize something as an obstacle to our growing may well be to acquiesce in oppression, especially in if we live in oppressive or humiliating circumstances. The alternative may be what Milan Kundera (1984) describes as an "unbearable lightness of being," a feeling of living among chance happenings and fortuitous encounters, without clear possibilities. Or it may be a mere submission to fatalism, to what Kundera's characters call *"Es muss sein!"* (p. 193), a sense of overriding necessity. Or—and this is what I am reaching toward— it can be a life lived in tension and a kind of ardor, with the dialectical struggle never quite resolved. Indeed, we would not need to be wide-awake to our lives if it could be resolved.

When I ponder my own history, I realize that I can never quite overcome the unease caused by the tension between my unalloyed love for, say, the works of Flaubert, Baudelaire, Melville, Cézanne, Debussy, and Stevens and my recognition that theirs are male imaginings and soundings that, like any other category of speaking, demand a diversity of decodings and interpretings, not reverential uncoverings of what seems at first to be objectively illuminating, objectively *there*. It was my presumed, but also learned, capacity to uncover their works in that fashion that gave me the feeling of being one with those artists. Following the rules, I thought, I could make their visions mine. Today I, along with many others, feel unease because the very metaphor of uncovering no longer serves nor does the idea of a preexistent vision. I am now obligated to achieve those works as meaningful by paying heed to them through a range of shifting perspectives, including those created by my own embodied consciousness. How do I break through the circles I am likely to create? What do I do about what Gadamer calls my "prejudgments"? (1976, p. 9). It is with that sort of unease and in the midst of interrogation that I find my freedom, it seems to me, because the initiatives I find myself required to take open spaces in which I must make choices and then act upon the choices I make. I recall Martin Buber speaking about teaching and about the importance of "keeping the pain awake" (1957, p. 116); and I suggest that the pain he had in mind must be lived through by teacher as well as student, even as the life stories of both must be kept alive. This, it seems to me, is when real encounters occur—when human beings come together as being living in time.

In this time of interest in narrative and storytelling as a way of knowing (Bruner, 1986, pp. 13–14), my hope is that the story disclosed here will move readers to tap their own stories, their experiences in finding projects by which to create identities. It is important for me, for example, to summon up the ways in which I was demeaned in my early days of college teaching by being told I was too "literary" to do philosophy. That seemed to mean that I was thought ill equipped to do the sort of detached and rigorous analysis of language games and arguments that for a long time dominated the academic world. I could not objectify nor separate my subjectivity from what I was perceiving. I could not separate my feeling, imagining, wondering consciousness from the cognitive work assigned for me to do. Nor could I bracket out my biography and my experiences of embeddedness in an untidy, intersubjective world. Only now, trying to understand the contexts of the dominant preoccupations and their connections with issues of gender, trying to name the relationship between academic norms and the demands of an advanced technological society, trying to grasp the real meaning of instrumental rationality in a universe of suffering children and desperate mothers and thousands of sickening poor, can I begin to identify what stopped me from the kind of analysis that was expected of me earlier. Gaining perspective on it now, pondering a better state of things, I can try to achieve my freedom in an expanded sphere. I hope it is one in which I can act as teacher and as practitioner to transform what is inhuman, what alienates people from themselves.

Still, caught in turmoils of interrogation, in what Buber called the pain, I am likely to feel the pull of my old search for certainty. I find myself now and then yearning after the laws and norms and formulations, even though I know how many of them were constructed in the interests of those in power. Their appeal to me was not only due to the ways in which they provide barriers against relativism. It was also due to my marginality: I wanted so much to be accepted in the great world of wood-panelled libraries, authoritative intellectuals, sophisticated urban cafés. My response to the criticisms I received early on was to turn away from the local and particular in my life, to strive for an incarnation of values that promised to transcend gender and class and race. And, indeed, some people continue to frequently remind us today of how they believe self-interest and provincialism can best be overcome through mastery of a monological "cultural literacy" justified by an almost transcendent notion of "national community" (Hirsch, 1987, p. 137). Rejecting that belief for a range of reasons, I can still feel drawn to the idea that there is such a thing as "view from nowhere" (Putnam, 1985, p. 27). I always liked feeling like one of Plato's prisoners released from the cave and standing in the blinding light of disembodied reason. Knowing better, I even liked the idea of the objectively universal, the overwhelmingly True.

It took time for me to realize that the Great White Father, along with the eternal verities, was as much a construct as the indifferent God paring his nails in Joyce's *Portrait of the Artist as a Young Man*. But that did not leave me quiescent in the face of loss. I think of the "forlornness" about which Jean-Paul Sartre used to write, describing what it signifies to be alone with no excuses (1947). A kind of homesickness accompanies such knowledge, even when the individual realizes that he or she is not literally alone but caught up in intersubjectivity. That is why so many people including our students still turn eagerly toward the stable, the monolithic, and the monological. We all want a foothold in the face of collapsing hierarchies, when the world is increasingly viewed as "continuously changing, irreducibly various, and multiply configurable" (Smith, 1988, p. 183). The debate over the proper role (and even the right to existence) of the National Endowment for the Arts is evidence of this, as is the defensiveness we see with respect to the traditional canon in the humanities or the resistance to curricula "of difference."

It has taken many shocks of awareness for me to realize how I existed within a tradition (or a "conversation") as within a container. Merleau-Ponty, warning against such a constrained existence, reminds us of the importance of keeping our ideas open to the field of nature and culture which they must express: "The idea of going straight to the essence of things is an inconsistent idea if one thinks about it. What is given is a route, an experience which gradually clarifies itself, which gradually rectifies itself and proceeds by dialogue with itself and with others. . . . What saves us is the possibility of a new development" (1964, p. 21). The dialogue can be generated and enriched by the writing some of us try to do, the journals we keep along with others. Even now, it helps me to be in search of words, to break with immersion by seeing and saying. Of course, as I work in a dialogical relation with students, I want to communicate what this can mean; but at the same time, I want them to make their perspectives available so that both I and they can see from many vantage points, make sense from different sides. I want us to work together to unconceal what is hidden, to contextualize what happens to us, to mediate the dialectic that keeps us on edge, that may be keeping us alive.

That is why I have to keep summoning up the experiences that gave me moments of being and the ones that buried me in cotton wool, in the hope that I arouse others to couch some of their stories in similar ways. I have to communicate what it signifies to treat the texts we and our students read together as "open" in Umberto Eco's sense. The reader in the presence of an open work, writes Eco, supplies her or his own existential credentials, a sense of conditioning particularly her or his own, a defined culture, a "set of tastes, personal inclinations, and prejudices." The reader's own perspective, in other words, affects and modifies comprehension of the work. Moreover, "the form of the work of art gains its aesthetic validity precisely in proportion to the number of different perspectives from which it can be viewed and understood" (1984, p. 490). There are important connections between this view and Robert Scholes's treatment of interpretation in his *Protocols of Reading* as he describes the importance of protocols and the idea (taken from Barthes's *Pleasure of the Text* [1975] and similar to Freire's) of "rewriting the texts that we read in the texts of our lives, . . . and rewriting our lives in the light of those texts" (1989, p. 155).

Now I offer some examples, surely not unique, of how a tapping of perspectives while reading enabled me and still enables me to read my world differently. If we can teach our students to articulate what can be discovered in this way and to make it part of the dialogue in a classroom, this approach to reading may in time move us to wonder about going beyond reading the world to, as Freire says, "transforming it by means of conscious, practical work" (Freire, 1987, p. 35). But first we must find ways of being dialogical in relation to the texts we read together; reflecting, opening, to one another upon the texts of our lived lives.

In Chapter Seven, I quoted part of Elizabeth Bishop's poem "At the Fishhouses," in which she writes about a childhood experience with an old man repairing nets at a fishhouse, with the fir trees behind and with seals now and then appearing in the cold dark water. She speaks of how the water swings indifferently and icily above the stones, how its first "bitter" taste is like knowledge, and how it is

> drawn from the cold hard mouth
> of the world, derived from the rocky breasts
> forever, flowing and drawn, and since
> our knowledge is historical, flowing, and flown [(1955)
>   1983, pp. 65–66].

The very idea of there being a flow and a history to knowledge is to me a challenge and a critique, whatever Elizabeth Bishop intended. Not only systems but even discrete and formalized particles of knowledge are put to question here, as is ungrounded knowledge that is its own excuse for being. All this constituted a shock for me on my first and second reading, a rupture of some of the containers in which I had lived and thought I wanted to live.

And when students began pouring in their own inclinations and prejudices and memories (especially in response to the bitter taste and the salty clarity and the startling flow as from a stone fountain), I found something like a common text emerging among us, one that—in our diversity—we began to read and reread and even to rewrite.

Something similar happened when I read Bishop's poem "In the Waiting Room" (also quoted earlier), in which child Elizabeth about to turn seven, looking at the grown-up people sitting around a dentist's waiting room, feels "the sensation of falling off/the round, turning world" and thinks

> . . . you are an *I*,
> you are an *Elizabeth*,
> you are one of *them*.
> *Why* should you be one, too?
> I scarcely dared to look
> to see what it was I was [(1975) 1983, p. 159].

The interrogative mode; the painful particularity; the sensation of falling into space; all these introduce a vantage point that subverts the systematic, the complete. At once, at least for me and some of those with whom I learn, this poem enhances our consciousness of the ongoing dialectic. Feeling ourselves on a kind of verge, we all try to carve a space in which we can break the peculiar silences and choose.

In her novel *Cassandra*, Christa Wolf creates a narrator who tells us that the excluded always recognize and understand each other (1984). This thought makes me ponder the ways in which my own acquaintance with silence and the uncertainty I felt in seeking my own voice might help me begin to understand how the world is for people of minorities—black young men and women, newly arrived Hispanics, and others. Ralph Ellison's narrator in *Invisible Man* speaks of the importance of bestowing recognition rather than invisibility on others; and I understand that I can only recognize a person like the narrator and others whom I meet against my own lived situation. I need to try to see at once through their eyes and my own—if these individuals are willing to engage in dialogue, if they are willing to offer clues. I think, for example, of the clue that appears in *Invisible Man* in the narrator's beginning and ending his story "underground" (treating, as it might be, Dostoyevksy's *Notes from Underground* as open text). Reaching the concluding pages, I read: "In going underground, I whipped it all except the mind, the *mind*. And the mind that has conceived a plan of living must never lose sight of the chaos against which that pattern was conceived. That goes for societies as well as individuals. Thus, having tried to give pattern to the chaos which lives within the pattern of your certainties, I must come out, I must emerge" (Ellison, 1952, p. 502). Not only does Ellison's text raise questions that might affect readers' own inner eyes, the ones that render people recognizable or invisible. It allows us to discover (perhaps uncomfortably) a new intertextuality, enabling us in some way to rewrite *Notes from Underground*—as well as Emerson's "American Scholar" and Mark Twain's *Adventures of Huckleberry Finn*—within the texts of our lives.

How else have I found new perspectives in reading? Toni Morrison's works administer amazing shocks that can allow us to develop other modes of recognition against the background of our own lived lives. For example, recall the story of Pecola Breedlove in *The Bluest Eye* (1970) and the ways in which Pecola is destroyed by two of the dominant culture's master narratives: the "Dick and Jane" readers and the mythic image made of Shirley Temple with her blue eyes. Pecola is a little black girl, unloved by her mother, unsupported by her community, absolutely certain she is very ugly, wanting above all things to look like Shirley Temple with bright blue eyes. If her eyes were different, she thinks, she would be different; and perhaps her parents would no longer do bad things before such pretty eyes. Pecola is destroyed and steps over into madness; and we are left with the realization that an insistence that there is only one master story, only one kind of reputable human reality can be fatal to many people—to the variously disabled, to the visually or aurally impaired, certainly to abused little girls like Pecola. For Pecola, the standard of human reality is set by blue eyes; and although her view is alien to many readers in its particulars, it may still move us to rewrite parts of the texts of the world.

The vantage point on the unloved Pecola that is offered in the novel is that of two loved children who, in the words of the one that is the narrator, Claudia, defend their youthful behavior by considering "all speech a code to be broken by us, and all gestures subject to careful analysis" (p. 149). They are proud and arrogant because they have to be; unlike Pecola, they survive: "We tried to see her without looking at her, and never, never went near. Not because she was absurd or repulsive, or because we were frightened, but because we had failed her. Our flowers never grew." As the years go on and Pecola picks and plucks her way between the tire rims and milkweed, "among all the waste and beauty of the world, which she herself was," the narrators come to feel wholesome after cleaning themselves on Pecola: "Her simplicity decorated us, her guilt sanctified us, her pain made us glow with health, her awkwardness made us think we had a sense of humor. Even her waking dreams we used to silence our own nightmares" (p. 159). There are feelings not unlike these also described in Morrison's *Sula*. Sula's friend Nel thinks that Sula's return home is like getting an eye back because, for Nel, "talking to Sula had always been a conversation with herself. . . . Sula never competed; she simply helped others define themselves" (1975, p. 82).

Can it be that, in the struggle to define ourselves, strangers like Sula do indeed enter the dialectic when it comes to choosing who we are? I would like us to discover how we can all discover together against the diversity of our backgrounds, write together, draw upon each other's existential realities to create Arendt's in-between (1958, p. 182). "Everyone's liberation must be self-won," writes Catherine Stimpson (1989, p. 35); I know this, but I want to go further with her and with those around me to open terrains, to communities where our engagements can be wide and deep at once.

Of course, receptive as we try to be, we can only understand through the play of our own assumptions, our own prejudgments, our own memories, and perhaps, what Toni Morrison's Sethe in *Beloved* calls our "rememory" (1987, p. 191). There is no information or knowledge to be taken in or absorbed by empty consciousnesses. We can only attend from our own interpretive communities, if we can learn to name the appropriate strategies and make them understandable to those with whom we are trying to engage and somehow understand. We need to continue enlarging those communities until we create a secular realm with "a more open sense of community as something to be won and of audiences as human beings to be addressed" (Said, 1983, p. 152).

That means that what Elizabeth Fox-Genovese has called the elite culture must be transformed. This is the culture white male scholars tend to create, one that has "functioned in relation to women, the lower classes, and some white races analogously to the way in which imperialism functioned for colonized people. At worst, it denied the values of all others and imposed itself as an absolute standard." Fox-Genovese also points out that any canon, that is, "the power to speak for the collectivity, results from social and gender relations and struggles, not from nature. Those who fashioned our collective elite tradition were the victors of history" (1986, pp. 140–141). I am thrust back again into the contradictions of my life when I read that, and again, I am reminded of the differential meanings of literacy. As a set of techniques, literacy has often silenced persons and disempowered them. Our obligation today is to find ways of enabling the young to find their voices, to open their spaces, to reclaim their histories in all their variety and discontinuity. Attention has to be paid to those on the margins, the too frequently smothered voices from Latin America, the Middle East, and Southeast Asia.

This is not romantic or simply a matter of good will. We teachers will confront thousands and thousands of newcomers in the years ahead: some from the darkness and danger of the neglected ghettos, some exhausted from their suffering under dictators, some stunned by lives in refugee camps, some unabashedly in search of economic success. The texts are here. We have to make them accessible, offer the protocols, keep them open. We have to allow opportunities for students to structure their experiences by means of those texts, by means of books men and women have made. When Sartre, as I have mentioned, speaks of such works as gifts, he goes on to say:

> And if I am given this world with its injustices, it is not so I might contemplate them coldly, but that I might animate them with my indignation, that I might disclose them and create them with their nature as injustices, that is, as abuses to be suppressed. Thus, the writer's universe will only reveal itself in all its depth to the examination, the admiration, and the indignation of the reader; and the generous love is a promise to maintain, and the generous indignation is a promise to change, and the admiration is a promise to imitate; although literature is one thing and morality a quite different

one, at the heart of the aesthetic imperative we discern the moral imperative. For, since the one who writes recognizes, through the very fact that he takes the trouble to write, the freedom of his readers, and since the one who reads, by the mere fact of his opening the book, recognizes the freedom of the writer, the work of art, from whichever side you approach it, is an act of confidence in the freedom of men (1949, pp. 62–63).

Wishing he had said "human beings" rather than "men," I still find it deeply important that Sartre saw literature as an imaginary presentation of the world "insofar as it demands human freedom." I even find in that passage a source of paradigms for teaching, if teaching is indeed for finding openings, if we are concerned that choices be made. Both the reading experience and the teaching act are dialectical.

Finally, I want to suggest once more the sense in which literacy is and must be a social undertaking, to be sought in pluralist classrooms where persons come together "in speech and action" to create something in common among themselves (Arendt, 1958, p. 19). There will be a play of differences, inevitably, through which meanings can emerge. There will be, there ought to be, moments of recognition, moments of doubt. But there will also be endless interrogation as diverse persons strive to create themselves in their freedom. I think of *The Plague* again and Tarrou as he says that "all our troubles spring from our failure to use plain, clean-cut language. So I resolved always to speak—and to act—quite clearly. . . . That's why I decided to take the victims' side, so as to reduce the damage done" (Camus, 1948, p. 230). And, of course, that is the point of the novel: in times of pestilence, take the victims' side. These may be times of pestilence for us. That is why, like Tarrou, we need to be attentive and vigilant if we are to open texts and spaces, if we are to provoke the young to be free.

| **Art and Imagination**

The existential contexts of education reach far beyond the intent of Goals 2000. They have to do with the human condition in these often desolate days; and in some manner, they make such notions as world-class achievement and benchmarks seem superficial and limited, if not absurd. They extend beyond the appalling actualities of family breakdown, homelessness, and violence, and beyond the "savage inequalities" Kozol describes (1991). Our young, like us, their elders, inhabit a world of fearful moral uncertainty—a world where it appears that almost nothing can be done to reduce suffering, contain massacres, and protect human rights. The faces of refugee children in search of their mothers, of teen-age girls raped repeatedly by soldiers, of rootless people staring at burnt churches and libraries—all these may strike some as only a "virtual reality." Still others, who do look closely, often feel numbed and, reminded over and over of helplessness, are persuaded to look away. It has been said that Pablo Picasso's paintings of "weeping women" (Freeman, 1994) have become the icons of our time. They have replaced the public statues of men on horseback and of men in battle; they overshadow the emblems of what once seemed worth fighting for, perhaps dying for. When even the young confront loss and death, as most of us are bound to do today, "it is important that everything we love be summed up into something unforgettably beautiful . . ." (Leiris, 1988, p. 201). Leiris's matter of importance suggests one of the roles of the arts. To see sketch after sketch of women holding dead babies in their arms, as Picasso provoked us to do, is to become aware of a tragic deficiency in the fabric of life. If we know enough to make those paintings objects of our experience, to encounter them against the background of our lived lives, we are likely to strain toward conceptions of a better order of things in which there will be no more wars that make women weep like that, no bombs to murder innocent children. We are likely, in rebellion against such horror, to summon up images of smiling mothers and live and lovely children—"everything we love," metaphors for what *ought* to be.

Clearly, provoking this desire is not the single role of the arts when they become objects of our experience, although encounters with them frequently do move us to want to restore some kind of order, to repair, to heal. At the very least, participatory involvement with the many forms of art can enable us to *see* more in our experience, to *hear* more on normally unheard frequencies, to *become conscious* of what daily routines have obscured, what habit and convention have suppressed. Depending on our personal encounters, we might think yet again, for example, of what Pecola Breedlove in Toni Morrison's *Bluest Eye* has made us realize about the metanarrative implicit in the "Dick and Jane" basal readers or in the artifact called Shirley Temple that made so many invisible children yearn desperately to have blue eyes. We might recall the disclosures lived by so many as they became involved with the film *Schindler's List* (and the attending to the little girl with the red coat). We might try to retrieve the physical consciousness of unutterable grief aroused by Martha Graham's "Lamentation," with only the dancer's feet and hands visible outside the draped fabric and the agony expressed through stress lines on the cloth. When we see more and hear more, it is not only that we lurch, if only for a moment, out of the familiar and the taken-for-granted but that new avenues for choosing and for action may open in our experience; we may gain a sudden sense of new beginnings, that is, we make take an initiative in the light of possibility.

Our society's prevailing cynicism about the existence of deeply felt values, along with people's general feelings of resignation, cannot but create atmospheres in our schools at odds with the restlessness and the unpredictability associated with art experiences, be they creative or appreciative. At the same time, the neglect of the arts by those who identified the goals in Goals 2000 helped justify an administrative focus on the manageable, the predictable, and the measurable. While there have been efforts to include the arts in the official statements of national educational goals, the arguments have cohered with the arguments for education geared to economic competitiveness, technological mastery, and the like. The arguments for the teaching of the arts have also been supportive of the dominant arguments for a higher level than presently exists of skills development, academic achievement, standards, and preparation for the workplace.

One danger that threatens both teachers and students in such emphases is that they will come to feel anger at being locked into an objective set of circumstances defined by others. Young people find themselves described as "human resources" rather than as persons who are centers of choice and evaluation. They are, it is suggested, to be molded in the service of technology and the market, no matter who they are. Moreover, as many are now realizing, because great numbers of our young will find themselves unable to locate satisfying jobs, the very notions that all our children will get to participate in this kind of education and that they are human resources carry with them deceptions of all kinds. Perhaps it is no wonder that the dominant mood in many classrooms (if it is not one of cacophony, disinterest, and disorder) is one of passive reception. Umberto Eco's view of our desperate need to introduce a critical dimension where media and messages are concerned is that it is far more important to focus on the point of reception, which in this case is passive, than on the point of transmission. Finding a threat in "the universal of technological communication" and in situations where "the medium is the message," he calls for a return to serious individual resistance to messages: "To the anonymous divinity of Technological Communication, our answer could be: 'Not Thy, but *our* will be done'" (Kearney, 1988, p. 382).

As I view it, such resistance can best be evoked when imagination is released; but, as we well know, the bombardment of images from the divinity of Technological Communication frequently has the effect of freezing people's imaginative thinking. Instead of freeing audience members to take the initiative in reaching beyond their own actualities, in looking at things as if they could be otherwise, today's media present audiences with predigested concepts and images in fixed frameworks. Dreams are caught in the meshes of the saleable; possession of consumer goods is the alternative to gloom or feelings of pointlessness. Ideas of possibilities are trapped in predictability. But our imagination, as I have been illustrating, obviously deals in unpredictabilities, in the unexpected. It then requires reflectiveness on our part to acknowledge the existence of these unexpected and unpredictable vistas and perspectives in our experiences. The passive, apathetic person is all too likely to be unresponsive to ideas of the unreal, the as-if, the merely possible. And it is this passive person who bars the arts as frivolous, a mere frill, irrelevant to learning in the post-industrial world.

It is my conviction that informed engagements with the several arts is the most likely mode of releasing our students' (or any person's) imaginative capacity and giving it play. However, this will not, cannot, happen automatically or "naturally." We have all witnessed tourists' surface contacts with paintings as these mere sightseers hasten through museums. Without spending reflective time, without tutoring in or exposure to or dialogue about the arts, people merely seek the right labels, seek out the works by the artists they have heard they should see. There are some who watch a ballet only for the story, not for the movement or the music; some who fall into a reverie at concerts or focus only on appending pictorial illustrations to what they hear. The point is that simply being in the presence of art forms is not sufficient to occasion an aesthetic experience or to change a life.

Aesthetic experiences require conscious participation in a work, a going out of energy, an ability to notice what is there to be noticed in the play, the poem, the quartet. Knowing "about," even in the most formal academic manner, is entirely different from constituting an fictive world imaginatively and entering it perceptually, affectively, and cognitively. To introduce students to the manner of such engagement is to strike a delicate balance between helping learners to pay heed—to attend to shapes, patterns, sounds, rhythms, figures of speech, contours, and lines—and helping liberate them to achieve particular works as meaningful. And it is perhaps the refusal to control what is discovered as meaningful that strikes traditional educators as at odds with their conception of norms or their notions of appropriate cultural literacy. Indeed, this kind of refusal, which I see as essential, may well be at the root of certain administrators' preoccupation with national standards today.

If, however, we are to provide occasions for significant encounters with works of art, we have to combat both standardization and what Hannah Arendt called "thoughtlessness" on the part of all of those involved. Arendt had particularly in mind "the heedless reck-lessness or hopeless confusion or complacent repetition of 'truths' which have become trivial and empty" (1958, p. 5), a problem which continues to afflict us today. Her description recalls the behavior John Dewey had labeled as a "social pathology" thirty years earlier, a pathology manifested "in querulousness, in impotent drifting, in uneasy snatching at distractions, in idealization of the long estab-lished, in a facile optimism assumed as a cloak" ([1927] 1954, p. 170). Concerned about "sloppiness, superficiality, and recourse to sensations as a substitute for ideals," Dewey also made the point that "thinking deprived of its normal course takes refuge in acad-emic specialism" (p. 168). For Arendt, the remedy is "to think what we are doing." That is, we need to have and to teach self-reflec-tiveness originating in situated life, the life of persons in their plu-rality, open to one another in their distinctive locations, engaging with one another in dialogue. Provoked by the spectacle of the Nazi Adolf Eichmann, Arendt broached the same theme in a warn-ing against "cliches, stock phrases, [and] adherence to conven-tional, standardized codes of expression and conduct [which have] the socially recognized function of protecting us against reality, that is, against the claim on our thinking attention that all events and facts make by virtue of their existence" (1978, p. 4). Yet her warning was not a call for a new intellectualism, or a new concen-tration on higher-order skills. Instead, she was asking for a way of seeking clarity and authenticity in the face of thoughtlessness, and it seems to me that we must ask for much the same thing if we truly wish to open the young to the arts, if we are committed to the release of imagination.

Thoughtfulness is needed if we are to resist the messages of the media in the serious fashion Eco suggests, for it is difficult to think of young imaginations being freed without young learners' first finding out how to take a critical and thoughtful approach to the simulacra, the fabricated realities, presented to them by the media. To think in relation to what we are doing is to be conscious of our-selves struggling to make meanings, to make critical sense of what authoritative others are offering as objectively, authoritatively "real."

When we hold an image of what is objectively "the fact," it has the effect of reifying what we experience, making our experience resistant to reevaluation and change rather than open to imagination. I find a metaphor for the reification that must be overcome in the disease at the center of Camus's *Plague* (1948). The pestilence that strikes the town of Oran (submerged in habit and "doing business") thrusts most of the inhabitants into resignation, isolation, or despair. Gradually revealing itself as inexorable and incurable, it freezes people into place; it is simply *there*. Similarly, Dr. Rieux fights the plague for the most abstract of reasons at first, because that is his job; it is as logical an action as two and two equalling four. Only later, when the unspeakable tragedies he witnesses make him *think* about what he is doing, does he reconceive his practice and realize that the most important thing he can do is not be accepting of the pestilence because that is to be complicitous with it.

Likewise, Tarrou recognizes that the plague can be understood as a metaphor for people's indifference or distancing or (I would add) thoughtlessness. Trying to be a "saint without God," he finds the wit and, yes, the imagination to organize people into sanitary squads to fight the plague and, critically, make it the moral concern of all, because everyone carries the microbe for the plague of the body, the potential for the plague of indifference; it is, he tells Rieux, natural. He means what Arendt meant and Dewey and Eco and others who resist a society that has a lack of care, a lack of concern. As sources of moral plague, he has in mind evasions of complex problems, overly facile formulations of the human predicament, conventional solutions—all those factors I would say stand directly in the way of imaginative thinking and engagements with the arts. "Health, integrity, purity (if you like)—is a product of the human will," says Tarrou, "of a vigilance that must never falter." The message for us, of course, is that we (and those who are our students) must be given opportunities to choose ourselves as persons of integrity, persons who care. Tarrou also has a deep suspicion of turgid language that obscures the actualities of things, that too often substitutes abstractions for concrete particulars. This too is one of the modes of the thoughtlessness that Arendt urges us to remedy. She wants "plain, clear-cut language" and she wants to urge people, as does Tarrou, to attend to what is around them, "to stop and think" (1978, p. 4). Camus and Arendt affirm that such awareness and such openness to the world are what allow us to become conscious of alternative possibilities and—as we gain such a consciousness—allow us to become willing to risk encounters with Picasso's "weeping women," with Euripides' *Medea*, with *Moby Dick*, with Balanchine's *Prodigal Son*, with Mahler's *Songs of the Earth*.

There is another novel that enables its readers to envisage that what stands in the way of imagination is often the language spoken in classrooms in our technological, information age. As in the case of *The Plague*, I turn to this novel not in order to add to my knowledge or to find some buried truth, but because, as a work of literary art, it has made me see over the course of time what I might never have seen in my own lived world. It has, as it were, moved me to reach down for forgotten or repressed memories and insights and losses and to order them in accord with the ordering in the text. It has involved me in "rewriting the text of the work within the text of [my] life" (Barthes, 1975, p. 62).

Christa Wolf's novel *Accident: A Day's News* has moved me to clarify my own responses to the technical and the abstract in my experience. It may be because it has to do with the accident at Chernobyl some years ago, as experienced and responded to by a woman writer, a mother and grandmother living in the East German countryside. She is preoccupied both by her brother's brain surgery, taking place on the same day as the nuclear reactor accident, and by the consequences of that accident for her grandchildren and for children around the world. She spends no time wondering how she has responded or will respond to such a crisis; her preoccupation is with others—those she loves and the unknown ones whom she cannot for a moment forget—in a world of simultaneous technological beneficence and harm. It is particularly interesting, within the context of an ethic of care, to contain for a moment within our own experience a moral agent like Tarrou, trying to be a "saint without God," and a frightened young mother picturing what it means to pour away thousands of liters of milk for fear of poisoning the children in Germany while "the children on the other side of the earth are perishing for lack of those foods" (1989, p. 17).

It is also interesting to compare her reaction to two very different images, one immediately human and individual, the other more abstract. When the narrator asks her daughter to tell her about her grandchildren, she hears "that the little one had pranced about the kitchen, a wing nut on his thumb, his hand held high. Me Punch. Me Punch. I was thrilled by the image." But in contrast to this thrill, another sequence of mental pictures makes her think that she is "forced to admire the way in which everything fits together with a sleepwalker's precision: the desire of most people for a comfortable life, their tendency to believe the speakers on raised platforms and the men in white coats; the addiction to harmony and the fear of contradiction of the many seem to correspond to the arrogance and hunger for power, the dedication to profit, unscrupulous inquisitiveness, and self-infatuation of the few." But if it is so admirable, she wonders, "what was it that didn't add up in this equation?" (p. 17). It is this kind of picturing and questioning that may well be barred by the preoccupation with world-class achievement and human resources entailed by Goals 2000.

It does not have to be. Cognitive adventuring and inquiry are much more likely to be provoked by the grandmother's question about "this equation" and her wonder about people's tendency to believe men in white coats than they are by the best of curriculum frameworks or by the most responsible and "authentic" assessment. To set students' imaginations moving in response to a text like Wolf's may well be to confront the students with a demand to choose in a fundamental way, to choose between a desire for harmony along with the easy answer and a commitment to the search for alternative possibilities. Wolf's narrator, almost as if she were one of the weeping women, looks at the blue sky and (quoting some unnamed source) says, "Aghast, the mothers search the sky for the inventions of learned men" (1989, p. 27). She begins pondering the language and the difficulty of breaking through terms like "half-life" and "cesium," or "cloud" instead of polluted rain. And once again, we may be helped to feel a need to break through the mystifications of technology and the language to which it has given rise, a need to battle against disengagement in knowing and to speaking.

When Wolf's narrator ponders the motives of those who thought up the procedures for the "peaceful utilization of nuclear energy," she recalls a protest against a nuclear power plant and the rebukes and reprimands directed at the protestors for their skepticism that a scientific utopia was at hand. Then she lists to herself the activities which the men of science and technology "presumably do not pursue or which, if forced upon them, they would consider a waste of time: Changing a baby's diapers. Cooking, shopping with a child on one's arm or in the baby carriage. Doing the laundry, hanging it up to dry, taking it down, folding it, ironing it, darning it. Sweeping the floor, mopping it, polishing it, vacuuming it. Dusting. Sewing. Knitting. Crocheting. Embroidering. Doing the dishes. Doing the dishes. Taking care of a sick child. Thinking up stories to tell. Singing songs. And how many of these activities do I myself consider a waste of time?" (1989, p. 31).

Reading this, letting it help us pose a new set of questions, we cannot but consider the role such particularities might play in classroom conversation and in our efforts to awaken persons to talk about what ought to be. Wolf's narrator believes that the "expanding monstrous technological creation" may be a substitute for life for many people, a substitute gratification. She is quite aware of the benevolent aspects of technology: her brother, after all, is benefiting from advanced neurosurgery as she waits—and thinks. But she thinks about what we might well think about in our schools, about the less as well as the more benevolent consequences of technology for the ones we love. Her thinking may remind us once again of how important it remains for us to keep alive ideas, images of everything we love. Doing so, I want to believe, we may be able to create schoolroom atmospheres where young people are moved to find hope again and, even in small spaces, begin to repair.

This brings me back to my argument for the arts, so unconscionably neglected in the talk of educational goals for the year 2000. We need to recognize that the events that make up aesthetic experiences are events that occur within and by means of the transactions with our environment that situate us in time and space. Some say that participatory encounters with paintings, dances, stories, and all other art forms enable us to recapture a lost spontaneity. Breaking through the frames of presuppositions and conventions, we are enabled to recapture the processes of our becoming. Reflecting on our life histories, our projects, we may be able to resist making a "divinity" of the technological revolution, and we may gain a perspective on the men in white coats or even on our own desires for withdrawal and for harmony. Made aware of ourselves as questioners, as meaning makers, as persons engaged in constructing and reconstructing realities with those around us, we may communicate to students the notion that reality is multiple perspectives and that the construction of it is never complete, that there is always more. I am reminded of Paul Cézanne's several renderings of Mont St. Victoire and of his way of suggesting that it must be viewed from several angles, from multiple perspectives if it is to be achieved as a phenomenon in consciousness.

Cézanne made much of the insertion of the body into the landscapes he was making visible; and that itself may suggest a dimension of experience in which to ground our thinking and the thinking of those we teach. There are some who say that the aesthetics of dance, for instance, confront the question of what it means to be human. Arnold Berleant writes that "in establishing a human realm through movement, the dancer, with the participating audience, engages in the basic act out of which arise both all experience and our human constructions of the world. . . . It stands as the direct denial of that most pernicious of all dualisms, the division of body and consciousness. In dance, thought is primed at the point of action. This is not the reflection of the contemplative mind but rather intellect poised in the body, not the deliberate consideration of alternative courses but thought in process, intimately responding to and guiding the actively engaged body" (1991, p. 167). The focus is on process and practice; the skill in the making is embodied in the object. In addition, the dance provides occasions for the emergence of the integrated self. Surely, this view of the self ought to be taken into account in our peculiarly technicized and academicized time.

Berleant's remarks relate to painting as well, if painting is viewed (as it should be) in relation to the creator's and the perceiver's physical body, as it orients itself in space and time. Taking a participatory stance, we may enter the landscape or the room or the open street that is shown. Different modes of perception are asked of us, of course, by Raphael, Delacroix, Cézanne, Picasso, Edward Hopper, Mary Cassatt—but that ought to mean that we widen our sensitivity to perceived form, color, and space. Jean-Paul Sartre, making a point of significance for anyone concerned about the role of art and the awakening of imagination, tells us:

The work is never limited to the painted, sculpted or narrated object. Just as one perceives things only against the background of the world, so the objects represented by art appear against the

background of the universe. . . . If the painter presents us with a
field or a vase of flowers, his paintings are windows which are open
on the whole world. We follow the red path which is buried among
the wheat much farther than van Gogh has painted it, among other
wheat fields, under other clouds, to the river which empties into
the sea, and we extend to infinity, to the other end of the world,
the deep finality which supports the existence of the field and the
earth. So that, through the various objects which it produces or
reproduces, the creative act aims at a total renewal of the world.
Each painting, each book, is a recovery of the totality of being.
Each of them presents this totality to the freedom of the spectator.
For this is quite the final goal of art: to recover this world by giving
it to be seen as it is, but as if it had its source in human freedom
[1949, p. 57].

Sartre's insight sums up in many ways the significance of encounters with the arts for classrooms in which the young are moved to
imagine, to extend, and to renew. Surely, nothing can be more
important than finding the source of learning, not in extrinsic
demand, but in human freedom.

Everything I have discussed in this chapter directly concerns
what is today described as the active learner, here conceived as one
awakened to pursue meaning and to endow a life story with meaning. Yes, one tendency in education today is to shape malleable
young people to serve the needs of technology and the postindustrial society. However, there is another tendency that has to do with
the growth of persons, with the education of persons to become
different, to find their voices, and to play participatory and articulate parts in a community in the making. Encounters with the arts
and activities in the domains of art can nurture the growth of persons who will reach out to one another as they seek clearings in
their experience and try to be more ardently in the world. If the
significance of the arts for growth and inventiveness and problem
solving is recognized at last, a desperate stasis may be overcome
and hopes may be raised, the hopes of felt possibility. Muriel
Rukeyser's "Elegy in Joy" superbly suggests the feeling of possibility we might experience.

Out of our life the living eyes
See peace in our own image made,
Able to give only what we can give:

Bearing two days like midnight. "Live,"
The moment offers: the night requires
Promise effort love and praise.

Now there are no maps and no magicians.
No prophets but the young prophet, the sense of the world.
The gift of our time, the world to be discovered.
All the continents giving off their several lights,
the one sea, and the air. And all things glow. ([1949] 1992,
p. 104).

Art offers life; it offers hope; it offers the prospect of discovery; it offers light. Resisting, we may make the teaching of the aesthetic experience our pedagogic creed.

| **Texts and Margins**

We are reminded by the critic Denis Donoghue of how many people still consider the arts to be mere entertainments, without practical use. And "it is true enough that the arts will not cure a toothache [or] help very much in surmounting the pressures placed on us by the material world," he admits.

> But in another way, they are really momentous, because they pro-vide for spaces in which we can live in total freedom. Think of [life] as a page. The main text is central, it is the text of need, of food and shelter, of daily preoccupations and jobs, keeping things going. This text is negotiated mostly by convention, routine, habit, duty, we have very little choice in it. So long as we are in this text, we merely coincide with our ordinary selves. If the entire page were taken up with the text, we would have to live according to its non-conventional rhythms, even in our leisure hours; because they too are subjected to conventions [1983, p. 129].

Donoghue concludes that the arts are on the margins of most people's lives; the "margin" being "the place for those feelings and intuitions which daily life doesn't have a place for and mostly seems to suppress." Yet those who choose to live "within the arts . . . can make a space for themselves and fill it with intimations of freedom and presence" (p. 129). The idea of making spaces for ourselves, experiencing ourselves in our connectedness and taking initiatives to move through those spaces, seems to me to be of the first impor-tance. As Martin Heidegger says, things happen now and then "beyond what is" when an open place appears: "There is a clearing, a lighting" reaching beyond what we are sure we know (1971, p. 53). In Chapter Ten, I discussed the ways in general that art releases the imagination. In this chapter, I take those arguments further, looking at our need to learn a pedagogy that joins art education and aesthetic education so that we can enable our students to live within the arts, making clearings and spaces for themselves. I say "we" in the hope that there exists and that I can speak to a community of educators committed to emancipatory pedagogy, particularly in the domain of the arts. Such a community must include in its dialogue women and men of all classes, backgrounds, colors, and religious faiths, each one free to speak from a distinctive perspective, each one reaching from that distinctive perspective toward the making of some common world. And it must *share* unabashed love for the arts.

Hoping to challenge empty formalism, didacticism, and elitism, many of us teachers believe that the shocks of awareness to which the arts give rise leave us (*should* leave us) less immersed in the everyday and more impelled to wonder and to question. It is not uncommon for the arts to leave us somehow ill at ease or to prod us beyond acquiescence. They may, now and then, move us into spaces where we can envision other ways of being and ponder what it might signify to realize them. But moving into such spaces requires a willingness to resist the forces that press people into passivity and bland acquiescence. It requires a refusal of what Foucault called "normalization," the power of which imposes homogeneity and allows people "to determine levels, to fix specialties, and to render the differences useful by fitting them one to another" (1984a, p. 197). To resist such tendencies is to become aware of the ways in which certain dominant social practices enclose us in molds, define us in accord with extrinsic demands, discourage us from going beyond ourselves and from acting on possibility.

In truth, I do not see how we can educate young persons if we do not enable them on some level to resist such tendencies and to open clearings for communicating across the boundaries, for choosing, for becoming different in the midst of intersubjective relationships. In part, I argue for aware engagements with the arts for everyone, so that individuals in this democracy will be less likely to confine themselves to the "main text," less likely to coincide forever with what they are. Most commonly, what is worthy or respectable in this society's main text is identified with the white, middle-class values so long taken for granted as "American." Because they have been taken for granted, they have seldom been named; therefore, they have not been subject to examination or critique. The effect of this text on minorities is to make them feel like outsiders and invisible to the dominant culture. When Herbert Marcuse (1977, pp. 10–11) speaks of the qualities of art that allow it to indict established reality and evoke images of liberation, he may be suggesting, as I am here, the relevance of art in overcoming the inability to see others.

Moreover, as we integrate engagements with works of art, or the art world, into our pedagogy, it is also important that we heed Arthur Danto's reminder that "there cannot be an art world without theory, for the art world is logically dependent upon theory." An art theory detaches objects from the real world and make them "part of a different world, an *art* world, a world of *interpreted* things" (1981, p. 135). The art world is a *constructed* world, and therefore we must remember to view it as contingent and always open to critique. We must regard it as always open to expansion and revision. The canon, once defined by a certain number of men in time past, must always be skeptically conceived and kept open so that we no longer ignore the new and the different as they appear. It is increasingly evident that formulating a definition of "art" that suits everyone or making a universally acceptable decision as to what constitutes a work of art presents an insoluble problem. We can no longer placidly limit classroom choices to works ascribed greatness by narrow groups. However, neither can we simply list what we think to be "representative" samples from other traditions and call the result multiplicity. Today, we must allow the voices we realize were long silenced to sound: the voices of women, of ethnic minorities, of poets and musicians recognized outside the Western world, and we must make way for the untried and the unexpected. I believe it is by selecting out what they themselves have come to prize that teachers can offer their students opportunities for transformation of experience.

My concern over the canon, however, is not solely with our enabling persons to engage authentically and adventurously with a range of artists. I also have exploration of a range of media in mind—not just written and spoken language—vital as that is, being the stuff out of which riddles, poems, and stories are made and through which dreams are told, fictions invented, and novels given form—but also paint, pastels, clay, and stone; the melodies, dissonances, and pulses of sounds that are music; and the body in motion in dance, making shapes, exerting effort, articulating visions, and moving in space and time.

Pluralities of persons can be helped to go in search of their own images, their own visions of things, through carving, painting, dancing, singing, or writing. They can be enabled to realize that one way of finding out what they are seeing, feeling, and imagining is to transmute it into some kind of content and to give that content form. Doing so, they may experience all sorts of sensuous openings. They may unexpectedly perceive patterns and structures they never knew existed in the surrounding world. They may discover all sorts of new perspectives as the curtains of inattentiveness pull apart. They may recognize some of the ways in which consciousnesses touch and refract and engage with one another, the ways in which particular consciousnesses reach out to grasp the appearances of things.

When this happens to individuals, even very young individuals, they are clearly more attuned than they would otherwise be to grasping Alvin Ailey's reaching for a celebration at a riverside, the title character's weaving of tales in Isabel Allende's novel *Eva Luna* (1989), Stravinsky's rendering of the dash and shimmer of a firebird, Morrison's exploring in *Beloved* of the searing feeling of being a mother and sacrificing and then standing over the abyss thus created, Keith Haring's limning of stark shapes, or graffiti artists' imprinting of related works on city doors and walls. When students can share in learning the language of dance by moving as dancers move, entering the symbol system of novel writing and story weaving by composing their own narratives out of words, working with glass sounds or drums to find out what it signifies to shape the medium of sound, all these immediate involvements lead to a participant kind of knowing and a participant sort of engagement with art forms themselves. Aesthetic education ought to include adventures like these, just as it ought to include intentional efforts to foster increasingly informed and ardent encounters with artworks. Not incidentally, it ought to include the posing of the kinds of questions—aesthetic questions—that arise in the course of art experiences: Why do I feel spoken to by this work; excluded by that one? In what sense does this song actually embody Mahler's grief? What is it about Beethoven's "Ode to Joy" that makes me feel I am coming in touch with some transcendent reality? In what way does Márquez's novel *One Hundred Years of Solitude* (1970) reflect, refract, explain, interpret Colombian history? In what sense is Jamaica Kincaid's West Indian island in *Lucy* (1990) "real"? To pose aesthetic questions is to make the aesthetic experience itself more reflective, more critical, more resonant. Art education is deepened and expanded by what occurs in answering such questions.

By "art education," I mean, of course, the spectrum that includes dance education, music education, the teaching of painting and the other graphic arts, and (I would hope) the teaching of some kinds of writing. By "aesthetic education," I mean the deliberate efforts to foster increasingly informed and involved encounters with art. The point of enabling our students to both engage in art as a maker and experience existing artworks is to release them to be more fully present to, for example, an Edward Hopper city painting, a Cézanne landscape, a jazz composition, a Béla Bartók folk song, or a Joyce novel. Achieving this aim is, in part, what leads me to propose that art education be infused with efforts to do aesthetic education. We are fully present to art when we understand what is there to be noticed in the work at hand, release our imaginations to create orders in the field of what is perceived, and allow our feelings to inform and illuminate what is there to be realized. I would like to see one pedagogy feeding into the other: the pedagogy that empowers students to create informing the pedagogy that empowers them to attend (and, perhaps, to appreciate) and vice versa. I would like to see both pedagogies carried on with a sense of both learner and teacher as seeker and questioner, someone consciously "condemned to meaning" (Merleau-Ponty, [1962] 1967, p. xix) and thus reflective about his or her choosing process, turning toward the clearing that might (or might not) lie ahead. The ends in view are multiple, but they surely include the stimulation of imagination and perception, a sensitivity to various modes of seeing and sense making, and a grounding in the situations of lived life.

While most critics and teachers agree today that we are unlikely to come upon a fixed definition of *art* or a theory that accounts for all the art forms that have been and all that have yet to be, most would support Marcuse in his claim that art "breaks open a dimension inaccessible to other experience, a dimension in which human beings, nature, and things no longer stand under the law of the established reality principle." The languages and images in works of art, when persons are released to attend and let their energies go out to the art, make "perceptible, visible, and audible that which is no longer, or not yet, perceived, said, and heard in everyday life" (1977, p. 72). We can all recall experiences that validate Marcuse's claim. I remember, for example, the subversion of traditional orders of reality accomplished by Braque and Picasso when they enabled so many to realize the significance of looking through multiple perspectives at the lived world. I remember the astonishing disclosures in simultaneously viewing the ten or so serial visions of Rouen Cathedral rendered by Monet over three months. Like the poplar trees or the grain stacks in Monet's other serial paintings, the cathedral reveals changing shapes and even changing meanings of structure as the times of day, the play of shadows, and the slants of light change. When viewing the paintings of the grain stacks, we may feel a shifting, expressive rhythm of relationship, a play between a small and modest grain stack and a looming but protective one or between the shadow cast by the stacks and the glow of the sky beyond. It is not only seeing something in the visible world that we would not have suspected were it not for Monet that is of value to us, it is also recognizing that the vision—and the meaning and the pulsation—are functions of a certain way of attending on our part. Monet did not, after all, provide for us a window on a series of landscapes that were objectively out there and objectively "impressionist" in appearance. Just as in poetry, in painting, meanings are ways of relating to things. The meanings of those Monet landscapes (like the meanings of Velázquez's *Pope Innocent* or Edward Hopper's lonely city streets or Goya's *Disasters of War*) do not reside in the subject matter, in the canvas on the wall, or in our subjectivities when we come to them. Meaning *happens* in and by means of an encounter with a painting, with a text, with a dance performance. The more informed our encounter—by some acquaintance with the medium at hand, some use of critical lenses, and some consciousness of an art world (Danto, 1981, p. 5)—the more we are likely to notice and the more the work is likely to mean. If questions beat inside us about whether or not something is to be called good art or bad art, what context has to do with an artwork, and what constitute good reasons, we are likely to wonder and to perceive even more.

None of our encounters can happen, however, without the

release of imagination, the capacity to look *through* the windows of the actual, to bring as-ifs into being in experience. Imagination creates new orders as it brings "the severed parts together" (Woolf, 1976, p. 72), connecting human consciousness and works of visual art, literature, music, and dance. Imagination may be our primary means of forming an understanding of what goes on under the heading of "reality"; imagination may be responsible for the very texture of our experience. Once we do away with habitual separations of the subjective from the objective, the inside from the outside, appearances from reality, we might be able to give imagination its proper importance and grasp what it means to place imagination at the core of understanding. The American poet Hart Crane spoke of imagination as "a reasonably connective agent toward fresh concepts, more inclusive evaluations" (1926, p. 35). In his turn, the poet Wallace Stevens talked about the way imagination enhanced the sense of reality, about its being "the power of the mind over the possibilities of things" (1965, p. 31). Mary Warnock writes of how imagination is connected with emotions yet how necessary it is "for the application of thoughts or concepts to things" (1978, p. 202). She says that we must acknowledge that imagination and the emotions, including taste and sensibility, can be, and ought to be, educated. My argument here is that a powerful way of educating them is through initiation into the artistic-aesthetic domains.

For all his scientific intentions with respect to the effects of light on appearances, without imagination Monet could not conceivably have seen the facade of Rouen Cathedral in so many ways: as a stern embodiment of a dark faith, as a dancing radiant screen of promise, as a delicate lacy veil. Nor could we—without some capacity to transform those strokes of paint, those whites and golds and dark blues into a rendering of a cathedral, realize those distinctive visions within our consciousness. As we succeed in doing so, we are very likely to change some dimension of our perceiving and thus some dimension of our lives.

Wallace Stevens's poetry depicts imagination's centrality with peculiar acuity, perhaps especially to those who have themselves tried to write poems. When Stevens compares imagination to a "blue guitar" that (to the despair of certain listeners) does not "play things as they are" ([1937] 1964, p. 165), he cannot but evoke a resonance in those who know what it is to look at things as if they could be otherwise and who can attend to the oddity of a guitar colored blue, with strings that can sound an infinity of songs. When Stevens writes in another poem of "six significant land-scapes" and, letting his imagination play, realizes unexpected pos-sibilities in blue and white larkspur at the edge of a shadow, or in a pool shining "Like a bracelet/Shaken in a dance," or in the moon in a white gown, its folds "Filled with yellow light./ . . . Its hair filled/With certain blue crystallizations/From stars/Not far off" ([1916] 1964, pp. 73–74), he creates new connections between selves and things, and he maps readers' landscapes anew. The remarkable verses that follow remind readers that things are shaped and sculpted and that

> Not all the knives of the lamp-posts,
> Nor the chisels of the long streets,
> Nor the mallets of the domes
> And high towers
> Can carve
> What one star can carve,
> Shining through grape-leaves [pp. 74–75].

It is not necessary to be a sculptor to share the feeling of discovery by entering a new space, bringing together images of knives, chis-els, and mallets so that the star itself can become a carver, a sculp-tor, as it shines through leaves. It is not only our thoughts of starlight that may be changed through such figurative work. So may our idea or image of the sculptor, becoming an image of one who makes unpredictable forms. In the last stanza of the poem, Stevens lets meaning like this culminate somehow and explode:

> Rationalists, wearing square hats,
> Think, in square rooms,
> Looking at the floor,
> Looking at the ceiling.
> They confine themselves
> To right-angled triangles.
> If they tried rhomboids,
> Cones, waving lines, ellipses—
> As, for example, the ellipse of the half-moon—
> Rationalists would wear sombreros [p. 75].

All this meaning, too, is wrought by means of metaphor and through the kind of disclosure of unexpected relationships that brings something new into a reader's world. Experiencing the poem either from without or from within, the reader cannot but feel released from a confinement and a one-dimensionality that both depend on having a rationalist's gaze. When the rationalists are challenged to try rhomboids and cones, they are being lured to allow their lines and squares to move through a spectrum of shapes to the ellipse of the half-moon. They are not being asked to give up thinking or attending to their texts but to exchange their mortarboards for sombreros, at least now and then. They are being challenged to attend to things with a greater sense of play and panache, of the dialectic of the moon and the square room and of margin and text.

Many people can summon up kindred experiences if they allow themselves occasional adventures on the margins, if they let themselves cut free from anchorage through choice and action, through "belonging to the world" (Merleau-Ponty, [1962] 1967, p. 456). I am not suggesting that engagement with the arts ought to lead to denials of the work that has to be done or to distractions from doing it. Nor am I suggesting that the margins of experience are places for giving way to indulgence and sensuous extremes. As I view them, the arts offer opportunities for perspective, for perceiving alternative ways of transcending and of being in the world, for refusing the automatism that overwhelms choice.

These alternative ways may be grim and, at first glimpse, ugly. They may take the form of such images as these, in Elizabeth Bishop's "Night City":

> No foot could endure it,
> shoes are too thin.
> Broken glass, broken bottles,
> heaps of them burn [(1976) 1983, p. 167].

And where the tears and guilt are burning, there is a tycoon who "wept by himself" and "a blackened moon." But this is a view from a plane, we are reminded, through a dead sky; and the poem ends hauntingly, with a parenthesis: "(Still, there are creatures,/careful ones, overhead./They set down their feet, they walk/green, red; green, red)" (p. 168).

Like the violated children in Charles Dickens's novels, the battered women in Charlotte Perkins Gilman's works, the little ones tormented in Dostoyevsky's world—where, as Ivan Karamasov tells his brother, "it is a peculiar characteristic of many people, this love of torturing children and children only" ([1880], 1945, p. 286)— the execution of the guerrilla fighters in *The Disasters of War*, and the photographs of terror from the Holocaust, there are images and figures that speak directly to our indignation, to some dimension of ourselves where we connect with others. They open our eyes, they stir our flesh, they may even move us to try to repair our world.

I recently saw a painting of the German terrorist Ulrike Meinhof, fallen on her back after what seems to have been her hanging. Her dim pallid profile and her wounded neck appear in an airless setting where there is neither clarity nor breathing space. The painter is Gerhard Richter, who worked from photographs in his rendering of the work he calls "Red Battalion," showing the members of Baader-Meinhof gang—all of whom are now dead. "Art," he writes, "is always to a large extent about need, despair, and hopelessness . . . and we often neglect this content by placing too much importance on the formal, aesthetic side alone" (Kuspit, 1990, p. 129). Donald Kuspit comments that the "dialectic of concreteness and hazy suggestiveness" in Richter's dim depiction of photographed reality "emphatically articulates the major fact about the deaths: their incomprehensibility, the suspicion that surrounds them. . . . This is what makes them catalytic of 'infinite,' morbid speculation, including pessimistic observation of how seemingly 'open' images of events can in effect be used to rewrite history by closing it down. This incomprehensibility issues in the slippery, hidden mood of the paintings" (pp. 131–132). Richter himself apparently sees all ideologies and many beliefs as life threatening, and he regards the Baader-Meinhof gang as victimized by ideological behavior per se. We look, we wonder, and the questions come and batter us. Images like Richter's may perhaps evoke both a kind of outrage as we view what ideology and terror finally ask of us and a fundamental doubt, a responsiveness to pallid pointless death.

One of the functions of the arts is not only to make us see "according to our deserts" (Conrad, [1898] 1967), not only to change our everyday lives in some fashion, but to subvert our thoughtlessness and complacencies, our certainties even about art itself. Prone as we are to oppose aesthetic experience to the controls and limitations imposed by technicism, we may be too likely to find occasions for shelter in the arts, mere fulfillment of unmediated desire. Because we teach children whose spontaneity we want so badly to preserve, we choose too frequently to find only purity and radiance in domains that touch the depths as well as the heights of being human in the world.

It is because I believe it so important for those of us who teach to be reminded of this that I value encounters with artists like Joseph Beuys so much, and with Robert Wilson and Philip Glass and William Balcon and Toni Morrison and Martha Clarke and John Quare. Their association with the avant-garde or the postmodern is not the important thing. What is important, apart from the complex quality and, often, the eerie beauty of their works, is the problematic that each embodies, the restiveness with limits, the sense of some approximation of "the ellipse of the half-moon." I think, for example, of Jenny Holzer, whose work recently won a first prize at the Venice Biennale, and her mobile neon messages that sculpted the spirals of the Guggenheim Museum not long ago—red and white electric signs with phrases and words colliding and overlapping and the meanings rising and falling. Truisms were spelled out by the tubes and inscribed on marble stools, truisms sometimes as vague as Richter's images, sometimes startlingly and embarrassingly clear. There are one-liners—"The Family Is Living on Borrowed Time"; "Abuse of Power Comes as No Surprise"—that are parodies and simplifications of what appears on the walls of buildings and bus stops (Waldman, 1989). Then there are the introspective first-person messages she calls "Laments": "With only my mind to protect me I go into Days"; "What I fear is in a box with fur to muffle it. Every day I do nothing important because I am scared blank and lazy" (p. 18).

When I watched the glowing messages move by, become cliché, become collage, become conceptual art, minimal art, I was also watching a language of signs rendering the visible world invisible at a moment when I was celebrating the slow emergence of my world into visibility. "I try not," Holzer says, "to make [this art] completely random or sloppy, but there still has to be a wild part in it. In the writing you have to go off into the stratosphere and then come back down. That's what I like, when things spin out of control but then are pulled back so that they're available to you. I want them to be accessible, but not so easy that you throw them away after a second or two" (Waldman, 1989, p. 15). Appreciative as I am of Holzer's moving between randomness and control, of her using language to move beyond the tangible, I am caught in questions again about meaning and reference, and I find the questions almost as important as the moments of disclosure. Some of the same questions arise, I realize, when I try to penetrate the mythic, the secret parts of Toni Morrison's *Beloved*, or when I go back to William Faulkner's story "The Bear" or what "confidence" and "trust" actually signified in his strange tale called "The Confidence Man."

Of course, we need to use criticism, if only to help us elucidate, to help us notice what is there to be noticed, but we also have to find out what critics individually assume: through what critical perspectives are we looking at the works we are trying to make clear? We have to at once resist the pull of expertise and be conscious of "hype" and fetish making and the ways in which the market determines value and choice. Today, we who are teachers have an obligation to be aware of and wary of efforts that would determine from "above" (or from some apocryphal center of things) what is acceptable in the world of art and what has to be branded unacceptable because it is, say, charged with being pornographic, impious, homosexual, unpatriotic, or obscene. To issue edicts like the ones we have recently read against certain artworks, to utter proscriptions and prescriptions may be within the law. If, however, we stand by the view that experience always holds more than can be predicted, and that imagination creates openings to the unpredictable, we cannot but be chilled by what recent prohibitions imply. Realizing, too, that creative and appreciative encounters in the arts depend upon imaginative energies, we can only anticipate from such prohibitions a lulling and a limiting consequence that is miseducative in the deepest sense. We are bound to ponder, as authentically and critically as we can, what a Robert Mapplethorpe exhibition means to us as persons and what its banning means. What do the works of those like Andrés Serrano and Karen Finley and those who burn the flag mean to us when they are challenged? We may have pondered similarly when *Marat/Sade* and the musical *Hair* presented nudity upon the stage. We do not necessarily want to expose children to Mapplethorpe or Finley, although there may well be ways of doing so. We do, however, want to learn our-selves—and enable children to learn—what it is to make judgments on the grounds of lived experience and, at the same time, in rela-tion to community norms. Trying to open students to the new and the multiple, we want ourselves to break through some of the crusts of convention, the distortions of fetishism, the sour tastes of narrow faiths.

Such openness requires us to be in continuing quest of our-selves even as it requires that we do what we can to enable as many of the young as possible to crack the codes that prevent so many of them from engaging with works of art. Paintings, novels, and works of music are not likely to be realized by untutored consciousnesses when these artworks appear only in enclaves, in an esoteric or somehow timeless realm, assumed to be out of reach of many. John Dewey said that works of art are too frequently presented as if they have no roots in cultural life, as if they were specimens of fine art and nothing else. Art objects are made to seem remote to ordinary people, as are many fine fictions that reach beyond our daily hori-zons and much music that reaches beyond our accustomed gamut of sound. Set on pedestals, actual or figurative, art forms are removed "from the scope of common or community life" (Dewey, 1934, p. 6), and when they are deliberately set apart from ordinary experience, they serve largely as "insignia of taste and certitude" (p. 9). They confirm people in their elitism; they serve the inter-ests of social power. Walter Benjamin, with somewhat the same idea in mind, writes of such concepts as eternal value and mystery that have been attached to artworks and the "aura" of distance and uniqueness and tradition ([1955] 1978, pp. 222–223) that have made artworks inaccessible to the mass of people. John Berger, too, writes about the ways in which works of art are "enveloped in an atmosphere of entirely bogus religiosity. Works of art are discussed and presented as though they were holy relics: relics which are first and foremost evidence of their own survival" (1984, p. 21). Berger also makes the point that the visual arts have always existed in a preserve, magical or sacred or physical, and that later, moreover, "the preserve of art became a social one. It entered the culture of the ruling class, while physically it was set apart and isolated in their palaces and houses. During all this history, the authority of art was inseparable from the particular authority of the preserve" (p. 33).

Art is separated from the mass of people not only by the distance established when art is located in a "preserve" of some kind but also by the distance created by commodification, by esotericism, by false claims of realism, by artificial mystifications that excluded women, people of color, and the poor. Such separation is also caused by personal innocence or ignorance and by a reliance upon others who are innocent, ignorant, or conditioned by the media. Nor are the arts likely to open themselves naturally to young people who have been systematically demeaned and excluded from what others value as "goods" in their own world. Berger, for example, argues strongly against the view that the arts can be understood spontaneously, saying:

> The idea of innocence faces two ways. By refusing to enter a conspiracy, one remains innocent of that conspiracy. But to remain innocent may also be to remain ignorant. The issue is not between innocence and knowledge (or between the natural and the cultural) but between a total approach to art which attempts to relate it to every aspect of experience and the esoteric approach of a few specialized experts who are the clerks of the nostalgia of a ruling class in decline. (In decline not before the proletariat, but before the new power of the corporation and the state.) The real question is: to whom does the meaning of the art of the past properly belong? To those who can apply it to their own lives, or to a cultural hierarchy of relic specialists? [1984, p. 32].

Views such as this inform my argument for a pedagogy that integrates art education and aesthetic education. Yes, it should be education for a more informed and imaginative awareness, but it should also be education in the kinds of critical transactions that empower students to resist both elitism and objectivism, that allow them to read and to name, to write and to rewrite their own lived worlds.

It is clear enough, of course, that there can be great enjoyment of music, paintings, film, dance, and (to a lesser extent) literature grasped in moments of immediacy, without the interaction of outer and inner visions so essential if works of art are to be brought fully alive. It is clear enough, as well, that there is always a danger of imposing alienating standards, of suggesting a single "right" way of looking at a Monet poplar painting, of discerning the mirrored king and queen behind the artist in Velázquez's always problematic *Las Meninas,* of making sense of the madwoman in *Jane Eyre,* of interpreting the film *The Third Man.* But to take an opposing

view and teach with the suggestion that it is all, in any case, subjective, a matter of taste, is equivalent to the kind of permissiveness
that leads to mindless relativism. To judge the worth of *War and
Peace* by its fidelity to the Napoleonic Wars, or of *A Streetcar Named
Desire* by its fidelity to New Orleans or the "truth" it tells about some
kinds of pathology, is to avoid the aesthetic potentialities in each
work, to refuse the illusion and to treat the work as just another
window on the world.

Dewey used to remind his readers of how necessary it was for
their imaginative and perceptual energies to reach toward a painting or a poem if it were to be transmuted into an aesthetic object
for the one perceiving it. He continued to insist that the aesthetic
is not an intruder from without, not an affair "for odd moments"
(1934, p. 54). Donoghue speaks of the "cherishing bureaucracy"
and the temptation to assimilate, manage, or domesticate the arts
(1983, p. 71). As he sees it, the "State" or those in control seem to
be saying that artists can do what they like, because nothing they
do makes any difference to anyone (p. 74). And, indeed, artists will
not make any real difference if people rush by paintings, go into
reveries in concert halls, skim through works of fiction, come in
contact with art forms without involvement, as if the works in the
various domains were indeed commodities. Dewey wrote about
how important it always is to *attend* actively, to order the details and
particulars that gradually become visible the more we look into
integral patterns or "experienced wholes." He argued that "there
is work done on the part of the percipient as there is on the part
of the artist. The one who is too lazy, idle, or indurated in convention to perform this work will not see or hear. His 'appreciation' will be a mixture of scraps of learning with conformity to
norms of conventional admiration and with a confused, even if
genuine, emotional excitation" (1934, p. 54). There might be
recognition, he said, in the sense of an attaching of correct labels,
but there would not be the energizing encounter that counteracts
passivity. There would not be the launching of perceivers into the
making of meanings, the grounded interpretations that make for
wide-awakeness.

Most of us recognize the delicate balance that must be
achieved between the spontaneity, even careless rapture, of the initial response to a painting, dance performance, or fiction and the

work that is so necessary if the painting, dance, or fiction is to be realized. What we as teachers can communicate about that work and the energies to be released are the crucial issues for us, not necessarily a general cultural literacy or an adeptness at identifying great artists and works of art. Learning to overcome passivity and induration and learning to notice what is to be noticed may lead on and on to new disclosures. Jean-Paul Sartre said this clearly with regard to literature: if the reader "is inattentive, tired, stupid, or thoughtless, most of the relations will escape him. He will never manage to 'catch on' to the object. . . . He will draw some phrases out of the shadow but they will seem to appear as random strokes" (1949, p. 43). Conversely, when we read at our best, we project beyond the words a theme or a meaning. We realize through the language something that is never given *in* the language, whether that language is an Emily Dickinson poem or a Sartre play. We are helped to see that the artist tries to oblige the reader or the percipient to create what the artist discloses, to become an accomplice in freedom with that artist, an accomplice in releasing possibilities. It is this sort of action that is at the core of aesthetic education, this sort of action that may (it seems to me) save our human lives.

If we can enable more young persons to arouse themselves in this way, to make sense of what they see and hear, and to attend to works in their particularity, they may begin to experience art as a way of understanding. While we distinguish between the analytic, abstract rationality we often associate with knowing and the peculiar relational activity that brings us personally in touch with works of art, we may nevertheless well call art a way of knowing. The experience and knowledge gained by this way of knowing opens new modalities for us in the lived world; it brings us in touch with our primordial landscapes, our original acts of perceiving.

Since encounters with the arts can never be endpoints, they may challenge us to new encounters in experience. We may have the experience Merleau-Ponty describes when he talks about "a route" being given to us, "an experience which gradually clarifies itself, which gradually rectifies itself and proceeds by dialogue with itself and with others" (1964a, p. 21). It is hard for me to conceive of a better argument for the relevance of the arts in schools—if it is indeed the case, as so many people believe, that boredom and a sense of futility are among the worst obstacles to learning. To feel oneself en route, to feel oneself in a place where there are always the possibilities of clearings, of new openings, this is what we must communicate to the young if we want to awaken them to their lived situations and enable them to make sense of and to name their worlds.

At the heart of what I am asking for in the domains of the teaching of art and aesthetics is a sense of agency, even of power. Painting, literature, theater, film—all can open doors and move persons to transform. We want to enable all sorts of young people to realize that they have the right to find works of art meaningful against their own lived lives. Moreover, because the world that the arts illumine is a shared world, because the realities to which the arts give rise emerge through acts of communication, the encounters we are enabling students to seek are never wholly autonomous or private. Moving from one's own explorations of pictorial space to a conscious encounter with a Braque painting, looking up from one's own poem to read a Robert Frost or a Muriel Rukeyser poem—one can always enter into dialogue with those around. The languages can be explored; the reasons given; the moments of epiphany celebrated; the differing vantage points articulated. Communities of the wide-awake may take shape, even in the corridors of schools.

If we are indeed to make the margins visible and accessible, if we are to encourage dialectical movements from margin to text and back, we ought to open larger and larger meeting places in schools. We ought to reach out to establish ateliers, studios, and other places where music can be composed and rehearsed, where poems and stories can be read, where drawings and paintings and sculptures can be made. There might be new collaborations among questioners, as teachers and students both engage in perceptual journeys, grasp works and words as events in contexts of meaning, and undertake common searches for their own places and significance in a history to which they too belong and which they invent and interpret as they live.

What we are about can be, must be, life-enhancing, as more and more living beings discover what it is to make a shape or an image, to devise a metaphor, or to tell a tale for the sake of finding their own openings into the realms of the arts. No matter how alienating or shocking some of the images and affirmations they confront (and are urged to confront), they must learn that these works are not to be equated with actualities like war-wounded children, young men left broken on the side of the road, bodies scarred by torturers, or the eyes of people behind bars, but are to confirm that we must not evade, deny, or take for granted these actualities, that we must not be willing to remain passive, to coincide forever with ourselves. We must, instead, seek more shocks of awareness as the time goes on, more explorations, more adventures into meaning, more active and uneasy participation in the human community's unending quest.

Part Three

Community
in the Making

Chapter Twelve

The Passions of Pluralism

There have always been newcomers in the United States; there have always been strangers. There have always been young persons in our classrooms that most teachers did not, could not, see or hear. In recent years, however, invisibility has been refused on many sides. Old silences have been shattered; long-repressed voices are making themselves heard. Yes, we are in search of what John Dewey called "the Great Community" ([1927] 1954, p. 143), but at the same time, we are challenged as never before to confront plurality and multiplicity. Unable to deny or obscure the facts of pluralism, we are asked to choose ourselves with respect to unimaginable diversities. To speak of passions in such a context is not to refer to the strong feelings aroused by what strikes many as a confusion and a cacophony. Rather, it is to have in mind the central sphere for the operation of the passions: "the realm of face-to-face relationships" (Unger, 1984, p. 107). It seems clear that the more continuous and authentic personal encounters can be, the less likely will it be that categorizing and distancing take place. People are less likely to be treated instrumentally, to be made "other" by those around. In this chapter, I speak of pluralism and multiculturalism but with concrete engagements in mind, actual and imagined: engagements with persons young and old, suffering from exclusion, powerlessness, poverty, ignorance, or boredom. I speak with imagination in mind and metaphor and art.

Speaking of passions, engagements, and imagining can become a way of speaking of an expanding community that takes shape when diverse people, speaking as *who* and not *what* they are, come together in both speech and action to constitute something in common among themselves. "Plurality" is "the condition of human action because we are all the same, that is, human, in such a way

155

that nobody is ever the same as anyone else who ever lived, lives, or will live." Even though we are on a common ground, we have different locations on that ground, and each one "sees or hears from a different position" (Arendt, 1958, p. 57). Any object—a classroom, a neighborhood street, a field of flowers—shows itself differently to each spectator. The reality of that object arises out of the sum total of its appearances to all who view it. Thinking of those spectators as participants in an ongoing dialogue, each one speaking out of a distinct perspective and yet open to those around, I find a kind of paradigm for what I have in mind. I discover another in the work of Henry Louis Gates, Jr., who finds that "the challenge facing America in the next century will be the shaping, at long last, of a truly common public culture, one response to the long-silenced cultures of color" (1992, p. 176). More recently, he has evoked philosopher Michael Oakeshott and his notion of a conversation with different voices. Education, Gates suggests, might be "an invitation into the art of this conversation in which we learn to recognize the voices, each conditioned by a different perception of the world." After all, "common sense says that you don't bracket out 90 percent of the world's cultural heritage if you really want to learn about the world" (1991, pp. 711–712).

Yet for many of us, what is common sense for Gates represents an attack on the coherence of what we think of as our heritage, our canon. The notion of attending to different voices conditioned by different perspectives summons up the specter of relativism; and relativism, according to Clifford Geertz, is the "intellectualist Grande Peur [great fear]." It makes people uneasy because it appears to subvert authority; it eats away at what is conceived as objectively real. "If thought is so much out in the world as this," Geertz asks, as the uneasy might ask, "what is to guarantee its generality, its objectivity, its efficacy, or its truth?" (1983, p. 153). There is irony in Geertz's voice here. He knows that "for our time and forward, the image of a general orientation, perspective, *Weltanschauung*, growing out of humanistic studies (or, for that matter, out of scientific ones) and shaping the direction of the culture is a chimera." And he suggests that the "radical variousness of the way we think now" means that if this society is to have an integrated cultural life it must make "it possible for people inhabiting different worlds to have a genuine, and reciprocal, impact upon one another" (p. 161). As we keep experiencing attacks on what is familiar, experiencing "the irruption of otherness, the unexpected" (Clifford, 1988, p. 13), we may well find that our ability to tolerate the unexpected relates to our tolerance for multiculturalism.

For all that, teachers must be well aware that Arthur Schlesinger, Jr., among others who must also be taken seriously, sees a "disuniting of America" (1992) in the making if shared commitments shatter, if we lose touch with the democratic idea. Proponents of what is called "civism" (Pratte, 1988, p. 104) are concerned that pluralism threatens the existence of a democratic ethos intended to transcend all differences. This ethos encompasses the principles of freedom, equality, and justice, as well as regard for human rights; and there is fear that the new relativism and particularism will subvert the common faith. Then there are those like E. D. Hirsch, Jr., who see the concept of a shared background knowledge among people undermined by variousness and the multicultural emphases that distract from what they believe we ought to have in common. When what they call cultural literacy is undermined, the national community itself is eroded (Hirsch, 1987). At the extreme, of course, are those on the far right who find a conspiracy in challenges to the so-called Eurocentric canon and in what they construct as "politically correct," by which they mean a new orthodoxy built out of oversensitivity to multicultural concerns (D'Sousa, 1991, p. 239). As for the religious fundamentalist right, says Robert Hughes, one of the motives driving men like Jesse Helms is to establish themselves as defenders of what they define as the "American Way," now "that their original crusade against the Red Menace has been rendered null and void" (1992, p. 21). Not only do they argue for their "Way" against the grants of the National Endowment for the Arts to avant-garde artists but they also attack such "deviations" as multiculturalism. It is important to hold this in mind as we try to work through a conception of pluralism to an affirmation of the struggle to attain the life of "free and enriching communion" that John Dewey identified with democracy ([1927] 1954, p. 189).

The seer of the life of communion, according to Dewey, was Walt Whitman. Whitman wrote about the many shapes arising in the country in his time, "the shapes of doors giving many exits and entrances" and "shapes of democracy . . . ever projecting other

shapes." In "Song of Myself" (in total contradiction to the fundamentalist version of the "American Way"), he wrote:

> Through me many long dumb voices,
> Voices of the interminable generations of prisoners and
> slaves,
> Voices of the diseas'd and despairing and of thieves and
> dwarfs,
> Voices of cycles of preparation and accretion,
> And of the threads that connect the stars, and of wombs
> and of the father-stuff,
> And of the rights of them the others are down upon. . . .
> Through me forbidden voices [(1855) 1931, p. 53].

Whitman was, from all appearances, the seer of a communion arising out of "many shapes," out of multiplicity. There is no suggestion of a melting pot here; nor is there a dread of plurality.

For some of us, our new feelings that our own stories are worth
telling, the reminders of the "long dumb voices," and the talk of
"the rights of them the others are down upon" cannot but draw our
attention to the absences and silences that are as much a part of
humankind's history as the articulate voices, the shimmering faces,
and the images of emergence and success. Bartleby, the clerk who
"prefers not to," may suddenly become exemplary. (Melville, [1853]
1986). What of those who said no, who found no place, who made
no mark? Do they not say something about a society that closed too
many doors, that allowed people to be abandoned like "wreckage
in the mid-Atlantic"? What of those like Tod Clifton, the former
youth leader who ends up selling Sambo dolls in front of the public library in Ralph Ellison's *Invisible Man*? When the police try to
dislodge him, he protests; and they kill him. The narrator, watching, wonders: "Why did [Tod] choose to plunge into nothingness,
into the void of faceless faces, of soundless voices, lying outside history? . . . All things, it is said, are duly recorded—all things of importance, that is. But not quite; for actually it is only the known, the
seen, the heard, and only those events that the recorder regards as
important are put down. . . . But the cop would be Clifton's histo-
rian, his judge, his witness, his executioner (1952, p. 379).

The many who have similarly ended up "lying outside history" have diminished the community, leaving an empty space on the common ground and leaving undefined an aspect of reality. It is true that we cannot know all the absent ones; but they must be present somehow in their absence. Absence, after all, suggests an emptiness, a void to be filled, a wound to be healed, a flaw to be repaired. Envision the landscape of denial painted by E. L. Doctorow at the beginning of *Ragtime*.

> Teddy Roosevelt was President. The population customarily gathered in great numbers either out of doors for parades, public concerts, fish fries, political picnics, social outings, or indoors in meeting halls, vaudeville theatres, operas, ballrooms. There seemed to be no entertainment that did not involve great swarms of people. Trains and steamers and trolleys moved them from one place to another. That was the style; that was the way people lived. Women were stouter then. They visited the fleet carrying white parasols. Everyone wore white in summer. There was a lot of sexual fainting. There were no Negroes. There were no immigrants [1975, pp. 3–4].

This picture appeals to wonder but also to indignation, demanding a kind of repair. Doctorow is writing about New Rochelle in 1906; but the past he presents reaches into the present, into *our* present, whether or not we ride trolleys anymore. The story has to do with a decent, intelligent black man named Coalhouse Walker, who is cheated, never acknowledged, never understood, scarcely *seen*, and who begins his own fated strategy of vengeance that ends when promises are broken and he is shot down in cold blood. Why is he unseen? Why were there no Negroes, no immigrants? More than likely because of the condition of the minds of those in power, minds that bestowed upon many others the same invisibility that Ellison's narrator encounters. But that mental condition must have been partly due to the play of power in discourse as well as in social arrangements. We may wonder even now what the assimilation or initiation sought by so many educators in those days signified when there were so many blanked-out spaces—"no Negroes . . . no immigrants," oftentimes no full-grown women.

Looking back at the gaps in our own lived experiences, we might think of silences like those Tillie Olsen had in mind when she spoke of literary history "dark with silences," the "unnatural silences" of women who worked too hard or were too embarrassed to express themselves (1978, p. 6) and of others who did not have the words or had not mastered the proper ways of knowing. We might ponder the plight of young island women, like Jamaica Kincaid's Lucy from Antigua, forced to be "two-faced" in a postcolonial school: "outside, I seemed one way, inside I was another; outside false, inside true" (1990, p. 18). For years, we knew no more about people like her (who saw "sorrow and bitterness" in the faces of daffodils because of the Wordsworth poem she had been forced to learn) than we did about the Barbadians that Paule Marshall ([1959] 1981) has described, people living their fragmented lives in Brooklyn. We had little consciousness of what Gloria Anzaldua (1987) calls "borderlands," or *la frontera,* on which so many Latinos live or of the Cuban immigrants in *The Mambo Kings Sing Songs of Love,* the musicians whose music is never heard outside their clubs, their enclosed world (Hijuelos, 1989). Who of us truly wondered about the builders of the railroads, those Maxine Hong Kingston calls "China men," chopping trees in the Sandalwood Mountains and the Sierra Nevada? Who of us could fill the gaps left by such a person as Ah Goong, whose very "existence was outlawed by the Chinese Exclusion Acts"? His family, writes Kingston, "did not understand his accomplishments as an American ancestor, a holding, homing ancestor of this place. He'd gotten the legal or illegal papers burned in the San Francisco earthquake and fire; he appeared in America in time to be a citizen and to father citizens. He had also been seen carrying a child out of the fire, a child of his own in spite of the laws against marrying. He had built a railroad out of sweat, why not have an American child out of longing?" (1989, p. 151). Did we pay heed to a person like Michelle Cliff, an Afro-Caribbean woman who felt that speaking in words that were not her own was a form of speechlessness (1988)? How many of us have been willing to read about and suffer the experiences most recently rendered in Art Spiegelman's two-volume comic book, *Maus*? Spiegelman tells about his father, the ill-tempered Vladek who is a survivor of Auschwitz, and his resentful sharing of his Holocaust memories with his son. Every character in the book is an animal: the Jews, mice; the Germans, cats; the Poles, pigs. That

depiction is a reminder, not simply of a particular culture's disso-
lution, when all that is left of "Anja's parents, the grandparents, her
big sister Tosha, little Bibi, and our Richieu is the photos" (1991,
p. 115), but a reminder of the need to recognize that everything is
possible, something normal people (including schoolteachers)
either do not know or do not want to know.

To open up our experience (and, yes, our curricula) to existential possibilities of multiple kinds is to extend and deepen what
each of us thinks of when he or she speaks of a community. If we
break through and disrupt our surface equilibrium and uniformity,
it does not mean that a particular ethnic or racial tradition will, or
ought to, replace our own. Toni Morrison, for example, writes that
she pursues her freedom as a writer in a "genderized, sexualized,
wholly racialized world"; but this does not keep her from developing a critical project "unencumbered by dreams of subversion or
rallying gestures at fortress walls" (1992, pp. 4–5). In her case, the
project involves exploring the ways in which what we think of as our
Americanness is, in many ways, a response to an African presence
far too long denied. Morrison is not interested in replacing one
domination by another, but she is interested in showing others what
she sees from her own perspective—and in this showing, enriching
all others' understanding not only of their own culture but also of
themselves. She speaks of themes familiar to us all: "individualism,
masculinity, social engagement versus historical isolation; acute and
ambiguous moral problematics; the thematics of innocence coupled with an obsession with figurations of death and hell." Morrison queries what Americans are alienated from, innocent of,
different from. "As for absolute power, over whom is this power
held, from whom withheld, to whom distributed? Answers to these
questions lie in the potent and ego-reinforcing presence of an
Africanist population" (p. 45). Even as Americans once defined
their moral selves against the wilderness, they began to define their
whiteness against what Melville called "the power of blackness"
(p. 37); they understood their achievement of freedom against slavery. Whether white Americans choose to see their history that way
or not, Morrison introduces a vision only she could create, and it
offers all of us alternative vantage points on the world. Indeed, the
tensions people feel when faced with multiculturalism may be

partially due to the suspicion we all often define ourselves against some unknown, some darkness (in many forms, not only of skin color), some "otherness" that we chose to thrust away, to master rather than to understand. In this regard, Morrison says something that seems to me unanswerable: "My project is an effort to avert the critical gaze from the racial object to the racial subject; from the described and imagined to the describers and imaginers; from the serving to the served" (p. 90).

To take this view is not to suggest that curricula should be tailored to the measure of specific cultural groups of young people. Nor is it to suggest, as the Afrocentrists do, that emphasis should be laid on the unique experiences, culture, and perspectives of African Americans and their link to African roots. There is no question that what history has overlooked or distorted must be restored—whether it has to do with African Americans, Hispanics, Asians, women, Jews, Native Americans, Irish, or Poles and so on—but the exclusions and the deformations have not kept artists like Morrison, Ellison, and James Baldwin from plunging into and learning from Western literary works anymore than it has prevented scholars like Gates and Cornel West and Alain Locke from working for more and richer interchanges between African American and Euro-American cultures. For example, Morrison begins her new book with a verse from T. S. Eliot and goes on to pay tribute to Homer, Dostoyevsky, Faulkner, James, Flaubert, Melville, and Mary Shelley. It is difficult to forget James Baldwin's reading Dostoyevsky and haunting the public library, to turn our attention from West's critiques of Emerson, to ignore Ellison's writing about Melville and Hemingway even as he drew attention to what he called "the Negro stereotype," which was "really an image of the irrational, unorganized forces in American life" (Ellison, 1964, p. 55). We might think of Maya Angelou as well, of her years of self-imposed silence as a child and the reading she did through those years. We might recall Alice Walker engaging with Muriel Rukeyser and Flannery O'Connor, drawing energy from them, even as she went in search of Zora Neale Hurston and Bessie Smith and Sojourner Truth and Gwendolyn Brooks. Walker "also loved Ovid and Catullus . . . the poems of e. e. cummings and William Carlos Williams" (Walker, 1983, p. 257). And we are aware that, as time goes on, more and more

Afro-American literature (and women's literature, and Hispanic American literature) is diversifying our experience, changing our ideas of time and life and birth and relationship and memory.

My point is that we need openness and variety as well as inclusion. We need to avoid fixities, even the stereotypes linked to multiculturalism. To view a person as in some sense "representative" of Asian culture (too frequently grouping together those of Japanese, Koreans, Chinese, and Vietnamese culture in addition to ignoring each individual's differences) or Hispanic, Afro-American, or Euro-American culture is to presume an objective reality called "culture," a homogeneous and fixed presence that *can* be adequately represented by existing subjects. But do Amy Tan's maternal characters (1989) embody the same reality as Maxine Hong Kingston's "woman warrior" (1989)? Does Richard Wright's Bigger Thomas in *Native Son* (1940) stand for the same thing as Miss Celie stands for in *The Color Purple* (Walker, 1982)? We do not *know* the person in the front row of our classroom, or the one sharing the raft, or the one drinking next to us at the bar by her or his cultural or ethnic affiliation.

Cultural background surely plays a part in shaping identity; but it does not determine identity. It may well create differences that must be honored; it may occasion styles and orientations that must be understood; it may give rise to tastes, values, even prejudices that must be taken into account. It is important to know, for example, without embarrassing or exoticizing her, why a person like Jamaica Kincaid's Antiguan Lucy feels so alienated from a Wordsworth poem and whether or not (and against what norms) it is necessary to argue her out of her distaste for daffodils. It is important to realize why, as in Bharati Mukherjee's *Jasmine* (1989), Hindus and Sikhs are so at odds with one another, even in this country, and to seek out ways in which (consulting what we believe to be the Western principle of justice) they can be persuaded to set aside hostility. Or perhaps, striving to sympathize with what they feel, we can communicate our own caring for their well-being in such a fashion as to move them provisionally to reconceive their views of one another. Freire makes the point that every person ought, on some level, to cherish her or his culture, but that culture should never become an absolute, closing the person against the new culture surrounding her or him. When this happens, "you would even find it hard to learn new things which, placed alongside your personal history, can be meaningful" (Freire and Macedo, 1987, p. 126).

What one does want, however, is a feeling of ownership of one's personal history. In the dominant U.S. culture, because of its brutal and persistent racism, it has been painfully difficult for Afro-American young people to affirm and be proud of what they choose as personal history. Poverty, hopelessness, the disruption of families and communities, and the ubiquity of media images all make it difficult to place new things against a past too often made to appear a past of victimization, shadows, and shame. To make it worse, the mystification that proceeds on all sides gives rise to a metanarrative of what it means to be respectable and successful in the United States—a metanarrative that too often seems to doom minorities to life on the outermost borders, or as Toni Morrison writes in *The Bluest Eye*, "outdoors," where there is no place to go: "Outdoors was the end of something, an irrevocable, physical fact, defining and complementing our metaphysical condition. Being a minority in both caste and class, we moved about anyway on the hem of life, struggling to consolidate our weaknesses and hang on, or to creep singly up into the major folds of the garment" (1970, p. 18).

It happens that *The Bluest Eye*, because of its use of the first paragraph of the basal reader *Dick and Jane*, dramatizes as few other works do the coercive and deforming effect of the dominant culture's official story, the metanarrative of secure suburban family life. As the novel plays itself out, everything that occurs is the obverse of the basal reader's story with its themes of pretty house, loving family, play, laughter, friendship, cat, and dog. At the close of the preface to the main story, ostensibly written after Pecola's baby and rapist father have died, after the seeds Pecola has planted do not flower, after Pecola goes mad, the narrator, Claudia, says, "There is really nothing more to say—except why. But since *why* is difficult to handle, one must take refuge in *how*" (p. 9). In the process of telling how, from her own view when very young and then a little older, Claudia also orders the materials of her own life—her own helplessness, her own longings—arranging them in relation to Pecola, whom she could not help, and in relation to the seeds that would not flower and those around her "on the hem of life." She weaves her narrative in such a fashion that she establishes an important connection to the past and reinterprets her own ethnicity, in part through what Michael Fischer calls "the arts of memory" (1986). Whatever meaning she can draw from the connections she makes feeds into an ethic that may be meaningful in the future, an ethic that takes her beyond her own guilt at watching Pecola search the garbage: "I talk about how I did *not* plant the seeds too deeply, how it was the fault of the earth, the land, of our town. I even think now that the land of the entire country was hostile to marigolds that year. . . . Certain seeds it will not nurture, certain fruit it will not bear, and when the land kills of its own volition, we acquiesce and say the victim had no right to live. We are wrong, of course, but it doesn't matter. It's too late." As Charles Taylor and Alasdair MacIntyre have both written, when we understand our lives we do so in narrative form, and clearly, our stories while different are nonetheless connected by the same need to make sense, to make meaning, to find a direction.

To help the diverse students we know articulate their stories is not only to help them pursue the meanings of their lives—to find out *how* things are happening and to keep posing questions about the why. It is to move them to learn the new things Freire spoke of, to reach out for the proficiencies and capacities, the craft required to be fully participant in this society, and to do so without losing the consciousness of who they are. But that is not all. Stories like the one Claudia tells must be able to break through into what we think of as our tradition or our heritage. They will if we can do what Cornel West has in mind when he speaks about the importance of acknowledging the "distinctive cultural and political practices of oppressed people" without highlighting their marginality in such a way as to further marginalize them. For example, he calls attention to both the resistance of African Americans and that of other long-silenced people to the dominant culture and to African Americans' multiple contributions to the dominant culture over the generations. We might think of the music—gospel, jazz, ragtime; we might think of the black churches; we might summon up the civil rights movement and the philosophies and dreams that informed it; we might ponder—looking back, looking around—the images of courage, the images of survival. West goes on to say: "Black cultural practices emerge out of a reality they cannot *not* know—the ragged edges of the real, of necessity; a reality historically constructed by white supremacist practices in North America. . . . These ragged edges—of not being able to eat, not to have shelter, not to have health care—all this is infused into the strategies and styles of black cultural practices" (1989, p. 93). In other words, as we seek multi-culturalism, Afro-American culture in all its variousness should *not* be defined mainly in terms of oppression and discrimination. While one of the many reasons for opening spaces in which African Americans can tell their own stories is that they, far more than those from other cultures, can explain the ways in which poverty and exclusion have mediated their own sense of the past, and while it is also true that experiences of pain and abandonment have led to a search for roots and, on occasion, to a revision of recorded history, what is crucial is the provision of opportunities for telling *all* the diverse stories, for interpreting membership as well as ethnicity, for making inescapable the braids of experience woven into the fabric of U.S. plurality.

In the presence of an increasingly potent Third World, against the sounds of increasingly eloquent postcolonial (and, now, post-totalitarian) voices, we can no longer pretend that the "ragged edges" are an exception. We can no longer talk in terms of seam-less totalities under such rubrics as "free world," "free market," "equality," or even "democracy." Like the "wreckage in the mid-Atlantic," like the "faceless faces," like the "unnatural silences," lacks and deprivations have to be made aspects of our plurality as well as of our cultural identity. Publics, after all, take shape in response to unmet needs and broken promises. Human beings are prone to take action in response to the sense of injustice or to the imagination's capacity to look at things as if they could be other-wise. The democratic community, always a community in the mak-ing, depends not so much on what has been achieved and funded in the past. It is kept alive; it is energized and radiated by an aware-ness of future possibility. To develop a vision of such possibility, a vision of what might and ought to be, is very often to be made aware of present deficiencies and present flaws. The seeds did not flower; Pecola and her baby could not be saved. But more and more persons, paying heed, may move beyond acquiescence. They may say, as Claudia does, "We are wrong, of course," yet go on to overcome the thought that it "doesn't matter." At that moment, they may reach beyond themselves, choose themselves as who they are, and reach out to the common to repair.

Learning to look through multiple perspectives, young people may be helped to build bridges among themselves; attending to a range of human stories, they may be provoked to heal and to transform. Of course there will be difficulties in at once affirming plurality and difference and working to create community. Since the days of de Tocqueville, Americans have wondered how to deal with the conflicts between individualism and the drive to conform. They have wondered how to reconcile the impassioned voices of cultures not yet part of the whole with the requirements of conformity, how not to lose the integrity of those voices in the process, how not to allow the drive to conformity to determine what happens at the end. The community many of us hope for now is not to be identified with conformity. As it is shown in Whitman's way of saying, it is a community attentive to difference, open to the idea of plurality. That which is life-affirming in diversity must be discovered and rediscovered, as what is held in common becomes always more many-faceted, open and inclusive, and drawn to untapped possibility.

No one can predict precisely the common world of possibility we will grow to inhabit, nor can we absolutely justify one kind of community over another. Many of us, however, for all the tensions and disagreements around us, would reaffirm the value of principles like justice and equality and freedom and commitment to human rights, since without these we cannot even argue for the decency of welcoming. Only if more and more persons incarnate such principles, choosing to live by them and engage in dialogue in accord with them, are we likely to bring about a democratic pluralism and not fly apart in violence and disorder. Unable to provide an objective ground for such hopes and claims, all we can do is speak with others as eloquently and passionately as we can about justice and caring and love and trust. Like Richard Rorty and those he calls pragmatists, we can only articulate our desire for as much intersubjective agreement as possible, our "desire to extend the reference of 'us' as far as we can" (Rorty, 1991, p. 23). But as we do so, we have to remain aware also of the distinctive members of the plurality, appearing before one another with their own perspectives on the common, their own stories entering the culture's story, altering it as it moves through time. We want our classrooms to be just and caring, full of various conceptions of the good. We want them to be articulate, with the dialogue involving as many persons as possible, opening to one another, opening to the world. And we want our children to be concerned for one another, as we learn to be concerned for them. We want them to achieve friendships among one another, as each one moves to a heightened sense of craft and wide-awakeness, to a renewed consciousness of worth and possibility.

With voices in mind and the need for visibility, I think of Muriel Rukeyser's call for human solidarity. In her vision, we are to "widen the lens and see/standing over the land myths of identity, new signals, processes."

> Carry abroad the urgent need, the scene,
> to photograph and to extend the voice,
> to speak this meaning.
> Voices to speak to us directly. As we move.
> As we enrich, growing in larger motion,
> this word, this power [1938, p. 7].

Yes, we need to seek this power, the unexplored power of pluralism and the wonder of an expanding community.

Chapter Thirteen

Standards, Common Learnings, and Diversity

Academic rigor, high standards, common learning, technical proficiency, excellence, equity, and self-development—these themes have arisen over and over since the founding of the public schools. Considering them in present moment of hope tinged with anxiety, we teachers find ourselves (at least on occasion) pondering the nature of our democratic society, wondering about the future of our world. Yes, there are the clear definitions of Goals 2000, but there is also a cacophony of voices all around. Diverse publics challenge our teaching; often, they scapegoat. They demand not only improvements but guarantees; they want things to be stable and predictable; they want the schools to repair cultural deficiencies; they want their own interests to be secured. Oftentimes, poverty itself is blamed on ineffective schooling; ethnic discrimination, class factors, poor housing, and family break-ups are set aside. At other times, schools—particularly those in poor neighborhoods—are simply thought to be ineffectual in the face of such obstacles. For all the optimism of movements for reform, that moment of hope among educators that I just cited, often a hopelessness infects those who administer and those expected to learn.

As I suggested in Chapter Twelve, the United States calls itself the strongest of powers, the paradigm of free-market economies, the appointed representative of the free Western world. Yet we cannot but take note of the unease accompanying our educational system. Why the cries of such intense alarm about schools? Why the fearsome specter of "mediocrity"? Why the fear of multiculturalism? Why the rationalizations for censorship? Why the official efforts to bar discussions of values and sex education and moral education? Why the endless campaigns for school prayers? Why the preoccupation in a day of whole language and portfolio assessment with quantifiable mastery? It sometimes appears that the measurement people have joined forces with modern incarnations of the Puritan divines, trying to defend against an impinging wilderness, to keep the demons at bay.

The wilderness has many aspects, of course; the demons have many faces. What is happening makes me wish, more and more desperately, for authentic dialogue among educators. It is time our own voices are heard with greater clarity, the voices of those who engage with the young in their concreteness and particularity. Children's and teachers' stories and journals are breaking through classroom depersonalization. We are less likely to talk of children in the aggregate within our schools. But this change has not broken through into the public space, where we teachers are very seldom asked to testify and are seldom inclined to speak voluntarily for ourselves. Everyone needs to hear articulate practitioners ask in public what the purposes of U.S. education really ought to be in these times, what it *means* to be concerned about children's futures and "to decide whether we love our children enough not to expel them from our world and leave them to their own devices, not to strike from their hands their chance of undertaking something new, something unforeseen by us, but to prepare them in advance for the task of renewing a common world" (Arendt, 1961, p. 196). How do we comprehend that task? How do we understand "a common world"? Our discussions of standards and curriculum frameworks and outcomes still have not touched seriously upon the matter of our purposes as a society: upon what it means to educate live persons, to empower the young not simply to make a living and contribute to the nation's economic welfare but to live and, along with others, remake their own worlds.

No matter what our personal inclinations, teachers especially can no longer obliterate the diverse voices, unashamed of their distinctiveness, speaking life stories and cultural stories sometimes at odds with or contemptuous of the sacred writs of mainstream life. Nor can anyone hide any longer from the troubling fact that industrialized, technological societies have turned out to be fundamentally unequal ones when it comes to status and reward, that they parcel out unequal life chances. We realize now that success depends only occasionally on capacity or even on merit. We realize how often it depends upon original advantage, on contingency or luck. So how do public schools, presumably dedicated to equality in the midst of pluralism, even out the playing field? How do they provide more opportunities for personal, distinctive growth? How do we as teachers, cautioned against thinking in terms of predictions and predeterminations, provoke all our students to learn how to learn in a world we and they already know is neither equitable nor fair?

In spite of the infrequency of academic and administrative attention to the world of public schools, scholarly and policy discourse has been affected by such perplexities. In the fields within the humanities, becoming more specialized and esoteric each day, scholars now wonder how they can open structuralist and deconstructionist and hermeneutic enclaves to one another. They ponder the nature of their limited audiences, sometimes concluding that the mass of people must, after all, be left to the functional literacy level of airport bookstores, television programs, and MTV. Or they speculate about what would happen in their particular academic lives if they were to make the move of reaching out and were to extend their subject matters to include (and perhaps absorb) "the moving image" ("Moving Image," 1985) or the culture of rock. On occasion, they ponder the rising challenges to their canon, to the hold of white men on whatever is defined as tradition. As increasing numbers of Afro-American and Hispanic scholars appear, the traditional academics ask themselves what this change will signify for their conception of literacy, regularly identified as that which holds the culture together in some semblance of coherence. Scientists and technical experts try to legislate the kinds of scientific and technical literacy ordinary citizens ought to be expected to master; but this seldom reaches down to schools, except in the form of crisis prescriptions. Ought the hopelessly uninformed, it may be muttered, be trusted to make decisions about DNA research, genomes, heart transplants, arms sales, life support systems, health care, gun control, AIDS? Or ought they be taught to rely on those with proven expertise in each field, on individuals who can understand the methodologies and the notations, who know how to calculate the risks? What sort of scientific literacy ought to be disseminated? How much of it should be taught?

Responses to such concerns cannot but affect our views of education as well as democracy. Again, I want to affirm that actual practitioners in their diverse communities ought to pose their own questions about what democratic education and democratic citizenship mean and ought to mean in the postmodern time. What, after all, is demanded of people in an age of random terror, massacres, rapes of the innocent? We are beginning to discover that superior technical competencies, like basic skills themselves, are insufficient in the face of holocausts, famines, budget deficits in the trillions, unimaginable wealth controlled by corporate interests (in entertainment and sports, as well as in traditional businesses and industries). What kinds of intelligences are required to remedy homelessness and addiction? What do we have to know, what do the schools have to teach to overcome divisiveness and group hostility? We have only to recall the Los Angeles riots and ask what sorts of investigations we can undertake to see that they do not break out again. Then what of media simulations, the constant rain of images, the confusion of illusion with the generally agreed upon real? What happens to the rule of law when guilt or innocence is, in a way, voted on by the television audience? What happens to democracy when call-in talk shows supplant democratic dialogue? Again, how do we learn to think about it? How do we teach others to think about it? It is surely not sufficient (or even decent) to settle for equipping those we think of as "Deltas" (to use Huxley's term, [1932] 1950) with a short range of closed capacities, while reserving the higher cognitive skills for the superior, ostensibly gifted few. Nor does it make sense to restrict what we call excellence merely to the testable or to suggest that the raising of standards for all the young will provoke them and their teachers to produce in such a fashion that what they produce will ensure this nation's technical, military, and economic supremacy.

Of course, I believe in doing what we can to overcome shoddiness and carelessness and passivity and lack of style. But I am convinced that through reflective and impassioned teaching we can do far more to excite and stimulate many sorts of young persons to reach beyond themselves, to create meanings, to look through wider and more informed perspectives at the actualities of their lived lives. It seems eminently clear to me that a return to a single standard of achievement and a one-dimensional definition of the common will not only result in severe injustices to the children of the poor and the dislocated, the children at risk, but will also thin out our cultural life and make it increasingly difficult to bring into existence and keep alive an authentically common world. Granted, multiple perspectives make it all the more difficult to define coherent purposes in what many believe to be a dangerously fragmented culture, devoid of significant guidelines and generally accepted norms. Multiplicity makes it difficult as well to think about how we can love our children in Arendt's terms and remain true to what we have come to know as practitioners.

Because so much of what we do depends upon perceived and interpreted context, it may be helpful to turn to some works of imaginative literature in order to evoke images of the actual demands that are made on schools today. Obviously, journalistic and social scientific sources abound; there are numerous descriptions of the ecosystems and social systems that "interfere" with the educational system. But perhaps these descriptions are too numerous, too familiar by now. They may no longer prompt us to ask ourselves what we, personally, see and feel. Instead, the metaphors, the worlds, offered by certain modern novels may release the imaginations of some of those who read them. If that occurs, those readers may be moved to think afresh and in their own terms about such matters as rigor and the new curriculum, about the possibilities of releasing the young to become different—to go beyond where they are. It will surely be admitted that imagination has seldom been tapped within the long debates and discussions about educational "reforms." The participants, with few exceptions, have functioned within the limits of the official language; they have acceded to the conceptual taken-for-granted and have seldom wondered whether things might be otherwise than proposed.

The three novels I want to mention are not utopian or even political, nor do they touch upon education per se. They simply have the capacity to make one "see, finding encouragement, consolation, fear, charm—all you demand—and, perhaps, also that glimpse of truth for which you have forgotten to ask" (Conrad, [1898] 1967, pp. ix–x). The first thing to "see," briefly since we have viewed it once before, is the image of the "noxious cloud" in Don DeLillo's novel *White Noise* (1985). An invisible cloud from a deadly chemical, it leaves the people in the Midwestern college town over which it has settled confronting death, feeling a weight they can neither interpret nor understand. Yet after the first panic and the fleeing to shelters, they react by living pretty much as they have all along, even as they wait for the effects of the cloud to occur, whatever they may be and whenever they may happen. Realistic or not, the images in this novel might well move certain ones of us to ponder what can be done to enable the young to become scientifically literate enough to take action with regard to such invisible menaces as noxious clouds, radiation, and pollution. I am not talking about educating young physicists necessarily. I am talking about giving students an acquaintance with the kind of thinking that is tentative and hypothetical, the kind of knowing that involves a backing up of what is said, a consulting of evidence, a drawing of inferences, and a linking of what is found and inferred to conceptions of what is appropriate, decent, just, and humane. Some readers (along with me), regarding DeLillo's townspeople at end of the novel as they "wait together" in the supermarket with shopping carts stocked with goods and tabloid headlines to pass the time (p. 596), will wonder what can be done to arouse the young from consumerism and passivity and extraterrestrial fantasies—at least to the extent of devising significant projects for themselves that call them to surpass what is and to reach toward a better order of things.

Another image I have in mind is to be found in Anne Tyler's *Accidental Tourist* (1985). The main character, Macon, is a man so disengaged, so submerged in the familiar, so afraid of the strange, that he inhabits a world like a cocoon where there are only old childish games to play and the thin correct language of an ingrown family come back together in adulthood to hide in the mundane. Macon writes travel books for businessmen who do not want to feel away from home when they take business trips. For them, Macon finds all the McDonald's there are in London and Paris, the Holiday Inns, the places where no one has to face the challenging or the strange. If it were not for the unmanageable dog Macon owns and the unexpected adventures the dog leads to, he would remain the very paradigm of what Christopher Lasch calls the "minimal self" (1984), shrunken, privatist, lacking any sense of agency.

Readers who recognize that image of attenuated adulthood, of a life lived in a wholly private sphere, may be moved as I am to wonder how we can educate children to discover in lived situations openings that are not for mere accommodation. How can we teach so as to provoke questioning of the taken-for-granted, the kind of questioning that involves simultaneously critical and creative thinking and attentive engagement with actualities? How can the young Macons all around us be aroused to move into public spaces and bring something common into existence among themselves, something that makes learning personally and intersubjectively worthwhile? I do not mean only expanded disciplinary learning (although I always hope for that). I mean collaborative efforts to resolve real perplexities. I mean a coming together to improve a neighborhood, open a playground, house some homeless people, put on a street concert, assist at a day care center, invent a tutoring program. None of this, it is clear, can take place mindlessly and be effective. Each effort requires the activation of a range of capacities, even literacies. It is not just a question of finding alternatives to a McDonald's or a Holiday Inn when in a distant place, not just a matter of reading newspapers (as Macon and his family refuse to do) and keeping in touch with events in the world. It is a matter of going intentionally in search of something and seeking out the kind of understandings needed for the search, for moving toward what is not yet known. In this search, a refusal of the comfortable is always required, a refusal to remain sunk in everydayness. The alternative very often may be boredom, a sense of futility, or even despair. It may be unintentionally becoming an accidental tourist, avoiding deliberate engagement with life. Any significant curriculum or mode of teaching must, it seems to me, take account of all the ideas raised by this image.

The third image I have in mind comes from Milan Kundera's *Unbearable Lightness of Being* (1984). It is the polarity of two kinds of life: a restless, uncommitted, decontextualized, "light" way of life (the way of the émigré very often, the wanderer on the roads) and life under a *weight*. The weight may be that of official doctrine, or what Kundera calls the "grand march" of the doctrinaire. Or it may be the weight of sentimental pieties, slogans, and stereotypes. Both weights are associated with "kitsch" and denials, that is, "folding screens set up to ward off the fear of death." Totalitarian "kitsch," Kundera tells us, prohibits people from speaking; democratic "kitsch" can so lull and mystify that it leaves individuals with nothing authentic to say. We are experiencing democratic kitsch when we hear the word "awesome" taking the place of judgment among the young, when we realize how conversation is eroding among adults. Not accidentally, in totalitarian countries it happens that the voices and books that speak seriously about freedom or human rights are the voices and books of dissent, the expressions of men and women aware of limits and boundaries, affirming their own humanity by resisting, trying to break through. In our own country, with the exception of certain black women writers, few spokespersons articulate much concern for human rights or freedom in any concrete sense. People generally feel themselves *to be* free, and our themes have frequently to do with a kind of vagabondage, with being on the edge. In films, in fiction, and in ordinary life, the young (outside of cults and fundamentalist religions) feel unconstrained when it comes to dyeing their hair, having sex, trying drugs, experiencing pornography. They know no limits; they hang loose and feel there is nothing truly important to say. Such phenomena as Live Aid concerts and sympathy for far-off famine victims are not for me signs of overcoming "lightness"; nor do they even signify serious commitments or what existentialists call the "courage to be."

Reading Kundera can draw our attention to the split in our own society, then, in our case a split between fundamentalism, or perhaps the ethos of the moral majority, and an uncommitted and noncommittal decontextualized mode of existence in which people jog around the edge of things without any particular end in view. Kundera can make readers think as well of the moral vacuum in the cost-benefit talk of official spokespeople, where budgetary and deficit considerations replace concern for human deprivation, humiliation, and need. There are times when he makes me see a connection between the youngster with the punk haircut passing the head shop (well-meaning and drug-free though the particular youngster I am seeing at the moment may be) and the government economist or budget-balancer (preoccupied with national "welfare" though he or she may be). Neither is concerned for values; neither really cares. And then I am reminded of how much of value discussion today has been, in any case, taken over by those who—in the name of family values, domestic virtues, and purity—march against abortion, birth control, and the building of neighborhood methadone centers or hospices for people with AIDS. The arguments of those who espouse, or say they espouse, "collective respon-sibility for the disadvantaged" (Norton, 1985) or affirmative action or expanded support for education and the arts are too often either weary or diagrammatic. They are seldom of the sort that might awaken the young to stir out of their enclaves, to care.

Lightness and weight—value-free and dogma-heavy—those are the extreme poles of the dialogue we should be having. How can we create classroom situations in which significant dialogue might be encouraged once again, the live communication out of which there might emerge some consciousness of interdependence as well as a recognition of diverse points of view? In the Deweyan tradition, as we know, there is an emphasis on the devising of situ-ations in which preferences might somehow be released. Prefer-ences differ from impulses or merely unreflected-on desires; thus, the idea is that if the young were enabled to identify alternative possibilities and to choose themselves in accord with what they thought preferable, they might have *reasons* for learning to learn on their own initiative, reasons to investigate whether the world is as predefined as it has been made to seem. Dewey wrote that "the self is not something ready-made, but something in continuous for-mation through choice of action" (1916, p. 408); and we are aware that action (unlike behavior) is conceived of as the reflective tak-ing of initiatives, the making of new beginnings, the moving toward what cannot be precisely predicted but what is often thought of as possibility.

Of course, there are practitioners concerned with enabling stu-dents of very different potentials to discover appropriate courses of action by means of which to shape identities for themselves. To find one's right action may be to discover the self as someone with a sense of agency, the author of a life lived among others and not merely a passive observer or an accidental tourist or a member of a crowd. Acknowledging themselves as situated in a particular place in a social world, given opportunities to find out what can emerge from communication with others, the young may be sometimes enabled to escape the weight of kitsch as well as an unbearable lightness. They may find themselves unexpectedly able to deal with the forces that seem to determine and condition, that make them feel powerless (and, in their powerlessness, irresponsible and dis-engaged). Freedom is an achievement in the midst of life and with other human beings. People achieve whatever freedom they can achieve through increasingly conscious and mindful transaction with what surrounds and impinges, not simply by breaking out of context and acting in response to impulse or desire. And it seems clear that most people find out who they are only when they have developed some power to act and to choose in engagements with a determinate world. As civil rights workers found out not so long ago, as women keep finding out, as minorities discover over and over, freedom has to be gradually achieved and nurtured in situations that have been made intelligible but that have to be continually named and understood. The pedagogical implications of this view are multiple, and it is hard to conceive of a set of educational purposes that does not include a concern for human freedom and sense of agency in the face of a more and more controlled and administered world.

Noxious clouds and unreadable threats, consumerism, privatism and the shrinkage of the self, the void of rootlessness and negative freedom, the weight of dogmas and pieties, the absence of dialogue, the loss of a public space—what do they all have to do common learnings, academic rigor, hierarchies, and even excellence? Catharine Stimpson writes that "excellence in the humanities—the works themselves, and our study of these works—ought to reveal a pulsating alliance of consciousness and vitality." (Reading that, I realize that I am more concerned about "consciousness and vitality" than I am about technical mastery and quantifiable skills.) She expects "the quest for excellence will generate—not a monolithic tradition that we can organize into a hierarchy of excellent, meritorious, mediocre, and lousy—but a multiplicitous tradition that we will judge, enjoy, and judge anew" (1984, p. 8); and I hope she is right.

It is tempting to move from this optimistic view to what we are discovering about the thousands of newcomers now entering our schools: immigrants from countless cultures, with their own distinctive symbol systems, their own ways of seeing and being in the world. It is also tempting to move to what we have been learning about "multiple intelligences" (Gardner, 1983) ranging from the logical-linguistic to the mathematical to the literary to the bodily kinesthetic to the musical—all potential modes of knowing how and of dealing with the appearances of things and with the experienced world. Surely, it must be wrong to neglect those potentials ordinary curricula do not permit us to heed, potentials that do not appear to contribute to the growth of technology or do not result in easily measurable achievements. I have in mind the craft and the "artistry" required to become, say, an opera singer (Howard, 1982); the interactions between motor and perceptual activity and the making of shapes in space and time that identify a dancer's "literacy"; the thinking that guides the hands of cabinetmakers and motorcycle mechanics and machinists, people who can relate themselves to wood, metal parts, and the interiors of complex machines.

Like a number of other educational and philosophical inquirers, I favor plurality and multiplicity over one-dimensional hierarchies. In our schools, I would try to seek out multiple excellences, to think of academic rigor in connection with the cultivation of qualities of mind in diverse domains. It still seems to me fruitful to consider mind, as Dewey did, as a verb denoting "all the ways in which we deal consciously and expressly with the situations in which we find ourselves" (1934, p. 263). Our dealings with situations, of course, are affected by our cultural membership and preunderstandings, by the world we share (and can share no matter how distinctively it may be interpreted), the world we have to create and recreate in common as we work and help others to work to decode it. However, even while attending to particular qualities of mind, we can allow for and even celebrate multiplicity of perspective.

The British philosopher Richard S. Peters has written about excellences as "connected with the manner in which we conduct various activities. We discuss or think critically . . . we paint or cook creatively and integrity is shown in our moral life or in a work of art" (1975, p. 121). That is, specifiable capacities, if fully developed, *become* excellences: to think critically, for example, to work creatively, to display foresight and persistence and strength of character. The qualities I have named in this chapter with potential for becoming excellences are tentativeness; regard for evidence; simultaneously critical and creative thinking; openness to dialogue; and a sense of agency, social commitment, and concern. They have potential also for "consciousness and vitality."

To concern ourselves with "the manner in which we conduct various activities" is different from concerning ourselves primarily with the same quantifiable or measurable substantive for everyone. Nevertheless, like Peters and others, I tend to believe that the qualities of mind we cherish can best be developed, not in vacuo, but through specific kinds of experiences, most often with subject matters. It seems likely that there are connections between a gradually incarnated sense of what ought to be, of possible attainment (within a field of knowledge, a discipline, a form of life) and a consciousness of agency, of existing consciously and responsibly in the world.

However, I doubt that an insistence on a vision of normalized, common reality—to be accepted and mastered by everyone in the same way—will provoke young persons' desires to transcend, to be (as individuals) the best they know how to be. Moreover, most of us have become aware of the exclusivity of what we have thought of as heritage or tradition. Tradition can longer be treated as though it were naturally Northern, Western, and male. To take, even for a moment, the perspective of a young student from a different culture than one's own is to recognize the provisional nature of our understanding of human history, time, death, power, even love. Many non-Hispanic teachers discovered Gabriel Márquez, Carlos Fuentes, Jorge Amado, Manuel Puig, and even Jorge Luis Borges only a few years ago; and, surely, fictional realities like the one presented in Márquez's *One Hundred Years of Solitude* or the multiple ones in Borges's *Fictions* have shocked many of us into an awareness of our own one-dimensionality, if not of the degree to which we inhabit a constructed social reality. Surely, the same will be true when we read Far Eastern and Indian cultures and literatures. When Vietnamese, Chinese, Thai, and African young faces confront white teachers, or any teachers of a different heritage from the students, we must know we can no longer confine what we call the humanities or history to Western forms and events. Many of us, in addition, female as well as male, have been provoked to alter our ways of seeing by the introduction of women's life stories and experiences into accounts of history and culture and economic development. Not only is the composition of the pictures transmitted to us being altered, along with its contours and colors and even the media through which it transmitted, but new vantage points have brought with them and ought to continue to bring with them fundamental reconceptualizations of the nation's heritage, of true cultural literacy, and of our emergent curriculum.

The curriculum unquestionably needs expanding and deepening so that more and more options are provided where the study of texts and images and formulations are concerned. Teachers are becoming aware that they need to think more deeply about enabling more students to be personally present to their own learning processes and self-reflective with regard to them. Interpretive approaches to knowing, now so evident in the natural and social sciences as well as the humanities, are beginning to become relevant to teaching and learning. Interpretation, of course, focuses on the disclosure of meanings *for* particular subjects (or inquirers, or students) in particular fields. They may also be intersubjective meanings, embodying visions of persons as members of communities. They may move ongoingly between the local, the immediate, and what Clifford Geertz calls "the most global of global structures," a continuing reaching toward a wider and wider context. Geertz, along with others stressing multiplicity as "the hallmark of modern consciousness," calls for a "sort of ethnography of thought work . . . [which] will deepen even further our sense of the radical variousness of the way we think now, because it will extend our perception of that variousness beyond the merely professional realms of subject matter, method, technique, scholarly tradition, and the like, to the larger framework of our moral existence" (1983, p. 161). He too is preoccupied with the life of meaning and with interpretation; he too is convinced that different concerns and different questions constitute openings into existing symbol systems for different people.

Surely, we all have memories of our worlds opening outward through encounters we have had with other human beings, with texts, with works of art, with games, and with structured disciplines. If we were fortunate, we were able to develop open capacities—meaning the kinds of capacities that enabled us to move on our own from particular texts to other texts and other modes of representation. There must be analogues in that experience for what might happen to diverse young persons today, students who should be allowed to affirm and name their own local worlds by means of their encounters and at once reach beyond those local worlds toward what they do not yet know. It cannot be absolutely necessary for every person to read *Hamlet* or *Middlemarch* or Lewis Thomas's *Lives of a Cell* (although I would consider carefully before I withheld any of these). What is important is that whatever is chosen is read and attended to with care and integrity, with both critical and creative thinking, with persistence, and with a regard for what that engagement *ought* to be so it can feed into a wider knowing how and, at length, into situations where the young can teach themselves.

Where standards and rigor are concerned, it is profoundly important to communicate to young people the connection between the discipline or the effort they exert and the possibilities of vision. Recall what Dewey wrote of the effort and understanding it requires really to apprehend the cathedral of Notre Dame or a Rembrandt painting, to go beyond "mere seeing" and mere attaching of the correct name to what is seen: "There is work to be done on the part of the percipient as there is on the part of the artist. The one who is too lazy, idle, or indurated in convention to perform this work will not see or hear. His 'appreciation' will be a mixture of scraps of learning with conformity to norms of conventional admiration" (1934, p. 54). Others (critics and educators and philosophers) have beckoned in the same fashion, pulling us beyond carelessness, beyond stupidity, with a promise that all sorts of vistas lie ahead if the work is authentically performed.

The overcoming of induration is significant for ways of knowing other than the aesthetic or the interpretive; and it is obvious that students have to be introduced to many ways of explaining, judging, schematizing, drawing inferences, and analyzing. Moreover, the validation of any mode of inquiry ought to be found in its contribution to the life of meaning and to communication in the intersubjective world. As we ponder educational purposes, we might take into account the possibility that the main point of education (in the context of a lived life) is to enable a human being to become increasingly mindful with regard to his or her lived situation—and its untapped possibilities. The languages and symbol systems we make available ought to provide possibilities for thematizing very diverse human experiences and, not incidentally, for diverse introductions to the conversation among people that carries the culture on in time. Since the languages at hand must live up to certain standards if those using them are to make their own experiences intelligible, we ought to enable students to enter into the needed languages responsibly and reflectively so they can name themselves and name their worlds. Such naming, of course, can never be complete, and part of learning is to recognize the lacks and deficiencies that always have to be repaired and that require one to reach on and on.

What I have been calling the common, then, has to be continually brought into being. We may indeed use representative texts and works of art at certain times; we may use paradigm cases in the various domains; we may even use the popular arts. There is always a flux in the things and ideas of this world, and there is always the need to catch that flux in networks of meaning. Whatever the networks, the focus should be one that dislodges fixities, resists one-dimensionality, and allows multiple personal voices to become articulate in a more and more vital dialogue.

Arendt once made the point that the problem of our culture is not so much that there is a lack of public admiration for poetry and philosophy but that such admiration "does not constitute a space in which things are saved from destruction by time." We may have reached the point where we in education are charged with bringing such a space into existence. Arendt went on to say that the reality of such a space will rely

> on the simultaneous presence of innumerable perspectives and aspects in which the common world presents itself and for which no common measurement or denominator can ever be devised. For though the common world is the common meeting ground of all, those who are present have different locations in it. . . . Being seen and heard by others derive their significance from the fact that everybody sees and hears from a different position. . . . Only where things can be seen by many in a variety of aspects without changing their identity, so that those who are gathered around them know they see sameness in utter diversity, can worldly reality truly and reliably appear [1958, p. 57].

I like to see that "worldly reality" as analogous to common learnings; and I like to identify "the innumerable perspectives" with the multiple life experiences of those we hope will learn to learn—and do so with increasing eagerness, craft, and sense of standard and style.

There *can* be spaces of excellence where diverse persons are moved to reach toward the possible. Through the exercise of imagination, individuals can gain that sense of significance that enables them to realize that "there is always more to experience, and more in what we experience than we can predict" (Warnock, 1978, p. 202). Made aware of this, young people may be moved to exert themselves, to surpass, to transcend. In the dialogue about educational purposes, standards and common learnings both may be viewed as an emergent from human choosing. It may be that fundamental to our purposes, finally, will be the achievement of human freedom within a human community. Clearly, that has much to do with our wondering about the future of our world.

Chapter Fourteen

Multiple Voices
and Multiple Realities

Almost half a century has passed since Albert Camus declared to us that although we long for clarity and wish for a principle that would explain everything there is, only professional rationalists offer abstract and generalized certainties. And when they do, "that universal reason, practical or ethical, that determinism, those categories that explain everything are enough to make a decent man laugh. They have nothing to do with the mind" (1955, p. 21). Today, many voices speak about the enormous multiplicity of modern consciousness, helping us see that "the image of a general orientation . . . growing out of humanistic studies (or, for that matter, out of scientific ones) . . . is a chimera. Not only is the class basis for such a unitary humanism completely absent, gone with a lot of things like adequate bathtubs and comfortable taxies; but, even more important, the agreement on the foundations of scholarly authority, old books and older manners, has disappeared" (Geertz, 1983, p. 161). Geertz's hope, of course, is that we can create the conditions under which there can be an interplay of "a disorderly crowd of not wholly commensurable visions," the nearest we can get to a general consciousness. The hope lies in the possibility of our developing a vocabulary in which our many differences can be formulated, a vocabulary in which we "can give a credible account of themselves to one another" (p. 161). I add my supplemental hope that these accounts can be offered from the vantage points of people's lived experiences, from what has been called each person's "life-world" (Husserl, 1962, pp. 91–100).

It is from those particular standpoints, after all, that we become conscious of the newcomers who throng as never before through the streets and through the schools. It is from those standpoints that most of us have been shocked into an awareness of voices most of us scarcely heeded in earlier times: not only the voices of women and members of minority groups and gay people and disabled people, but those of children, patients in hospitals and hospices, addicts, and wanderers, those in search of shelter or cure or a bit of happiness, a bit of joy. Although scholars in some fields have indeed broken out of the enclaves of specialization, an actual multidisciplinary viewing of an endlessly variegated world is only now becoming conceivable. Whether it has been the impact of hermeneutics or of a reconceptualization of the human sciences, whether it has been a recognition of heteroglossia as opposed to monologic utterance, we have become wary of single languages of truth and fixed categories. We are appreciative now of storytelling as a mode of knowing (Bruner, 1986, pp. 11ff.), of the connection between narrative and the growth of identity, of the importance of shaping our own stories and, at the same time, opening ourselves to other stories in all their variety and their different degrees of articulateness.

As I have been describing, this awareness of the significance of story, and of understanding rather than mere conceptualization, seems to have led a number of educators and others to inquiries in which the perspectives of the human sciences are deepened and expanded by imaginative literature. I have recalled, for example, how we may read about the history, demographics, and economics of slavery in this country, but we may also read Toni Morrison's *Beloved,* and in the course of achieving it as meaningful, find ourselves possessing a new perspective of slavery, perhaps also a stunned outrage, perhaps also more about our own lives and experiences of loss even as we perceive more about the world of slavery once we are enabled to look at it through our own lived situations. Literature does not replace historical description, but engagement with it does tap all sorts of circuits in reader consciousness, until it is possible to see slavery in relation to such ongoing contemporary violations as child abuse. We begin moving between immediacies and general categories, as reflective practitioners are bound to do when they try to make sense. We see; we hear; we make connections. We participate in some dimensions that we could not know if imagination were not aroused. "Only the imagination can get us out of the bind of the eternal present, inventing or hypothesizing or pretending or discovering a way that reason can then follow into an infinity of options, a clue through the labyrinth of choice, a golden string, the story, leading us to the freedom that is properly human, the freedom open to those whose minds can accept unreality" (Le Guin, 1989, p. 45). Having accepted "unreality," we can turn back to the variegated social realities we share and, perhaps, find them enhanced, expanded, corrigible.

However, no novelistic reality can ever be complete or wholly coherent; nor can it settle anything. We are left, therefore, with our open questions—about practice, about learning, about educational studies, about community. They may be the sorts of questions that lead us on more and more far-reaching quests.

I have also been describing those who respond to images of multiplicity with nightmares of anarchy and total cacophony. When such observers look around and hear the contesting voices, the clashing interpretations, they perceive what strikes them as a slippage, a shaking of the foundations. The language community seems to these observers to be fundamentally in danger. They erect walls of cultural literacy and plan "excellence networks." They deliver jeremiads about the "closing of the American mind" (Bloom, 1987) and calls to turn the eyes of *our* minds to a super-sensible realm again, to find our anchorage in something objective and enduring, transcending cacophony and heteroglossia, as well as the stranger in our midst. The federal voices and the corporate voices chime in, lamenting the lack of appropriate technical training. Many times ignoring exclusion, abandonment, and felt alienation among students, they deliver monologues calling for more monologues, for concentration on particular sorts of linear technical skill development. They focus on competence for the new age, on reactive approaches to the new technologies.

Yes, we teachers are aware of the new "market demands" the young are expected to meet. We realize how many parents remain hungry for success and respectability—and how they will guide their young to safe acquiescence. Yes, we have to confront the drugs that intervene so horrendously in young lives, the AIDS epidemic, the homelessness, the deterioration of families and neighborhoods, the teenage pregnancies, the hectic rhythms, the malaise. Even in the midst of confrontation, however, we yearn to communicate what we feel to be worthwhile. We ache to share our notions of the desirable with the young, even as we equip them with the rudiments of learning and the tricks of the trade they need to become "functionally literate." We want them to grasp the *shapes* of our geography, the *story* of our democracy. Oftentimes, we want to make accessible an art form of some kind: parts of a Rossini opera, a Hawthorne short story, van Gogh's sunflowers or those crows against the sky.

Yet by now, most of us are finding out how necessary it is to discover how the things we want to teach appear to young people who are often so unlike our remembered selves. Listening to them, we frequently find ourselves dealing as never before with our own pre-judgments and preferences, with the forms and images we have treasured through most of our lives. What we have learned to treat as valuable, what we take for granted may be challenged in unexpected ways. We find ourselves stopped in our tracks—to wonder, to protest sometimes, to lash out in anger or contempt, to retreat now and then to think about our own thinking. Meeting with a group of high school adolescents who had just completed a research project on New York City museums, I was stopped in my tracks when an African American teenager from the Bronx abruptly asked, "You ever been in the Cloisters, lady?" "Of course," I murmured properly (and, more than likely, smugly). "I'll tell you about the Cloisters, lady," he said. "The Cloisters sucks." My initial response was shock and, I am sure, a degree of outrage. The Cloisters, I thought, the very apex of medieval longing and faith, the embodiment of a kind of beauty I had long since appropriated as *mine.* My next thought was that there was no reason to assume that the Cloisters was of interest to the boy. What was a white unicorn to him? A medieval man in iron armor? Jewel-like flowers planted in a circle? Gothic art itself? My third thought had to do with whether his appreciating the Cloisters really mattered—and why, and to whom. It did occur to me that I might do something to make the Cloisters accessible to him, to help him enter a glowing anteroom of *my* world by sharing something with him, offering him a kind of token of membership in mainstream informed society. It only struck me later, I must admit, that there were things about his world—imagery, movement, sound, story—that I might ask him about, if he chose to listen, if he cared. Meanwhile he was resisting and refusing, and I am not sure in the name of what. I do not even know if he had alternative possibilities in mind.

If he did (and I would like to think so), he might well have encountered the Cloisters as emblematic of the excluding power of the dominant society. If that were the case, it would be very important to understand how such emblematic images are mediated by the consciousness of the one who feels himself to be excluded, discriminated against, shamed. For Michel Foucault, power is not experienced as either possessed or lacked except in the face of some recalcitrance on the part of persons (1982, p. 221). A person does not fully see or live through the impacts of discrimination unless he or she has desires that discrimination (or poverty, or abandonment) prevents him or her from fulfilling. The power relationship for Foucault is to a degree a function of freedom: people have to be somewhat aware of alternative possibilities they want to pursue if they are to feel themselves blocked or manipulated. Most of us recognize by now what Foucault means when he says that we are caught up in the complex play of mechanisms he describes as the "technology of power" (1980, p. 159). The term does not describe power exerted by one individual or several at the apex of a structure trying to further their own interests. Rather, it characterizes a mode of discourse at a particular time, a set of procedures used in producing statements ostensibly adding up to some "truth" or a system of examinations used to determine what is acceptable and what is required if individuals are to be "normalized." Foucault also makes the point that power relations ordinarily take shape over time in piecemeal fashion. Therefore, what results is not the homogenization we are inclined to associate with schooling but "a complex play of supports in mutual engagement, different mechanisms of power which retain all their specific character. Thus where children are concerned at the present time, the interplay of the family, medicine, psychiatry, psychoanalysis, the school and justice does not have the effect of homogenizing these different instances but of establishing connections, cross-references, complementarities, and demarcations between them which assume that each instance retains to some extent its own special modalities" (1980, p. 159).

If power is not conceived as a superstructure, if there are discontinuities as the institutions and discourses concerned mesh with one another, then we cannot see any individual simply as an object totally conditioned by the whole. There are gaps, and these potentially open spaces may be identified as spaces for thought, which, Foucault says, "is not what inhabits a certain conduct and gives it its meaning; rather it is what allows one to step back from this way of acting or reacting, to present it to oneself as an object of thought and question it as to its meanings, its conditions, and its goals. Thought is freedom in relation to what one does, the motion by which one detaches oneself from it, establishes it as an object, and reflects on it as a problem" (1984b, p. 388). To say this is to place emphasis on human consciousness and its vantage points. To be able to "step back" is to have the capacity to break with immersion in the habitual, in the everyday. It is similar to but not identical with what we customarily call critical thinking; it also connects with Paulo Freire's idea of "reading the world." For Freire, "reading the word is not preceded merely by reading the world, but by a certain form of *writing* it or *rewriting* it, that is, of transforming it by means of conscious, practical work" (Freire and Macedo, 1987, p. 35). Freire adds to that view, the important proviso that the "word universe" of learners should be filled with the meanings of their own existential experiences and not those of the teachers. As teachers and teacher educators, as re-viewers of educational studies, we have to choose for ourselves the relation between thinking and transformative action, just as we have to decide on the value of provoking students to speak in their own voices in a world where other voices define the mainstream.

If, in any event, we were to take seriously the notion of detaching ourselves now and then from what we do, we would be breaking with what we ourselves take for granted, perhaps opening ourselves to a pluralism of diverse visions. Can we do the same for the teenager from the Bronx? Can we enable him to name his own recalcitrance, to see it in a dialectical relation to the structures that oppose (or seem to oppose) his becoming? Can we attune ourselves sufficiently to his word universe or create classroom conditions that make that universe audible? Can we enable him, at least, to chart a field of possibilities for himself and for those with whom he shares a world? For all we know, I realize, his word universe is infused with media language, commercial talk, soap opera dialogue, MTV lyrics. He may well have internalized the image of the successful man (the boss, the proprietor, the landlord, his oppressor) as his ego ideal. Can we free him to attend to his own "anxieties, fears, demands, and dreams" (Freire and Macedo, 1987, p. 35), to his authentic and unashamed reading of his truly lived world? The same questions hold true for those with different groundings and different hopes: the ones who feel "entitled" to all there is and who are said to be disinterested and almost pathologically bored; the young girls and women who have hesitated (out of embarrassment, out of lack of confidence) to consult their own ways of knowing; the ones whose fathers once worked in factories but are now reduced to a kind of service work that makes them feel rootless in the world; the newly arrived Thais and Koreans and Laotians and Russian Jews and Haitians, each with a life story, a distinctive background knowledge, and a desire and a dread when it comes to reading the world.

Understandably, given the social scientific orientations of many of us as teachers and teacher educators, we have focused on large conceptualizations, both interpretive and functionally rational; we have centered our attention on historical and social developments affecting aggregates of human beings over time. Many of us have been attracted to ideology critiques; we have spent many hours countering the mystifications associated with the old myths of the common school, equal opportunity, and meritocracy. Our re-viewing over the years has more often than not engaged us with the philosophies of continental Europe. We have studied a variety of critical theories and worked hard to enable ourselves and teachers-to-be to comprehend the ways in which educational institutions have served the interests of prevailing socioeconomic forces, how they have treated students as "resources," means to ends beyond themselves. We have studied the bureaucracies characteristic of the administered societies we inhabit; we have looked at the impacts of popular culture and media on our own as well as our students' consciousness. We have had to acknowledge the seductiveness of the consumer society's promises and the unpleasant fact of the young's widespread compliance with advertisers' demands. We know enough to understand the fallacies in basically determinist or functionalist explanations of what happens in the schools; we know enough to point out the coercions of consciousness that occur all around, not just in advertising. Also, we realize better than we did the inequities that still prevail in our society when investment in appropriate education for all is concerned. All too frequently, the spectacles of injustice and racism discourage us from pondering a better social order, and we lapse (or, in some cases, relapse) into a cynical opinion of the likelihood of democracy or a pluralist society that is in some degree just.

Our dominant function in recent years has been, as was the function of thinkers during the European Enlightenment, analytical and critical. We have played roles akin to those played by Locke, Hume, Voltaire, Montesquieu, Rousseau, and Condorcet as they challenged sophistries and illusions more than two centuries ago. The repressions they exposed derived from the excesses of the churches, armies, and kings of that age. William Blake's "London" made brilliantly clear how overt the violations were:

> In every cry of every Man,
> In every Infant's cry of fear,
> In every voice, in every ban,
> The mind-forg'd manacles I hear.
>
> How the Chimney-sweeper's cry
> Every black'ning Church appalls;
> And the hapless Soldier's sigh
> Runs in blood down Palace walls [(1793) 1958, p. 52].

The Enlightenment *philosophes* wielded their pens in the assurance that the cold blades of logic and rationality could cut through the superstitions and idolatries that held people captive. They thought and spoke in terms of abstract categories; they dealt in essences, ideals that were givens. This made it possible to speak of all men as endowed by their Creator with "certain inalienable rights." It allowed the rationalist thinkers to refer to natural and moral "laws" in a harmonious, mathematized universe—sometimes seen as macrocosm in relation to the microcosm of the human mind.

William Blake and the Romantics who followed him (including Schelling, Hegel, and the other systematic philosophers) rejected the tenets of deism and rationalism. And certainly, beginning with Kierkegaard, the existential thinkers affirmed and reaffirmed the significance of subjectivity and partiality of perspective.

Nevertheless, one of the climactic events in all twentieth-century academic fields has been the recognition of the need to reconceive the Enlightenment or the "enlightenment project" (MacIntyre, 1981, pp. 49–59) as it may be called. Our interest in the Frankfurt School and critical theory led many of us to such works as *Dialectic of Enlightenment* (Horkheimer and Adorno, 1972), which let us examine the "mass deception" of the "culture industry" through the eyes of Horkheimer and Adorno and also made us grasp the ways in which the Enlightenment rationalized the early extremes of capitalism and may have generated the forces that made Auschwitz and Hiroshima technically (and morally) conceivable. Some of us were struck by the explanations of alienation and oppression we discovered in the Marxist literature; others of us were drawn to a neo-Marxist position, based partly on a realization that the instrumental rationality (Habermas, 1971) derived from rationalism was as characteristic of modern socialist societies as it was of capitalist ones. All were bureaucratized; all were administered; all were afflicted with the technologies of power Foucault describes. Today the questions raised by the environmental movement and those involved with human ecology are making us challenge ideas of progress, growth, and control over nature that were fundamental in Enlightenment thought. André Gorz and Ivan Illich are not alone in talking about the "poverty of affluence" and in identifying the connection between "living better and producing less" (Gorz, 1980, p. 28), a connection aimed at the heart of consumer societies as well as at some of the major preoccupations of the late eighteenth century.

Theodor Adorno and Walter Benjamin were, for years, suspicious of what postmodernist thinkers were to call the "metanarrative" (Lyotard, 1987, p. 84), of the type that embodies a desire for all-encompassing explanation and that becomes (as Enlightenment narrative often did) a kind of prescriptive filter through which all individual statements had to pass. This is somewhat different from a metanarrative or master story that purports to give a "true" rendering of what is thought to be "real." Adorno writes that "the whole is the false" (1974, p. 50). Benjamin, viewing history in endless tension with the harmonious and the Messianic, suggest that "nothing historical can relate on its own account to anything Messianic. Therefore, the Kingdom of God is not the *telos* of the historical dynamic;

it cannot be set up as a goal" ([1955] 1979, p. 312). When Richard Rorty affirms the futility of trying "to find foundations to which one might cling, frameworks beyond which one must not stray" (1979, p. 316), he, too, is taking issue with metanarrative, encompassing metaphors, and notions of a "Kingdom of God." Like other social philosophers today, Rorty questions efforts to posit common ratio- nalities that bind all human beings, sets of rules "which will tell us how rational agreement can be reached on what would settle the issue on every point where statements seem to conflict." Rorty has said that he sees in skepticism regarding common rationalities few implications for conceptions of curriculum in schools (although he might for universities). Still, many thinkers among us have been see- ing connections between their own rejections of totalizing views and Rorty's conceptions of solidarity and relativism (1991). It may be that the re-viewing required of us will focus on the pragmatic reaffirma- tion of the pragmatists' "justification of toleration, free inquiry, and the quest for undistorted communication" (1991, p. 29) and on the accompanying conviction that people who have experienced differ- ent conditions (as the Hungarians have, and the East Germans) would never choose the securities of authoritarianism over what they think of as democracy with its pragmatic habits of mind. Acknowl- edging the relativism of his belief, which he attributes to habits deriv- ing from the Enlightenment tendency to justify things by appeals to a transcendent, transcultural Reason, Rorty says that the best we can do is to tell our stories in solidarity and in the light of shared beliefs. He fully realizes that the values and beliefs he is talking about were forged in the Enlightenment; but he is saying we can live by them without returning to Enlightenment modes of justification. Such val- ues, and the hopes to which they give rise, cannot and need not be demonstrated to be objectively superior to other values. The point is to try to live by them and make more and more inclusive the num- ber of people to which "we" refers.

Habermas introduces another idea when he writes of philoso- phy's role in promoting self-reflectiveness in the sciences (1984). More recently, he has laid much stress on the importance of the life-world and of the need to reach in that world some under- standing that touches on cognitive interpretations and moral expectations. This understanding requires, however, "a cultural tra- dition that ranges across the whole spectrum, not just the fruits of science and technology." Habermas would have philosophy take the role of interpreter on behalf of the life-world and, by so doing, launching an interplay between "the cognitive-instrumental, moral-practical, and aesthetic-expressive dimensions that has come to a standstill today" (1987, p. 313). Insisting that philosophy remains the "guardian of rationality," Habermas suggests that pragmatism and hermeneutics have joined forces to mediate between the everyday world and cultural modernity. They do so by attributing "epistemic authority to the community of all who cooperate and speak with one another" (p. 314). This, for me, summons up the idea of dialogue or multilogue that seems so important when it comes to the achievement of reciprocal understanding. Habermas, however, returns to those he calls the "master thinkers" and talks of grounding the validity of what different persons say unconditionally in rational norms. Justification cannot, for him, be regarded as a function of life-styles or habitual practices. It is necessary to return to a universal notion of procedural rationality.

However, an alternative to this return may be a shared decision to live in accord with shared norms that are continually remade and revised in the light of differing perspectives. I think of such norms and principles as equality, ones that have been misused repeatedly by those in power but that can be and are being reinterpreted in the light of presently lived experience. In *Choosing Equality,* for example, a challenge is levied against the old notion that "inclusion—entering the race—constitutes sufficient opportunity." This, the authors say, becomes a rationale for meritocracy and masks how limited inclusion is in practice. They propose setting different standards, measuring our commitment to equality by the results: "From a fully democratic perspective, therefore, we interpret the concepts of equal opportunity and equity quite differently. The concepts should mean not only the right to be included in the system but also the right to stay in the system and be provided the appropriate conditions for learning. If equality of result is the goal, equal opportunity requires a continuum of means as well as chances, which are extended, not exhausted by obstacles to learning" (Bastian and others, 1986, p. 30).

John Rawls revaluates the concept of justice itself as well as meritocracy. With a meritocratic form of social order, writes Rawls, the culture of poorer people is impoverished "while that of the governing and technocratic elite is securely based on the service of the national ends of power and wealth. Equality of opportunity means an equal chance to leave the less fortunate behind in the personal quest for influence and social position" (1972, pp. 106–107). For Rawls, "the confident sense of their own worth should be sought for the least favored and this limits the forms of hierarchy and the degrees of inequality that justice permits." Moreover, educational resources should not be allocated primarily according to their return in trained abilities, "but also according to their worth in enriching the personal and social life of citizens, including here the least favored" (p. 107). A similar rethinking of the value of freedom can be found as more and more people move away from the notion of negative freedom to a concept of freedom *for,* associated, as it was for John Dewey, with the power to act and the power to choose, with the "capacity to become different" (1931, p. 293). Dewey also appended that, "like all other possibilities, this possibility has to be actualized; and, like all others, it can only be actualized through interaction with objective conditions" (p. 297). Conditions have to be created, he meant, if the potentiality is to be actualized—conditions of cooperation, mutuality, support.

I say these things about the possibility of shared commitments not because I believe we can override pluralism or rediscover a "general orientation" or some renewed faith in a "universal reason." I say them in the belief that a re-viewing ought to involve us in the continuing constitution and renewal of a common world, if we can keep in mind the idea that such a world may come into being in the course of a continuing dialogue, which we ourselves can provoke and nurture in the midst of change. Hannah Arendt, rejecting conformism and leveling of all sorts, believed that nothing can keep a community together when people lose their interest in a common world. "Education is the point at which we decide whether we love the world enough to assume responsibility for it and by the same token save it from that ruin which, except for renewal, except for the coming of the new and young, would be inevitable. And education, too, is where we decide whether we love our children enough not to expel them from our world and leave them to their own devices" (1961, p. 196). As we have seen, Arendt herself made it continually clear that this active world only comes into being when people come together in "action and speech," retaining their "agent-revealing capacity" (1958, p. 182), and speaking from their life-worlds. And action always signifies a new beginning, a new initiative, so that fixed and final frameworks remain inconceivable.

The central questions will continue to haunt us. How can we reconcile the multiple realities of human lives with shared commitment to communities infused once again with principles? How can we do it without regressing, without mythicizing? How, like Tarrou in *The Plague,* can we move ourselves and others to affirm that "on this earth there are pestilences and there are victims, and it's up to us, so far as possible, not to join forces with the pestilences" (Camus, 1948, p. 229)? How can we, in every predicament, "take the victims' sides, so as to reduce the damage done" (p. 230)? Reminded by these questions of what we learned in the 1960s about community and about the ways in which individuality is constituted by membership, by coming together, we need to think again about overcoming our and others' peculiar silences where commitments are concerned. We need, in our re-viewing, to recapture some of the experiences of coming together that occurred in the peace movement and the civil rights movement. We need to articulate what it signifies for some of us to support people with AIDS, to feed and house homeless persons in some dignified way, to offer day-long support to the very young in store-front schools, to bring into being teacher communities in our working spaces. Many of us have learned how the very act of being together has enabled us to create our identities as subjects, not simply the objects of feelings and aspirations. Yes, this thought is evocative of the work of the great pragmatists, Dewey and George Herbert Mead among others; but it is also being made present to us today by the work being done on women's ways of knowing (Belenky, Clinchy, Goldberger, and Tarule, 1986), so long repressed in literature and philosophy. Our very realization that the individual does not precede community may summon up images of relation, of the networks of concern in which we teachers still do our work and, as we do so, create and recreate ourselves. More and more of us, for all our postmodern preoccupations, are aware of how necessary it is to keep such visions of possibility before our eyes in the face of rampant carelessness and alienation and fragmentation.

It is out of this kind of thinking, I still believe, that the ground of a critical community can be opened in our teaching and in our schools. It is out of such thinking that public spaces may be regained. The challenge is to make the ground palpable and visible to our students, to make possible the interplay of multiple voices, of "not quite commensurable visions." It is to attend to the plurality of consciousnesses—and their recalcitrances and their resistances, along with their affirmations, their "songs of love." And, yes, it is to work for responsiveness to principles of equity, principles of equality, and principles of freedom, which still can be named within contexts of caring and concern. The principles and the contexts have to be *chosen* by living human beings against their own life-worlds and in the light of their lives with others, by persons able to call, to say, to sing, and—using their imaginations, tapping their courage—to transform.

References

Adorno, T. *Minima Moralia: Reflections from a Damaged Life*. London: New Left Books, 1974.

Allende, I. *Eva Luna*. New York: Bantam Books, 1989.

Anzaldua, G. *Borderlands/La Frontera: The New Mestiza*. San Francisco: Spinsters/Aunt Lute, 1987.

Arendt, H. *The Human Condition*. Chicago: University of Chicago Press, 1958.

Arendt, H. *Between Past and Future*. New York: Viking Penguin, 1961.

Arendt, H. *Men in Dark Times*. Orlando, Fla.: Harcourt, 1968.

Arendt, H. *Crises of the Republic*. New York: Harvest Books, 1972.

Arendt, H. *Thinking*, Vol. 1. Orlando, Fla.: Harcourt, 1978.

Bakhtin, M. M. *The Dialogic Imagination*. Austin: University of Texas Press, 1981.

Bakhtin, M. M. *Problems of Dostoevsky's Poetics*. Minneapolis: University of Minnesota Press, 1984.

Barthes, R. *The Pleasure of the Text*. (R. Miller, trans.) New York: Hill & Wang, 1975.

Bastian, A., and others. *Choosing Equality*. Philadelphia: Temple University Press, 1986.

Belenky, M., Clinchy, B., Goldberger, N., and Tarule, J. *Women's Ways of Knowing*. New York: Basic Books, 1986.

Benjamin, W. *Illuminations*. New York: Schocken Books, 1978. (Originally published 1955.)

Benjamin, W. "Theologico-Political Fragment." In *Reflections*. New York: Harvest Books, 1979. (Originally published 1955.)

Berger, J. *Ways of Seeing*. New York: Viking Penguin, 1984.

Berleant, A. *Art and Engagement*. Philadelphia: Temple University Press, 1991.

Beyer, L. E., and Liston, D. P. "Discourse or Moral Action? A Critique of Postmodernism." *Educational Theory*, Fall 1992, *42*(4).

Bishop, E. "At the Fishhouses." In *The Complete Poems, 1927–1979*. New York: Farrar, Straus & Giroux, 1983. (Originally published 1955.)

Bishop, E. "In the Waiting Room." In *The Complete Poems, 1927–1979*. New York: Farrar, Straus & Giroux, 1983. (Originally published 1975.)

Bishop, E. "Night City." In *The Complete Poems, 1927–1979*. New York: Farrar, Straus & Giroux, 1983. (Originally published 1976.)

Blake, W. "The Ecchoing Green." In J. Bronowski (ed.), *William Blake*. Harmondsworth, England: Penguin, 1958. (Originally published 1789.)

Blake, W. "London." In J. Bronowski (ed.), *William Blake*. Harmondsworth, England: Penguin, 1958. (Originally published 1793.)

Bloom, A. *The Closing of the American Mind*. New York: Simon & Schuster, 1987.

Bloom, H. *The Western Canon: The Books and Schools of the Ages*. Orlando, Fla.: Harcourt Brace Jovanovich, 1994.

Bourdieu, P. *Outline of a Theory of Practice*. Cambridge: Cambridge University Press, 1977.

Bruner, J. *Actual Minds, Possible Worlds*. Cambridge, Mass.: Harvard University Press, 1986.

Buber, M. *Between Man and Man*. (R. G. Smits, trans.) Boston: Beacon Press, 1957.

Camus, A. *The Plague*. (S. Gilbert, trans.) New York: Knopf, 1948.

Camus, A. *The Myth of Sisyphus*. (J. O'Brien, trans.) New York: Knopf, 1955.

Cliff, M. "A Journey into Speech." In A. Simonson and S. Walker (eds.), *The Greywolf Annual*, Vol. 5: *Multicultural Literacy*. St. Paul, Minn.: Greywolf Press, 1988.

Clifford, J. *The Predicament of Culture*. Cambridge, Mass.: Harvard University Press, 1988.

Conrad, J. *Heart of Darkness*. In *Great Works of Joseph Conrad*. New York: HarperCollins, 1967. (Originally published 1902.)

Conrad, J. Preface to *The Nigger of the Narcissus*. In *Great Works of Joseph Conrad*. New York: HarperCollins, 1967. (Originally published 1898.)

Crane, H. *Poetry*, Oct. 1926.

Danto, A. C. *The Transfiguration of the Commonplace*. Cambridge, Mass.: Harvard University Press, 1981.

Danto, A. C. "Philosophy as/and/of Literature." In J. Rajchman and C. West (eds.), *Post-Analytic Philosophy*. New York: Columbia University Press, 1985.

Darling-Hammond, L. "Educational Indicators and Enlightened Policy." *Educational Policy*, 1992, *6*(3), 235–265.

Darling-Hammond, L., and Ancess, J. "Authentic Assessment and School Development." In J. B. Baron and D. P. Wolf (eds.), *National Society for the Study of Education Ninety-Third Yearbook*. Chicago: University of Chicago Press, 1993.

DeLillo, D. *White Noise*. New York: Viking Penguin, 1985.

Dewey, J. *Democracy and Education*. New York: Macmillan, 1916.

Dewey, J. *The Quest for Certainty.* London: Allen & Unwin, 1929.

Dewey, J. *Philosophy and Civilization.* New York: Minton, Balch, 1931.

Dewey, J. *Art as Experience.* New York: Minton, Balch, 1934.

Dewey, J. *The Public and Its Problems.* Athens, Ohio: Swallow Press, 1954. (Originally published 1927.)

Dickinson, E. "The Gleam of an Heroic Act." In T. H. Johnson (ed.), *The Complete Poems.* Boston: Little, Brown, 1960. (Written 1887; originally published 1914.)

Doctorow, E. L. *Ragtime.* New York: Random House, 1975.

Donoghue, D. *The Arts Without Mystery.* Boston: Little, Brown, 1983.

Dostoyevsky, F. *The Brothers Karamazov.* (C. Garnett, trans.) New York: Modern Library, 1945. (Originally published 1880.)

D'Sousa, D. *Illiberal Education: The Politics of Race and Sex on Campus.* New York: Free Press, 1991.

Du Bois, W.E.B. *The Souls of Black Folk.* New York: New American Library, 1982. (Originally published 1903.)

Eco, U. *The Name of the Rose.* (W. Weaver, trans.) Orlando, Fla.: Harcourt, 1983.

Eco, U. *The Open Work.* (A. Cocogni, trans.) Cambridge, Mass.: Harvard University Press, 1984.

Eliot, G. *Middlemarch.* Harmondsworth, England: Penguin, 1964. (Originally published 1871–1872.)

Eliot, T. S. *Four Quartets* ("East Coker"). In *The Complete Poems and Plays.* Orlando, Fla.: Harcourt, 1958. (Originally published 1943.)

Ellison, R. *Invisible Man.* New York: Signet Books, 1952.

Ellison, R. *Shadow and Act.* New York: Signet Books, 1964.

Elmore, R. F., and Associates. *Restructuring Schools: The Next Generation of Educational Reform.* San Francisco: Jossey-Bass, 1990.

Faulkner, W. *The Sound and the Fury.* New York: Modern Library, 1946.

Fine, M. "Silence in Public Schools." *Language Arts,* 1987, *64*(2), 157–174.

Fischer, M.M.J. "Ethnicity and the Post-Modern Arts of Memory." In J. Clifford and G. E. Marcus (eds.), *Writing Culture.* Berkeley: University of California Press, 1986.

Fitzgerald, F. S. *The Great Gatsby.* New York: Simon & Schuster, 1991. (Originally published 1925.)

Foucault, M. *The Archaeology of Knowledge and the Discourse on Language.* (A. M. Sheridan Smith, trans.) New York: Pantheon Books, 1972.

Foucault, M. *The Order of Things.* New York: Vintage Books, 1973.

Foucault, M. "Intellectuals and Power." In D. F. Bouchard (ed.), *Language, Counter-Memory, Practice* (D. F. Bouchard and S. Simon, trans.). Ithaca, N.Y.: Cornell University Press, 1977.

Foucault, M. *Power/Knowledge.* (C. Gordon, L. Marshall, J. Mepham, and K. Sop, trans.) New York: Pantheon Books, 1980.

Foucault, M. "The Subject and Power." (M. Foucault and L. Sawyer, trans.) Afterword to H. L. Dreyfus and P. Rabinos, *Michel Foucault: Beyond Structuralism and Hermeneutics.* Chicago: University of Chicago Press, 1982.

Foucault, M. "The Means of Correct Training." (R. Howard, trans.) In P. Rabinow (ed.), *The Foucault Reader.* New York: Pantheon Books, 1984a.

Foucault, M. "Polemics, Politics, and Problemizations: An Interview." (L. Davis, trans.) In P. Rabinow (ed.), *The Foucault Reader.* New York: Pantheon Books, 1984b.

Fox-Genovese, E. "The Claims of a Common Culture: Gender, Race, Class, and the Canon." *Salmagundi,* Fall 1986, 72.

Freeman, J. *Picasso and the Weeping Women.* Los Angeles: Los Angeles Museum of Art, 1994.

Freire, P. *Pedagogy of the Oppressed.* (M. B. Ramos, trans.) New York: Herder & Herder, 1970.

Freire, P. "The Importance of the Act of Reading." In P. Freire and D. Macedo, *Literacy: Reading the Word and the World.* South Hadley, Mass.: Bergin & Garvey, 1987.

Freire, P., and Macedo, D. *Literacy: Reading the Word and the World.* South Hadley, Mass.: Bergin & Garvey, 1987.

Freud, S. *Civilization and Its Discontents.* New York: Hogarth Press, 1953.

Frost, R. "The Road Not Taken." In E. C. Latham and L. Thompson (eds.), *Robert Frost: Poetry and Prose.* New York: Holt, 1972. (Originally published 1916.)

Gadamer, H.-G. "Hermeneutics and Social Science." *Cultural Hermeneutics,* 1975, 2.

Gadamer, H.-G. *Philosophical Hermeneutics.* Berkeley: University of California Press, 1976.

Gardner, H. *Frames of Mind: The Theory of Multiple Intelligences.* New York: Basic Books, 1983.

Gates, H. L., Jr. "Goodbye, Columbus? Notes on the Culture of Criticism." *American Literary History,* Summer 1991, *3*(4), 711–727.

Gates, H. L., Jr. *Loose Canons: Notes on the Culture Wars.* New York: Oxford University Press, 1992.

Geertz, C. *Local Knowledge.* New York: Basic Books, 1983.

Gilmour, J. *Picturing the World.* Albany: State University of New York Press, 1986.

Goodman, N. *Languages of Art.* Indianapolis: Hackett, 1976.

Gorz, A. *Ecology as Politics.* Boston: South End Press, 1980.

Habermas, J. *Knowledge and Human Interests.* Boston: Beacon Press, 1971.

Habermas, J. *Theory of Communicative Action.* Boston: Beacon Press, 1984.

Habermas, J. "Philosophy as Stand-In and Interpreter." In K. Baynes, J. Bohman, and T. McCarthy (eds.), *After Philosophy: End or Transformation?* Cambridge, Mass.: MIT Press, 1987.

Hável, V. *Letters to Olga.* (P. Wilson, trans.) New York: Holt, 1983.

Hawthorne, N. *The Scarlet Letter.* New York: Viking Penguin, 1969. (Originally published 1850.)

Heidegger, M. *Being and Time.* (J. McQuarrie and E. Robinson, trans.) New York: HarperCollins, 1962.

Heidegger, M. *What Is Called Thinking?* (J. C. Gray, trans.) New York: HarperCollins, 1968.

Heidegger, M. *Poetry, Language, and Thought.* New York: HarperCollins, 1971.

Hijuelos, O. *The Mambo Kings Sing Songs of Love.* New York: Farrar, Straus & Giroux, 1989.

Hirsch, E. D., Jr. *Cultural Literacy.* Boston: Houghton Mifflin, 1987.

Horkheimer, M., and Adorno, T. W. *Dialectic of Enlightenment.* New York: Seabury Press, 1972.

Howard, V. R. *Artistry: The Work of Artists.* Indianapolis: Hackett, 1982.

Hughes, R. "Art, Morality, and Mapplethorpe." *New York Review of Books,* Apr. 23, 1992, p. 21.

Husserl, E. *Ideas.* (R. B. Gibson, trans.) New York: Collier/Macmillan, 1962.

Huxley, A. *Brave New World.* New York: HarperCollins, 1950. (Originally published 1932.)

Iser, W. *The Act of Reading.* Baltimore: Johns Hopkins University Press, 1980.

James, H. *The Portrait of a Lady.* New York: Viking Penguin, 1984. (Originally published 1881.)

James, W. "The Dilemmas of Determinism." In *The Will to Believe and Other Essays.* New York: Holt, 1912. (Originally published 1897.)

James, W. *Principles of Psychology.* 2 vols. New York: Dover Books, 1950. (Originally published in 1890.)

Kearney, R. *The Wake of Imagination.* Minneapolis: University of Minnesota Press, 1988.

Kierkegaard, S. "Stages on Life's Way." In R. Bretall (ed. and trans.), *Kierkegaard.* Princeton, N.J.: Princeton University Press, 1940.

Kincaid, J. *Lucy.* New York: Farrar, Straus & Giroux, 1990.

Kingston, M. H. *China Men.* New York: Vintage International Books, 1989.

Kozol, J. *Savage Inequalities.* New York: Crown, 1991.

Kundera, M. *The Unbearable Lightness of Being.* (M. H. Heim, trans.) New York: HarperCollins, 1984.

Kuspit, D. *The Aesthetic Dimension.* Boston: Beacon Press, 1990.

Lasch, C. *The Minimal Self.* New York: Norton, 1984.

Le Guin, U. K. *Dancing at the Edge of the World.* New York: Grove Press, 1989.

Leiris, M. "Faire-part." In E. C. Oppler (ed.), *Picasso's Guernica.* New York: Norton, 1988.

Levertov, D. *Oblique Prayer.* New York: New Directions Press, 1984.

Levi, P. *The Drowned and the Saved.* (R. Rosenthal, trans.) New York: Summit Books, 1988.

Lyotard, J.-F. "The Post-Modern Condition." In K. Baynes, J. Bohman, and T. McCarthy (eds.), *After Philosophy: End or Transformation?* Cambridge, Mass.: MIT Press, 1987.

MacIntyre, A. *After Virtue.* Notre Dame, Ind.: Notre Dame University Press, 1981.

Madison, G. B. *The Hermeneutics of Postmodernity.* Indianapolis: University of Indiana Press, 1988.

Malraux, A. *Man's Fate.* (H. M. Chevalier, trans.) New York: Modern Library, 1936.

Mann, T. *Tonio Kröger.* In J. W. Angell (ed. and trans.), *The Thomas Mann Reader.* New York: Knopf, 1950. (Originally published 1903.)

Mann, T. *Confessions of Felix Krull, Confidence Man.* (D. Lindley, trans.) New York: Signet Books, 1955.

Marcuse, H. *Negations.* Boston: Beacon Press, 1968.

Marcuse, H. *The Aesthetic Dimension.* Boston: Beacon Press, 1977.

Márquez, G. C. *One Hundred Years of Solitude.* Translated by Gregory Rabassa. New York: HarperCollins, 1970.

Márquez, G. C. *Love in the Time of Cholera.* (E. Grossman, trans.) New York: Knopf, 1988.

Marshall, P. *Brown Girl, Brownstones.* New York: Feminist Press, 1981. (Originally published 1959.)

Martin, J. R. *The Schoolhome.* Cambridge, Mass.: Harvard University Press, 1992.

Marx, K. *The Communist Manifesto.* In E. Burns (ed. and trans.), *Handbook of Marxism.* New York: International Publishers, 1935. (Originally published 1848.)

Melville, H. *Moby Dick.* Berkeley: University of California Press, 1981. (Originally published 1851.)

Melville, H. "Bartleby the Scrivener." In *"Billy Budd, Sailor" and Other Stories by Herman Melville.* New York: Bantam Books, 1986. (Originally published 1853.)

Merleau-Ponty, M. *The Primacy of Perception.* Evanston, Ill.: Northwestern University Press, 1964a.

Merleau-Ponty, M. *Sense and Non-Sense.* (H. L. Dreyfus and P. A. Dreyfus, trans.) Evanston, Ill.: Northwestern University Press, 1964b. (Originally published 1948.)

Merleau-Ponty, M. *Phenomenology of Perception.* (C. Smits, trans.) New York: Humanities Press, 1967. (Originally published 1962.)

Merleau-Ponty, M. *The Structure of Behavior.* Boston: Beacon Press, 1967.

Morrison, T. *The Bluest Eye.* New York: Bantam Books, 1970.

Morrison, T. *Sula.* New York: Bantam Books, 1975.

Morrison, T. *Beloved.* New York: Knopf, 1987.

Morrison, T. *Playing in the Dark: Whiteness and the Literary Imagination.* Cambridge, Mass.: Harvard University Press, 1992.

"The Moving Image." *Daedalus,* Fall 1985.

Mukherjee, B. *Jasmine.* New York: Grove Weidenfeld, 1989.

Murray, C., and Herrnstein, R. J. *The Bell Curve.* New York: Free Press, 1994.

Nietzsche, F. *Thus Spake Zarathustra.* In W. Kaufmann (ed. and trans.), *The Portable Nietzsche.* New York: Viking Penguin, 1958. (Originally published 1883–1892).

Noddings, N. *The Challenge to Care in Schools.* New York: Teachers College Press, 1992.

Norton, E. H. "What the Democrats Should Do Next." *New York Times,* Nov. 27, 1985, p. A23.

Oakeshott, M. *Rationalism in Politics and Other Essays.* London: Methuen, 1962.

Olsen, T. "I Stand Here Ironing." In *Tell Me a Riddle.* New York: Dell, 1961.

Olsen, T. *Silences.* New York: Dell/Delacorte, 1978.

Ozick, C. *Metaphor and Memory.* New York: Knopf, 1989.

Paley, G. "Ruthie and Edie." In *Later the Same Day.* New York: Viking Penguin, 1986.

Passmore, J. *The Philosophy of Teaching.* Cambridge, Mass.: Harvard University Press, 1980.

Percy, W. *The Moviegoer.* New York: Knopf, 1979.

Peters, R. S. "Education and Human Development." In R. F. Dearden, P. H. Hirst, and R. S. Peters (eds.), *Education and Reason.* London: Routledge, 1975.

Polakow, V. *Lives on the Edge: Single Mothers and Their Children in the Other America.* Chicago: University of Chicago Press, 1993.

Pratte, R. *The Civic Imperative.* New York: Teachers College Press, 1988.

Putnam, H. "After Empiricism." In J. Rajchman and C. West (eds.), *Post-Analytic Philosophy.* New York: Columbia University Press, 1985.

Rawls, J. *A Theory of Justice.* Cambridge, Mass.: Harvard University Press, 1972.

Reich, R. *Tales of a New America.* New York: Random House, 1987.

Rilke, R. M. *Possibility of Being: A Selection of Poems.* (J. B. Leishman, trans.) New York: New Directions, 1977. (Originally published 1905.)

Rorty, R. *Philosophy and the Mirror of Nature.* Princeton, N.J.: Princeton University Press, 1979.

Rorty, R. "Solidarity or Objectivity?" In *Objectivity, Relativism, and Truth.* Cambridge: Cambridge University Press, 1991.

Rukeyser, M. *The Book of the Dead.* New York: Covici-Friede, 1938.

Rukeyser, M. "Tenth Elegy: Elegy in Joy." In *Out of Silence: Selected Poems.* Evanston, Ill.: TriQuarterly Books, 1992. (Originally published 1949.)

Said, E. W. "Opponents, Audiences, Constituencies, and Community." In H. Foster (ed.), *The Anti-Aesthetic.* Port Townsend, Wash.: Bay Press, 1983.

Sarraute, N. *Childhood.* New York: Braziller, 1984.

Sartre, J.-P. *Existentialism.* (B. Frechtman, trans.) New York: Philosophical Library, 1947.

Sartre, J.-P. *Literature and Existentialism.* (B. Frechtman, trans.) Secaucus, N.J.: Citadel Press, 1949.

Sartre, J.-P. *Being and Nothingness.* (H. Barnes, trans.) New York: Philosophical Library, 1956.

Sartre, J.-P. *Nausea.* (L. Alexander, trans.) New York: New Directions Press, 1959.

Sartre, J.-P. *Search for a Method.* New York: Knopf, 1963.

Schlesinger, A. M., Jr. *The Disuniting of America: Reflections on a Multicultural Society.* New York: Norton, 1992.

Scholes, R. *Protocols of Reading.* New Haven, Conn.: Yale University Press, 1989.

Schön, D. A. *The Reflective Practitioner.* New York: Basic Books, 1983.

Schrift, A. D. "The Becoming Post-Modern of Philosophy." In G. Shapiro (ed.), *After the Future.* Albany: State University of New York Press, 1990.

Schutz, A. *Collected Papers,* Vol. 2: *Studies in Social Theory.* The Hague: Nijhoff, 1964a.

Schutz, A. "Making Music Together." In *Collected Papers,* Vol. 2: *Studies in Social Theory.* The Hague: Nijhoff, 1964b.

Schutz, A. *Collected Papers,* Vol. 1: *The Problem of Social Reality.* 2d ed. The Hague: Nijhoff, 1967.

Shange, N. *For Colored Girls Who Have Considered Suicide, When the Rainbow Is Enuf.* New York: Macmillan, 1977.

Shaughnessy, M. P. *Errors and Expectations.* New York: Oxford University Press, 1977.

Silone, I. *Bread and Wine.* New York: HarperCollins, 1937.

Sizer, T. *Horace's School: Redesigning the American High School.* Boston: Houghton Mifflin, 1992.

Smith, B. H. *Contingencies of Value*. Cambridge, Mass.: Harvard University Press, 1988.

Smithson, R. *The Writings of Robert Smithson: Essays with Illustrations*. (N. Holt, ed.) New York: New York University Press, 1979.

Spiegelman, A. *Maus II*. New York: Pantheon Books, 1991.

Steinbeck, J. *Grapes of Wrath*. New York: Viking Penguin, 1976. (Originally published 1939.)

Stevens, W. "The Man with the Blue Guitar." In *The Collected Poems of Wallace Stevens*. New York: Knopf, 1964. (Originally published 1937.)

Stevens, W. "Six Significant Landscapes." In *The Collected Poems of Wallace Stevens*. New York: Knopf, 1964. (Originally published 1916.)

Stevens, W. *The Necessary Angel*. New York: Vintage Books, 1965.

Stimpson, C. R. *The Humanities and the Idea of Excellence*. New York: American Council of Learned Societies, 1984.

Stimpson, C. R. *Where the Meanings Are: Feminism and Cultural Spaces*. New York: Routledge, 1989.

"Talk of the Town." *New Yorker*, Aug. 14, 1989, p. 23.

Tan, A. *The Joy Luck Club*. New York: Putnam, 1989.

Taylor, C. *Sources of the Self*. Cambridge, Mass.: Harvard University Press, 1989.

Tocqueville, A. de. *Democracy in America*, Vol. 1. New York: Vintage Books, 1945. (Originally published 1835.)

Tyler, A. *The Accidental Tourist*. New York: Knopf, 1985.

Unger, R. M. *Passion: An Essay on Personality*. New York: Free Press, 1984.

Waldman, D. *Jane Holzer*. New York: Abrams, 1989.

Walker, A. *The Color Purple*. New York: Washington Square Press, 1982.

Walker, A. *In Search of Our Mothers' Gardens*. Orlando, Fla.: Harcourt, 1983.

Walzer, M. *Interpretation and Social Criticism*. Cambridge, Mass.: Harvard University Press, 1987.

Warnock, M. *Imagination*. Berkeley: University of California Press, 1978.

Welty, E. *One Writer's Beginnings*. Cambridge, Mass.: Harvard University Press, 1984.

West, C. "Black Culture and Postmodernism." In B. Kruger and P. Mariani (eds.), *Remaking History*. Port Townsend, Wash.: Bay Press, 1989.

Whitman, W. "Song of Myself." In *Leaves of Grass*. New York: Aventine Press, 1931. (Originally published 1855.)

Wigginton, E. *The Foxfire Books*. New York: Doubleday, 1972.

Wolf, C. *Cassandra*. (J. V. Heurck, trans.) New York: Farrar, Straus & Giroux, 1984.

Wolf, C. *Accident: A Day's News*. (H. Schwarzbauer and R. Fakrorian, trans.) New York: Farrar, Straus & Giroux, 1989.

Woolf, V. *A Room of One's Own*. Orlando, Fla.: Harcourt, 1957. (Originally published 1929.)

Woolf, V. *To the Lighthouse.* London: Everyman's Library, 1962. (Originally published 1927.)

Woolf, V. *Three Guineas.* New York: Harvest Books, 1966. (Originally published 1938.)

Woolf, V. *Moments of Being: Unpublished Autobiographical Writings.* (J. Schulkind, ed.) Orlando, Fla.: Harcourt, 1976.

Wright, R. *Native Son.* New York: HarperCollins, 1940.

Index